Programming Language
Concepts and Paradigms

Prentice Hall International Series in Computer Science

C. A. R. Hoare, Series Editor

BACKHOUSE, R. C., *Program Construction and Verification*
BACKHOUSE, R. C., *Syntax of Programming Languages: Theory and practice*
DeBAKKER, J. W., *Mathematical Theory of Program Correctness*
BEN ARI, *Principles of Concurrent Programming*
BIRD, R. and WADLER, P., *Introduction to Functional Programming*
BJÖRNER, D. and JONES, C. B., *Formal Specification and Software Development*
BORNAT, R., *Programming from First Principles*
BUSTARD, D., ELDER, J. and WELSH, J., *Concurrent Program Structures*
CLARK, K. L. and McCABE, F. G., *micro-Prolog: Programming in logic*
CROOKES, D., *Introduction to Programming in Prolog*
DROMEY, R. G., *How to Solve it by Computer*
DUNCAN, F., *Microprocessor Programming and Software Development*
ELDER, J., *Construction of Data Processing Software*
ELLIOTT, R. J. and HOARE, C. A. R. (eds.), *Scientific Applications of Multiprocessors*
GOLDSCHLAGER, L. and LISTER, A., *Computer Science: A modern introduction (2nd edn)*
GORDON, M. J. C., *Programming Language Theory and its Implementation*
HAYES, I. (ed.), *Specification Case Studies*
HEHNER, E. C. R., *The Logic of Programming*
HENDERSON, P., *Functional Programming: Application and implementation*
HOARE, C. A. R., *Communicating Sequential Processes*
HOARE, C. A. R. and JONES, C. B. (ed.), *Essays in Computing Science*
HOARE, C. A. R. and SHEPHERDSON, J. C. (eds.), *Mathematical Logic and Programming Languages*
HUGHES, J. G., *Database Technology: A software engineering approach*
INMOS LTD, *occam Programming Manual*
INMOS LTD, *occam 2 Reference Manual*
JACKSON, M. A., *System Development*
JOHNSTON, H., *Learning to Program*
JONES, C. B., *Software Development: A rigorous approach (OOP)*
JONES, C. B., *Systematic Software Development using VDM (2nd edn)*
JONES, C. B. and SHAW, R. C. F. (eds.), *Case Studies in Systematic Software Development*
JONES, G., *Programming in occam*
JONES, G. and GOLDSMITH, M., *Programming in occam 2*
JOSEPH, M., PRASAD, V. R. and NATARAJAN, N., *A Multiprocessor Operating System*
LEW, A., *Computer Science: A mathematical introduction*
MacCALLUM, I., *Pascal for the Apple*
MacCALLUM, I., *UCSD Pascal for the IBM PC*
MARTIN, J. J., *Data Types and Data Structures*
MEYER, B., *Introduction to the Theory of Programming Languages*
MEYER, B., *Object-oriented Software Construction*
MILNER, R., *Communication and Concurrency*
MORGAN, C., *Programming from Specifications*
PEYTON JONES, S. L., *The Implementation of Functional Programming Languages*
POMBERGER, G., *Software Engineering and Modula-2*
REYNOLDS, J. C., *The Craft of Programming*
RYDEHEARD, D. E. and BURSTALL, R. M., *Computational Category Theory*
SLOMAN, M. and KRAMER, J., *Distributed Systems and Computer Networks*
SPIVEY, J. M., *The Z Notation: A reference manual*
TENNENT, R. D., *Principles of Programming Languages*
WATT, D. A., WICHMANN, B. A. and FINDLAY, W., *ADA: Language and methodology*
WELSH, J. and ELDER, J., *Introduction to Modula-2*
WELSH, J. and ELDER, J., *Introduction to Pascal (3rd edn)*
WELSH, J., ELDER, J. and BUSTARD, D., *Sequential Program Structures*
WELSH, J. and HAY, A., *A Model Implementation of Standard Pascal*
WELSH, J. and McKEAG, M., *Structured System Programming*
WIKSTRÖM, A., *Functional Programming using Standard ML*

Programming Language Concepts and Paradigms

David A. Watt
University of Glasgow, UK

with contributions by

William Findlay
University of Glasgow, UK

John Hughes
University of Glasgow, UK

Prentice Hall

New York London Toronto Sydney Tokyo Singapore

First published 1990 by
Prentice Hall International (UK) Ltd
66 Wood Lane End, Hemel Hempstead
Hertfordshire HP2 4RG
A division of
Simon & Schuster International Group

Ada is a registered trademark of the US Government Ada Joint
Program Office.
Miranda is a registered trademark of Research Software Ltd.
occam is a registered trademark of the INMOS Group of Companies.
Unix is a registered trademark of AT&T Bell Laboratories.

Printed and bound in the United States of America

Library of Congress Cataloging-in-Publication Data

Watt, David A. (David Anthony)
    Programming language concepts and paradigms/David A. Watt.
    p. cm. – (Prentice Hall international series in computer science)
    Includes bibliographical references.
    ISBN 0–13–728874–3
    1. Programming languages (Electronic computers) 2. Electronic
digital computers – Programming. I. Title. II. Series.
    QA76.7.W39   1989
    005.13 – dc20   89–39814
                                                CIP

British Library Cataloguing in Publication Data

Watt, David A. (David Anthony)
    Programming language concepts and paradigms.
    1. Computer systems. Programming languages
    I. Title
    005.13

    ISBN 0–13–728874–3

---

3   4   5   94 93 92

Contents

Preface

Programming languages have fascinated me ever since I first took a programming course in 1966. I consider myself fortunate that my first programming language was Algol-60. Once I got over my initial disbelief that the computer could 'understand' English words like **if**, **then**, **else**, **begin**, and **end**, I began to appreciate Algol-60's elegance and large measure of regularity. But I did soon notice some inconsistencies. If I could write the following integer expression:

> **if** leapyear **then** 29 **else** 28

then why not the following string expression?

> **if** female **then** 'Ms' **else** 'Mr'

I was unconsciously trying to apply the *type completeness principle*, which was properly formulated only much later. I also learned that some Algol-60 constructs have bizarre properties, Jensen's device being the most famous example. Still, my interest in programming languages was founded, and I began to appreciate the benefits of simplicity and consistency in language design.

Since then I have learned and programmed in about ten other languages, and I have struck a nodding acquaintance with many more. Like many programmers, I have found that certain languages make programming distasteful, a drudgery; others make programming enjoyable, even esthetically pleasing. A good programming language, like a good mathematical notation, helps us to formulate and communicate ideas clearly. My personal highlights were Pascal, Ada, and ML. Like Algol-60 these were, to me, more than just new languages for coding programs; they all sharpened my understanding of what programming is (or should be) all about. Pascal taught me structured programming and data types. Ada taught me modularity. ML taught me functional programming and polymorphism. Most of these concepts I had previously met and understood in principle, but I did not *really* understand them until I was able to write programs in languages in which the concepts were clearly visible.

Programming languages occupy a peculiarly central position in computer science. Programming itself is central, of course, but there are other reasons:

- There is a relationship with *databases* and *information retrieval*. Query languages share many concepts with programming languages, and with logic programming languages in particular. Furthermore, programming languages are now being designed that treat databases as ordinary data structures, allowing database transactions to be programmed easily.
- There is a relationship with *human–computer interaction*. Programming languages must be designed so that programs can be written and read by humans as well as processed by computers. Moreover, natural language processing has many similarities with programming language processing.
- There is a relationship with *operating systems*. Input–output support and storage management are needed to implement programming languages. Modern command languages and file systems share many concepts with programming languages.
- There is a relationship with *computer architecture*. Instruction sets and architectural features like hardware stacks have a significant influence on how effectively programming languages can be implemented. Modern computer engineers often attempt to tailor the architecture to the implementation of programming languages. Furthermore, a convergence between hardware and software is demonstrated by the development of hardware design languages, and the possibility of compiling programs directly into VLSI rather than machine code.

A programming languages trilogy

This is the first of a series of three books on programming languages:

- *Programming Language Concepts and Paradigms*
- *Programming Language Syntax and Semantics*
- *Programming Language Processors*

Programming Language Concepts and Paradigms explains the concepts underlying programming languages, and the major language paradigms that use these concepts in different ways; in other words, it is about language design. *Programming Language Syntax and Semantics* shows how we can specify the syntax (form) and semantics (meaning) of programming languages. *Programming Language Processors* studies the implementation of programming languages, examining language processors such as compilers and interpreters.

In these three books I am attempting something that has not previously been achieved, to the best of my knowledge: a broad study of all aspects of programming languages, using consistent terminology, and emphasizing connections likely to be missed by books that deal separately with these aspects of programming languages. For example, the concepts incorporated in a language must be defined precisely in the language's semantics. Conversely, a study of semantics helps us to discover and refine elegant and powerful new concepts, which can be incorporated in future language designs. A language's syntax underlies analysis of source programs by language processors; its semantics underlies object code generation and interpretation. Implementation is an important consideration for the language designer, since a language that cannot be implemented with acceptable efficiency will not be used.

The three books are designed to be read as a series. For readers who wish to study just one aspect of programming languages, however, each book is sufficiently self-contained to be read on its own.

Content of this book

Apart from its introduction and conclusion, this book falls naturally into three parts.

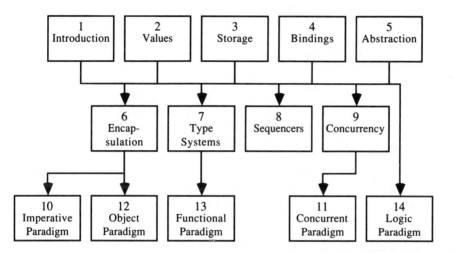

Chapters 2–5 explain the basic concepts that underlie almost all programming languages: values and types, variables and storage, bindings and scope, abstraction and parameterization. The emphasis in these chapters is on identifying the basic concepts and studying them individually.

Chapters 6–9 continue this theme by examining some more advanced concepts: encapsulation (including abstract types, objects and classes, packages, and generics), type systems (including monomorphism, overloading, polymorphism, type inference, and inheritance), sequencers (including exceptions), and concurrency (including conditional critical regions, monitors, and rendezvous). These concepts underlie recent advances in language design. Most of them have been properly integrated only into the more modern programming languages.

Chapters 10–14 survey the major programming paradigms, illustrated by overviews of several important languages. The emphasis is on how concepts have been selected and combined in the design of complete languages. The long-established imperative programming paradigm is compared and contrasted with the increasingly important concurrent, object-oriented, functional, and logic programming paradigms. These different paradigms are based on different selections of concepts, and give rise to sharply contrasting styles of language and of programming.

This book need not be read sequentially. Chapters 1–5 should certainly be read first, but the remaining chapters could be read in many different orders. Chapters 10–14 are largely self-contained; my recommendation is to read at least some of them after Chapters 1–5, in order to gain some insight into the way that complete languages are designed. The diagram above summarizes the dependencies between the chapters.

This book concludes, in Chapter 15, with some brief thoughts on how languages should be selected for particular projects, and on how new languages should be designed.

Examples and case studies

The concepts studied in Chapters 2–9 are freely illustrated by examples. The bulk of these are drawn from Pascal, ML, and to a lesser extent Ada. I have chosen these languages because they are fairly well known, because they offer sharp contrasts, and because they are basically well designed. (They are by no means perfect, but even their flaws are highly instructive!) I have assumed that the reader already knows Pascal or a Pascal-like language (e.g., Ada, Concurrent Pascal, Euclid, Modula, Modula-2, Pascal Plus, or Turing). Knowledge of ML or a related language (e.g., Miranda) would be an advantage, but is not essential since I briefly explain the relevant ML constructs as and when necessary.

The paradigms studied in Chapters 10–14 are illustrated by case studies of representative programming languages. These languages are examined only impressionistically. It would certainly be valuable for the reader to learn to program in some of these languages, in order to gain deeper insight, but this book makes no attempt to teach programming *per se*. The bibliography contains suggested reading on all of these languages.

Exercises

Each chapter is followed by a number of relevant exercises. These vary from short exercises, through longer ones (marked *), up to truly demanding ones (marked **) that could be treated as projects.

A typical exercise is to analyse some aspect of a favorite language, in the same way that Pascal and other languages are analysed in the text. Exercises like this are designed to deepen readers' understanding of languages that they already know, and to reinforce their understanding of particular concepts by studying how they are supported by different languages.

A typical project is to design some extension or modification to an existing language like Pascal. Now language design should not be undertaken lightly! These projects are aimed particularly at the most ambitious readers, but all readers would benefit by at least thinking about the issues raised.

Readership

This book and its two companions are aimed at junior, senior, and graduate students of computer science and information technology, all of whom need some understanding of the fundamentals of programming languages. The books should also be of interest to professional software engineers, especially project leaders responsible for language evaluation and selection, designers and implementors of language processors, and designers of new languages and extensions to existing languages.

To derive maximum benefit from this book, the reader should be able to program in at least two contrasting high-level languages. Language concepts can best be understood by comparing how they are supported by different languages. A reader who knows only Pascal (say) should learn a contrasting language, such as ML, at the same time as studying this book.

The reader will also need to be comfortable with some elementary concepts from discrete mathematics – sets, functions, relations, and predicate logic – as these are used to explain a variety of programming language concepts. The relevant mathematical concepts are briefly reviewed in Chapters 2 and 14, in order to keep this book reasonably self-contained.

The three books together attempt to cover all the most important aspects of a large subject. Where necessary, depth has been sacrificed for breadth. Thus the really serious student will need to follow up with more advanced studies. Each book has an extensive bibliography, and each chapter closes with pointers to further reading on the topics covered by the chapter.

Acknowledgments

First of all, I want to thank Bill Findlay and John Hughes for the chapters they have kindly contributed to this book. Their expertise, on concurrent programming and functional programming respectively, has made this book broader in scope than I could have made it myself.

Two persons have profoundly influenced the way I have organized this book. These are Bob Tennent and Peter Mosses.

Bob Tennent's own book *Programming Language Principles* was published by Prentice Hall International in 1981. Previous books (and some more recent ones!) on programming languages have tended to be *syntax-oriented*. They would examine several popular languages feature by feature, without offering much insight into the underlying concepts or suggesting how future languages might better be designed. Tennent's book is *semantics-oriented*. He first identifies and explains powerful and general semantic concepts, and only then analyses particular programming languages in terms of the concepts underlying them. Research into programming language semantics, by Christopher Strachey and others, has produced valuable insights into language design issues, and Tennent's book reflects these insights in an informal way. In this book I have attempted to follow Tennent's approach, but placing more emphasis on concepts that have gained in importance during the 1980s.

Peter Mosses' more recent work on semantics has produced new insights into the structure·of programming languages. I am fortunate to have collaborated with him and thus benefited from his insights. Each programming language has several *faeets* in terms of which it can be analysed. In the *functional facet*, values are computed and then immediately used. In the *imperative facet*, values are propagated through being held in storage. In the *binding facet*, values are propagated through bindings to identifiers. In the *communicative facet*, values are propagated by messages between concurrent processes. These four facets are predominant in the worlds of expressions, commands (statements), declarations, and concurrent processes, respectively. Mosses' analysis has suggested a structure for much of this book: Chapters 2, 3, 4, and 9 examine the various facets; Chapters 5 and 6 examine ways in which pieces of program with various facets are abstracted or encapsulated.

For providing a stimulating environment in which to think about programming language issues, I am grateful to colleagues and visitors in the Computing Science Department of Glasgow University, in particular Malcolm Atkinson, Peter Buneman, Kieran Clenaghan, Bill Findlay, John Hughes, and Phil Wadler. I have also been strongly influenced, in many different ways, by the work of Luca Cardelli, Frank DeRemer, Edsger Dijkstra, Tony Hoare, Jean Ichbiah, Mehdi Jazayeri, Robin Milner, and Niklaus Wirth.

I am particularly grateful to Tony Hoare, editor of the Prentice Hall International Series in Computer Science, for his encouragement and advice, freely and generously offered when I was still planning this book. Helen Martin, senior editor at Prentice Hall International, could not have been more helpful in guiding this book from initial planning through to production; and by their painstaking efforts Helen Simms and the copy editor helped me to remove what I hope were the last few errors. The reviewers by their constructive criticisms of an earlier draft have helped me to improve this book, as have Satnam Singh, Kevin Waite, and Brian Wichmann by reading and commenting on parts of the earlier draft.

Finally, the patience of my family – Helen, Susanne, and Jeffrey – deserves to be acknowledged above all. They have had to tolerate my closeting myself for hours at a time cutting, polishing, and repolishing the text, and (worse still) monopolizing the home computer. To them I dedicate this book.

Glasgow   D.A.W.
October, 1989

CHAPTER ONE

Introduction

1.1 Programming linguistics

The first high-level programming languages were designed during the 1950s. Ever since then, programming languages have been a fascinating and productive area of study. Programmers endlessly debate the relative merits of their favorite programming languages, sometimes with almost religious zeal. On a more academic level, computer scientists search for ways to design languages that combine expressive power with simplicity and efficiency.

The study of programming languages is sometimes called *programming linguistics* – by analogy with *(natural) linguistics*, which is the study of natural languages. An illustration of this analogy is that both programming languages and natural languages have *syntax* (form) and *semantics* (meaning). The analogy cannot be taken too far. Programming languages cannot be compared with natural languages in terms of their range, expressiveness, or subtlety. On the other hand, a natural language is nothing more nor less than what a group of people speak and write, so the natural linguist is restricted to analysing existing languages; whereas programming languages are consciously designed, and can be implemented on computers.

Programming linguistics therefore has several aspects, which we discuss briefly in the following subsections.

1.1.1 Concepts and paradigms

Every programming language is an artifact, and as such has been consciously designed. Some languages have been designed by a single person, for example Pascal. Others have been designed by large groups of persons, notably PL/I and Ada. Experience suggests that languages designed by single persons, or small groups, tend to be more compact and coherent than languages designed by large groups.

A programming language, to be worthy of the name, must meet certain requirements.

The programming language must be *universal*. That is to say, every problem

1

must have a solution that can be programmed in the language, if that problem can be solved at all by a computer. This might seem to be a very strong requirement, but even a very small language can meet it: any language in which we can define recursive functions will be universal. On the other hand, a language with neither recursion nor iteration would not be universal. There are certain application languages that are not universal, but it would be unreasonable to describe them as *programming* languages.

In practice, the programming language should also be reasonably *natural* for solving problems, at least problems within its intended application area. For example, a language whose only data types are numbers and arrays might be natural for solving numerical problems, but would be less natural for solving problems in commercial data processing or artificial intelligence.

A further fundamental requirement is for the programming language to be *implementable* on a computer. That is to say, it must be possible to execute every well-formed program in the language. Mathematical notation (in its full generality) is not implementable, because in this notation it is possible to formulate problems that cannot be solved by any computer. Natural languages also are not implementable, for entirely different reasons: they are too imprecise, and they tend to ambiguity.

In practice, the programming language should be capable of an acceptably *efficient* implementation. There is plenty of room for debate over what is acceptably efficient, especially as the efficiencies of language implementations are strongly influenced by currently available computer architectures. Fortran, C, and Pascal programmers might expect their programs to be as efficient, within a factor of 2–5, as the corresponding assembly-language programs. Prolog programmers have to accept an order of magnitude less efficiency, but would justify this on the grounds that this language is far more natural within its own application area; besides, they hope that new computer architectures will eventually appear that are more suited for executing Prolog programs than conventional architectures.

In this textbook we shall study the concepts that underlie the design of programming languages: values, storage, bindings, abstraction, encapsulation, type systems, sequencers, and concurrency. Programming language design itself is extremely difficult to do well, and is best left to experienced computer scientists. Nevertheless, as programmers we can all benefit by studying these concepts. Programming languages are our most basic tools, which we must thoroughly master. Whenever we have to learn a new language and discover how it can be effectively exploited to construct reliable well-structured programs, and whenever we have to decide which language is most suitable for solving a given problem, a basic understanding of language concepts is indispensable. A new language can be mastered most effectively if the underlying concepts it shares with other languages are well understood.

Just as important as the individual concepts are the ways in which they may be put together to form complete programming languages, and the styles of programming that these languages support: imperative programming, functional programming, logic programming, and so on. We shall also study these *paradigms* in this textbook.

1.1.2 Syntax and semantics

Every language has syntax and semantics:

- The *syntax* of a programming language is concerned with the *form* of programs, i.e., how expressions, commands, declarations, etc., are put together to form programs.
- The *semantics* of a programming language is concerned with the *meaning* of programs, i.e., how they behave when executed on computers.

A language's syntax influences how programs are written by the programmer, read by other programmers, and parsed by the computer. A language's semantics determines how programs are *composed* by the programmer, *understood* by other programmers, and *interpreted* by the computer. Syntax is important, but semantics is more important still.

In this textbook we shall pay little attention to syntactic issues. A given construct might be provided in several programming languages, with variations in syntax that are essentially superficial. Semantic issues are more important. We need to appreciate subtle differences in meaning between apparently similar constructs. We need to see whether a given language confuses distinct concepts, or supports an important concept inadequately, or fails to support it at all.

In this textbook we shall concentrate on semantic concepts. We study those concepts that are so fundamentally important that they are supported (or ought to be supported) by nearly every programming language.

In order to avoid distracting syntactic variations, wherever possible we shall illustrate each concept using the following languages: Pascal, ML, and Ada. The choice of Pascal needs justification, as it is now middle-aged, and its design defects are numerous. However, Pascal is very widely known, and its defects are themselves very instructive – many examples and exercises in this textbook suggest ways of tidying up Pascal. Ada is a descendant of Pascal, but ML makes a sharp contrast. Ada and ML are more modern than Pascal, but neither is by any means perfect. The ideal programming language has not yet been designed, and is never likely to be!

1.1.3 Language processors

This textbook is concerned only with *high-level* programming languages, i.e., languages that are (more or less) machine-independent. Such languages are implemented by *compiling* programs into machine language, by *interpreting* them, or by some combination of compilation and interpretation.

Any system for processing programs – executing them, or preparing them for execution – is called a *language processor*. Language processors include compilers, interpreters, and auxiliary tools like syntax-directed editors.

A programming language must be implementable, but this does not mean that programmers need to know in detail how a language is implemented in order to understand it thoroughly. Accordingly, implementation issues are ignored in this textbook, except where they have an important influence on language design.

1.2 Historical background

Today's programming languages are the product of developments that started in the 1950s. Numerous language concepts have been invented, tested, and improved by being incorporated in successive languages. With very few exceptions, the design of each language has been strongly influenced by experience with earlier languages. A brief historical survey gives us some impression of the development of the concepts introduced in this textbook and the ancestry of the major programming languages. It also reminds us that today's languages are not the *end* product of developments in language design; exciting new concepts and paradigms are still being developed, and the programming language scene ten years from now might turn out to be rather different from today's.

Figure 1.1 summarizes the dates and ancestry of several important languages. This is not the place for a comprehensive survey, so only the major languages can be mentioned. The major languages have often been partly influenced by earlier, minor languages, but there is not enough space here to trace all these influences.

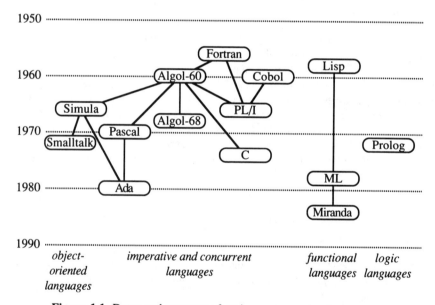

Figure 1.1 Dates and ancestry of major programming languages.

The earliest major high-level programming languages were *Fortran* and *Cobol*. Fortran introduced symbolic expressions, and subprograms with parameters; Cobol introduced the concept of data description. In other respects these languages (in their original forms) were fairly low-level; for example, control flow was largely governed by thinly disguised jump instructions. (Fortran and Cobol, and many other languages, have developed quite a long way from their original designs.)

The first major language designed for communicating algorithms, rather than just for programming a computer, was *Algol-60*. This introduced the concept of block structure, whereby variables, procedures, etc., could be declared wherever in the program they were needed. Algol-60 influenced numerous successor languages so strongly that they are collectively called *Algol-like* languages.

Fortran and Algol-60 were most useful for numerical computation, and Cobol for commercial data processing. *PL/I* was an attempt to design a general-purpose language by merging features from all three earlier languages. It also introduced rather low-level forms of exceptions and concurrency, and many other features. The resulting language was huge, complex, incoherent, and difficult to implement. Experience with PL/I showed that simply piling feature upon feature is a bad way to make a language more powerful and general-purpose.

A better way to gain expressive power is to choose an adequate set of concepts and to combine them systematically. This was the design philosophy of *Algol-68*; the programmer can for example define arrays of integers, arrays of arrays, arrays of procedures, etc., and likewise define procedures that take or return integers, arrays, procedures, etc. It was *Pascal*, however, that turned out to be the most popular of the Algol-like languages, because it is simple, systematic, and efficiently implementable. Pascal and Algol-68 were among the first languages with rich control structures, rich data types, and type definitions.

Pascal's powerful successor, *Ada*, introduced packages and generics – designed to aid the construction of large modular programs – as well as high-level forms of exceptions and concurrency. Like PL/I, Ada was intended by its designers to become *the* standard general-purpose language. Such a stated ambition is perhaps very rash, and Ada also attracted a lot of criticism. For example, Tony Hoare memorably remarked that Pascal, like Algol-60 before it, was a marked advance on its successors! Nevertheless, Ada was far better designed than PL/I, and a study of Ada is instructive.

Certain trends can be discerned in the history of programming languages. One has been a trend towards higher levels of *abstraction*. The mnemonics and symbolic labels of assembly languages abstract away from operation codes and machine addresses. Variables and assignment abstract away from storage fetch and update. Data structures abstract away from storage structures. Control structures abstract away from jumps. Procedures abstract away from subroutines. Block structure and modules achieve forms of encapsulation, which help to make programs modular. Generics abstract parts of the program away from the types of values on which they operate, in the interests of reusability.

Another trend has been a proliferation of programming paradigms. All the languages so far mentioned are *imperative* programming languages, characterized by the use of commands that update variables. The imperative programming paradigm is still the dominant one, but other paradigms are rapidly gaining popularity.

Smalltalk is based on classes of objects, an object being a variable that may be accessed only through operations associated with it. Smalltalk is an example of an *object-oriented* language, which is a highly structured kind of imperative language in which entire programs are constructed from such object classes. Object-oriented programming derives from concepts first tried in Simula, yet another Algol-like language.

That significant problems can be solved without resorting to variables was demonstrated at a remarkably early date by *Lisp*, a language that (in its pure form) is based entirely on functions over lists and trees. Lisp was the ancestor of the *functional* programming languages. *ML* and *Miranda* are modern functional languages; they treat functions as first-class values, and also incorporate advanced type systems.

As noted above, mathematical notation in its full generality is not implementable. Nevertheless, many language designers have sought to exploit subsets of mathematical notation in programming languages. A *logic* programming language is one based on a subset of mathematical logic. The computer is programmed to infer relationships between values, rather than to compute output values from input values. *Prolog* made logic programming popular. Prolog (in its pure form) is rather weak and inefficient, however, and it has been adulterated by nonlogical features to make it more usable as a programming language.

1.3   Further reading

Comparative studies of programming languages may be found in books by Horowitz (1987), Pratt (1984), and Wilson and Clark (1988). The history of programming languages up to the 1970s has been the theme of a major conference, reported in Wexelblat (1980).

The languages shown in Figure 1.1 are described in the following works:

Language	Description or overview	Textbook
Ada	Ichbiah (1983)	Watt *et al.* (1987)
Algol-60	Naur (1963)	
Algol-68	van Wijngaarden *et al.* (1976)	McGettrick (1978)
C	Harbison and Steele (1987)	Kernighan and Ritchie (1988)
Cobol	ANSI (1974)	Welland (1983)
Fortran	ANSI (1966), ANSI (1978)	Ellis (1982)
Lisp	McCarthy *et al.* (1965)	Winston and Horn (1984)
Miranda	Turner (1986)	Bird and Wadler (1988)
ML	Harper *et al.* (1988)	Wikström (1987)
Pascal	BSI (1982)	Findlay and Watt (1985)
PL/I	ANSI (1976)	Conway and Gries (1979)
Prolog		Malpas (1987)
Simula	Dahl *et al.* (1970)	Birtwistle *et al.* (1975)
Smalltalk	Goldberg and Robson (1983)	Goldberg and Robson (1983)

Exercises 1

Note: The longer exercises are marked *; projects are marked **.

1.1   Here is a whimsical exercise to get you started. Some programming languages are more verbose than others. For each language that you know, determine the length of the shortest possible program that *does nothing at all*. This is quite a good measure of the language's verbosity!

1.2*   The brief historical survey of Section 1.2 mentions only those programming languages that have been particularly influential, in the *author's* opinion. If a favorite language of yours has been omitted, develop an argument that your language is important enough to be included. Show where your language should be placed in Figure 1.1.

1.3*   Basic, Cobol, and Fortran are archaic, but still the most commonly used programming languages in the world. Can you explain this paradox?

CHAPTER TWO

Values

Data are the raw material of computation. In a very real sense, data are at least as important as programs. A large volume of data, such as a telephone directory, a dictionary, census data, or geological data collected by a satellite, might well have economic value exceeding that of the relatively simple programs that manipulate it. So it is not surprising that in computer science the study of data is considered as an important topic in its own right.

In this chapter we study the *types* of value that may be manipulated as data in programming languages, including primitive, composite, and recursive types; *type systems* that constrain the operations that may be performed on values; and the kinds of *expression* that may be used in programs to compute new values from old. (In Chapter 3 we shall study how values may be *stored*, and in Chapter 4 how they may be *bound* to identifiers.)

2.1 Values and types

The term *value* is often used rather loosely in computer science. In this book we shall classify as a value anything that may be evaluated, stored, incorporated in a data structure, passed as an argument to a procedure or function, returned as a function result, and so on. In other words, we define a value to be any entity that exists during a computation.

For example, in Pascal we find the following sorts of value:

- primitive values (truth values, characters, enumerands, integers, and real numbers)
- composite values (records, arrays, sets, and files)
- pointers
- references to variables
- procedure and function abstractions

The first three of these are fairly obvious; primitive, composite, and pointer values can be used in nearly all the ways mentioned above. However, it might seem surprising to include references to variables, and procedure and function abstractions, since these entities cannot be stored or incorporated in data structures. We count them as values because they can be passed as arguments. (We use *abstraction* as a collective term for procedures, functions, and similar entities in other languages.)

In ML we find the following sorts of value:

- primitive values (truth values, integers, real numbers, and strings)
- composite values (tuples, records, constructions, lists, and arrays)
- function abstractions
- references to variables

In ML, function abstractions and references to variables can be used in exactly the same ways as any other values.

We find it useful to group values into *types*, as suggested by the lists above. To take a simple example, we usually make a clear distinction between truth values and integers, and we regard addition and multiplication as suitable operations on integers but not on truth values.

What exactly *is* a type? The most obvious answer, perhaps, is that a type is a set of values. When we say that v is a value of type T, we mean simply that $v \in T$. When we say that an expression E is of type T, we are asserting that the result of evaluating E will be a value of type T.

However, not every set of values is suitable to be regarded as a type. We insist that all the values in a type exhibit uniform behavior under operations associated with the type. Thus the set {13, *true*, *Monday*} is not a type; but {*false*, *true*} is a type because its values exhibit uniform behavior under the operations of logical negation, conjunction, and disjunction; and {..., –2, –1, 0, +1, +2, ...} is a type because all its values exhibit uniform behavior under addition, multiplication, and so on. Thus we see that a type is characterized not only by its set of values but also by the operations on these values. We shall explore the nature of types further in Chapters 6 and 7.

Every programming language has both *primitive types*, whose values are atomic, and *composite types*, whose values are composed from simpler values. Some languages also have *recursive types*, a recursive type being one whose values may be composed from other values of the same type. We examine primitive, composite, and recursive types in the next three sections.

2.2 Primitive types

A *primitive type* is one whose values are atomic and therefore cannot be decomposed into simpler values.

The choice of primitive types in a programming language tells us much about that language's intended application area. A language intended for commercial data processing (e.g., Cobol) is likely to have primitive types whose values are fixed-length strings and fixed-point numbers. A language intended for numerical computation (e.g., Fortran) is likely to have primitive types whose values are real numbers (with a choice of precisions) and perhaps also complex numbers. A language intended for string process-ing (e.g., Snobol) is likely to have a primitive type whose values are strings of any length.

Similar primitive types often crop up in different languages under different names. For example, Pascal has `Boolean`, `Integer`, and `Real`; ML has `bool`, `int`, and `real`. However, these name differences are of no significance. For the sake of consis-tency, we shall use the following notation for the more common primitive types:

Truth-Value	=	{*false*, *true*}	(2.1)
Integer	=	{..., −2, −1, 0, +1, +2, ...}	(2.2)
Real	=	{..., −1.0, ..., 0.0, ..., +1.0, ...}	(2.3)
Character	=	{..., 'a', 'b', ..., 'z', ...}	(2.4)

We shall write the truth values consistently as *false* and *true*. In some languages they are denoted by literals such as **false** and **true**. In other languages they are denoted by predefined constant identifiers `false` and `true`.

Note that each of the types Integer, Real, and Character is implementation-defined; that is to say, it has a set of values that may be defined differently by each im-plementation of the programming language. Integer is an implementation-defined range of the whole numbers, Real is an implementation-defined subset of the (rational) real numbers, and Character is an implementation-defined set of characters. We see here that hardware limitations and variations have some influence even on high-level languages, causing problems for programmers who wish to write portable programs.

In Pascal and Ada, we can define a completely new primitive type by enumerating its values (more precisely, by enumerating identifiers that will denote its values). Such a type is called an *enumeration type*, and its values are called *enumerands*.

Example 2.1
Consider the Pascal type definition:

```
type Month = (jan, feb, mar, apr, may, jun,
              jul, aug, sep, oct, nov, dec)
```

This defines a new type, whose values are twelve enumerands:

Month = {*jan, feb, mar, apr, may, jun, jul, aug, sep, oct, nov, dec*}

These enumerands are distinct from the values of any other type.

Note that we must carefully distinguish between the enumerands (which for convenience we have written as *jan, feb*, etc.) and the identifiers that denote them in the program (`jan`, `feb`, etc.). This distinction is necessary because, for example, `dec` might later be redefined to denote something else (perhaps a procedure to decrement an integer), but the enumerand *dec* still exists and can be computed, e.g., by '`succ (nov.)`'.   □

In Pascal we can also define a subset of an existing type, by means of a *subrange type*. For example, the subrange type '`28..31`' has the set of values {28, 29, 30, 31}, a subset of Integer. The subset must be a range of consecutive values. We shall examine the more general notion of *subtype* in Section 7.6.

A *discrete primitive type* is a primitive type whose values have a one-to-one relationship with (a range of) integers. This is an important concept in Pascal and Ada, in which values of any discrete primitive type may be used in a variety of operations, such as counting, case selection, and array indexing. In most other languages, only integers may be used in these operations.

We are sometimes interested in the *cardinality* of a set (or of a type). We write '#*S*' to stand for the number of distinct values in *S*. For example:

```
# Truth-Value  = 2
# Month        = 12              (above)
# Integer      = 2 × maxint + 1  (in Pascal)
```

2.3 Composite types

A **composite type** (or *structured data type*) is a type whose values are composed or structured from simpler values. Programming languages support a wide variety of data structures: tuples, records, variants, unions, arrays, sets, strings, lists, trees, serial files, direct files, relations, etc. The variety may seem bewildering, but in fact these types can all be understood in terms of a small number of structuring concepts. These concepts are:

- Cartesian products (tuples and records)
- disjoint unions (variants and unions)
- mappings (arrays and functions)
- powersets (sets)
- recursive types (dynamic data structures)

The first four are discussed in this section. Recursive types will be discussed in Section 2.4.

Each programming language provides its own notation for describing composite types. Here we shall introduce mathematical notation that is simple, standard, and suitable for defining sets of values composed in the above ways. The notation is powerful enough to describe a variety of data structures.

2.3.1 Cartesian products

The simplest kind of value composition is the **Cartesian product**, whereby values of two (possibly different) types are paired. We use the notation $S \times T$ to stand for the set of all ordered pairs of values, such that the first value of each pair is chosen from set S and the second value from set T. Formally:

$$S \times T = \{ (x, y) \mid x \in S;\ y \in T \} \tag{2.5}$$

This is illustrated in Figure 2.1.

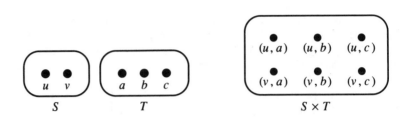

Figure 2.1 Cartesian product of two sets.

The basic operations on a pair are simply selection of its first component and selection of its second component.

We can easily infer the cardinality of a Cartesian product:

$$\#(S \times T) = \#S \times \#T \tag{2.6}$$

This motivates the use of the notation '×' for Cartesian product.

We can extend the notion of Cartesian product from pairs to triples, quadruples, and so on. In general, the notation $S_1 \times S_2 \times \ldots \times S_n$ stands for the set of all *n-tuples*, such that the first component of each *n*-tuple is chosen from S_1, the second from S_2, and so on.

The *tuples* of ML, the *records* of Cobol, Pascal, Ada, and ML, and the so-called *structures* of Algol-68 and C, can all be understood in terms of Cartesian products. A Pascal record type of the form:

```
record
    I₁  : T₁;
    ...
    Iₙ  : Tₙ
end
```

has values that are *n*-tuples in the set $T_1 \times \ldots \times T_n$.

Example 2.2
The following Pascal record type:

```
type Date = record
                m : Month;
                d : 1..31
            end
```

has the set of values Date = $\{jan, feb, \ldots, dec\} \times \{1, \ldots, 31\}$. These values are the following 372 pairs:

(*jan*, 1)	(*jan*, 2)	(*jan*, 3)	...	(*jan*, 31)
(*feb*, 1)	(*feb*, 2)	(*feb*, 3)	...	(*feb*, 31)
...	...	...	...	...
(*dec*, 1)	(*dec*, 2)	(*dec*, 3)	...	(*dec*, 31)

Note that some values in Date do not correspond to real dates. This type is only an approximate model for its real-world counterpart – a common phenomenon.

The identifiers m and d are used to access individual components of a record of type Date, e.g.:

```
var someday : Date;
...
someday.d := 29;   someday.m := feb
```

These commands access the second and first components of someday, respectively. The use of identifiers like m and d relieves the programmer of any need to remember the order of the components. ☐

ML has notation that corresponds directly to Cartesian products. The tuple type '$T_1 * \ldots * T_n$' has the set of values $T_1 \times \ldots \times T_n$.

Example 2.3
The following ML tuple type:

```
type person = string * string * int * real
```

has the set of values Person = String × String × Integer × Real.

A value someone of type person would be decomposed as follows:

```
val (surname, forename, age, height) = someone
...
if age >= 18 then … else …
```

Thus, to access the individual components of a tuple, the programmer must remember their positions within the tuple type. But the type definition gives no clue as to the intended use of each component, e.g., is the first component the person's forename or surname?

For such reasons, ML also provides record types:

```
type person = { surname  : string,
                forename : string,
                age      : int,
                height   : real   }
```

This is essentially similar to Pascal's notation. ☐

A special case of the Cartesian product is one where all tuple components are chosen from the same set. The tuples in this case are said to be *homogeneous*. We write:

$$S^n = S \times \ldots \times S \tag{2.7}$$

for the set of homogeneous n-tuples whose components are all chosen from set S. The cardinality of a homogeneous n-tuple is given by:

$$\#(S^n) = (\#S)^n \tag{2.8}$$

which motivates the superscript notation.

Finally, let us consider the very special case where $n = 0$. Equation (2.8) tells us that S^0 should have exactly one value. This value is the 0-tuple (), a tuple with no components at all. We shall find it useful to define a type consisting of this single value:

$$\text{Unit} = \{ () \} \tag{2.9}$$

Unit corresponds to the type known as `unit` in ML, and as **void** in Algol-68 and C. Note that Unit is *not* the empty set; it contains a single tuple that happens to have no components.

2.3.2   Disjoint unions

Another kind of value composition is the ***disjoint union***, whereby a value is chosen from either of two (usually different) types. We use the notation $S + T$ to stand for the set of values in which each value is chosen from either set S or set T, and in which each value is *tagged* to indicate which set it was chosen from. Formally:

$$S + T = \{ \textit{left } x \mid x \in S \} \cup \{ \textit{right } y \mid y \in T \} \tag{2.10}$$

Here values chosen from S have been tagged *left*, and values chosen from T have been tagged *right*. The tags serve only to distinguish which set each value was chosen from; therefore they must be distinct, but otherwise may be chosen freely.

Disjoint union is illustrated in Figure 2.2.

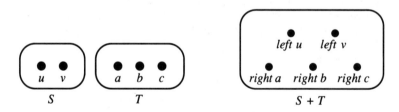

Figure 2.2 Disjoint union of two sets.

The basic operations on a value in $S + T$ are: (a) testing of its tag to determine whether it was chosen from S or T; and (b) *projection* to the original value in either S or T, as the case may be. For example, by testing the value *right b* we can determine that it was chosen from T, and therefore we can project it to the original value b in T.

We can easily infer the cardinality of a disjoint union:

$$\#(S + T) = \#S + \#T \tag{2.11}$$

This motivates the use of the notation '+' for disjoint union.

We can extend disjoint union to any number of sets. In general, the notation $S_1 + S_2 + \ldots + S_n$ stands for the set in which each value is chosen from *one* of $S_1, S_2,$

..., or S_n. Each value chosen from S_i may be tagged by i.

The *variant records* of Pascal and Ada, the *unions* of Algol-68, the so-called *constructions* of ML, and the so-called *algebraic types* of Miranda, can all be understood in terms of disjoint unions.

In its simplest form, a Pascal variant record type looks like this:

```
record
   case I : T of
      L₁ : (I₁ : T₁);
      ...
      Lₙ : (Iₙ : Tₙ)
end
```

where the literals L_1, ..., and L_n cover all the values of the discrete primitive type T. This variant record type has the set of values $T_1 + ... + T_n$, with each value from T_i tagged by the value of L_i.

Example 2.4
Consider the following Pascal variant record type:

```
type Accuracy = (exact, approx);
     Number   = record
                   case acc : Accuracy of
                      exact: (ival : Integer);
                      approx: (rval : Real)
                end
```

The set of values of this type is Number = Integer + Real. Its values are:

$$\{..., exact\ (-2), exact\ (-1), exact\ 0, exact\ 1, exact\ 2, ...\}$$
$$\cup\ \{..., approx\ (-1.0), ..., approx\ 0.0, ..., approx\ 1.0, ...\}$$

The tags here are the values *exact* and *approx*. As this example illustrates, in Pascal tags are values of any discrete primitive type chosen by the programmer.   □

In Pascal, a variant record's tag and variant components may be accessed in the same way as ordinary record components. This gives rise to a notorious insecurity. Consider a variable num of type Number. If num currently has the value *exact* 7, then num.acc will have value *exact*, and num.ival will have value 7. The program might attempt to access num.rval, which currently does not exist – a particularly unpleasant kind of run-time error. Assignment of *approx* to num.acc has the side effect of destroying num.ival and creating num.rval with an undefined value, so num's value has changed in one step from *exact* 7 to *approx undefined*.

The safest way to decompose a variant record is by using a *case* command:

```
var rounded : Integer;
...
case num.acc of
   exact:  rounded := num.ival;
```

```
approx: rounded := round (num.rval)
end
```

In ML, a so-called *datatype* declaration allows us to introduce a new disjoint union type. This is illustrated by the following example.

Example 2.5
Consider the ML type defined by:

```
datatype number  =  exact  of int
                   | approx of real
```

The set of values of this type is Number = Integer + Real. Its values are:

$$\{..., exact\,(-2), exact\,(-1), exact\,0, exact\,1, exact\,2, ...\}$$
$$\cup \{..., approx\,(-1.0), ..., approx\,0.0, ..., approx\,1.0, ...\}$$

similarly to Example 2.4. The tags here are the identifiers *exact* and *approx*. As this example illustrates, in ML tags are just identifiers (not values). ☐

Tagged values are called *constructions* in ML. Constructions are formed by expressions such as 'exact (i+1)' and 'approx (r/3.0)'. They can be decomposed only by *pattern matching*. If num is of type number, the following *case* expression computes the integer nearest to the number represented by num:

```
case num of
   exact i  => i
 | approx r => round (r)
```

Suppose that the value of num is *approx* 3.1416. This value matches the *pattern* 'approx r', so the subexpression 'round(r)' is evaluated with r bound to 3.1416, yielding 3. This controlled form of decomposition ensures that the insecurity of Pascal variant records does not exist in ML.

Example 2.6
In Pascal record types, the distinct concepts of Cartesian product and disjoint union are somewhat confused. Consider the following type definitions:

```
type Shape  = (point, circle, box);
     Figure = record
                 x, y : Real;
                 case figureshape : Shape of
                    point: ( );
                    circle: (radius : Real);
                    box:    (height, width : Real)
             end
```

The set of values of this type is Figure = Real × Real × (Unit + Real + (Real × Real)). Here are a few of these values:

(1.0, 2.0, *point* ())	– the point (1.0, 2.0)
(0.0, 0.0, *circle* 5.0)	– a circle of radius 5.0 centered at the origin
(1.5, 2.0, *box* (3.0, 4.0))	– a 3.0×4.0 box centered at (1.5, 2.0)

Each value in Figure is a triple. The first and second components of each triple are real numbers; the third component is a disjoint union. Within the latter, the tags are the values *point*, *circle*, and *box*. The unique value tagged *point* is the 0-tuple (); each value tagged *circle* is a single real number; and each value tagged *box* is a pair of real numbers. □

Notice that disjoint union is *not* the same as ordinary set union. The tags allow us to identify the source of any value in $S + T$, which is not the case in $S \cup T$ unless S and T happen to be disjoint. In fact, if $T = \{a, b, c\}$, then:

$$T \cup T = \{a, b, c\} = T$$
$$T + T = \{left\ a, left\ b, left\ c, right\ a, right\ b, right\ c\} \neq T$$

2.3.3 Mappings

The notion of a **mapping** (or **function**) from one set to another is extremely important in programming languages, and crops up in several guises. Consider a mapping m that maps every value x in set S to a value in set T. The latter value is called the *image* of x under m, and is conventionally written $m(x)$. We write:

$$m : S \rightarrow T$$

to state that m is a mapping from S to T.

Two different mappings from $S = \{u, v\}$ to $T = \{a, b, c\}$ are illustrated in Figure 2.3. The symbol $\mapsto$ is read as 'maps to'; thus $\{u \mapsto a, v \mapsto c\}$ stands for the mapping that maps u to a and v to c.

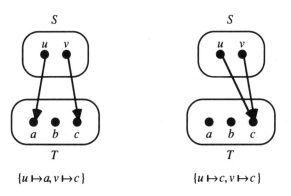

$$\{u \mapsto a, v \mapsto c\} \qquad \{u \mapsto c, v \mapsto c\}$$

Figure 2.3 Two different mappings in $S \rightarrow T$.

The notation $S \rightarrow T$ stands for the set of *all* such mappings. Formally:

$$S \rightarrow T = \{ m \mid x \in S \Rightarrow m(x) \in T \} \tag{2.12}$$

This is illustrated in Figure 2.4.

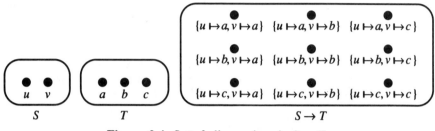

Figure 2.4 Set of all mappings in $S \rightarrow T$.

Let us deduce the cardinality of $S \rightarrow T$. For each value in S, the number of possible images under a mapping in $S \rightarrow T$ is just #T. There are #S values in S. Therefore:

$$\# \, (S \rightarrow T) \; = \; (\#T)^{\#S} \tag{2.13}$$

The *arrays* found in nearly every programming language can be understood in terms of mappings. An array in fact represents a *finite mapping*, i.e., a mapping from a finite set (called the array's *index set*) to some other set (called the array's *component set*). Conventionally, an array is implemented by storing all its components in a sequence, and access to components is implemented by mapping values in the index set to positions in that sequence.

Most programming languages restrict an array's index set to be a range of integers. Some languages even fix the lower bound of this range (typically at 0 or 1); other languages allow both bounds to be chosen by the programmer.

Pascal and Ada allow an array's index set to be any discrete primitive type. A Pascal array type of the form:

array [S] **of** T

has values that are finite mappings in the set $S \rightarrow T$.

Example 2.7
Consider the Pascal array type defined as follows:

```
type Color = (red, green, blue);
     Pixel = array [Color] of 0..1
```

The set of values of this array type is Pixel = Color $\rightarrow$ {0, 1}, where Color = {*red, green, blue*}. The values in Pixel are the following eight finite mappings:

{*red* ↦ 0, *green* ↦ 0, *blue* ↦ 0}	{*red* ↦ 1, *green* ↦ 0, *blue* ↦ 0}
{*red* ↦ 0, *green* ↦ 0, *blue* ↦ 1}	{*red* ↦ 1, *green* ↦ 0, *blue* ↦ 1}
{*red* ↦ 0, *green* ↦ 1, *blue* ↦ 0}	{*red* ↦ 1, *green* ↦ 1, *blue* ↦ 0}
{*red* ↦ 0, *green* ↦ 1, *blue* ↦ 1}	{*red* ↦ 1, *green* ↦ 1, *blue* ↦ 1}

If p is of type `Pixel` and c is of type `Color`, then `p[c]` accesses that component of p whose index is the value of c.   □

Most programming languages also have multidimensional arrays. A component of an *n*-dimensional array is accessed using *n* index values. We can think of an *n*-dimensional array as having a single index that happens to be an *n*-tuple.

Example 2.8
Consider the following Pascal two-dimensional array type:

   type Window = **array** [0..511, 0..255] **of** 0..1

The set of values of this type is Window = {0, ..., 511} × {0, ..., 255} → {0, 1}. An array of this type is indexed by a pair of integers. Thus `w[8,12]` accesses that component of w whose index is the pair (8, 12).   □

Is further generalization of array types possible? Certainly, the index set must be finite (indeed, small enough that all components can be stored). That rules out arrays indexed by unbounded-length strings or even by the full range of integer numbers. Moreover, the index set must be discrete. That rules out arrays indexed by real numbers. The usual implementation of arrays implies that there should exist an easy-to-compute mapping from the index set to a range of consecutive integers. Even with this restriction, we can envisage arrays indexed by records, for example: see Exercise 2.5.

Apart from arrays, mappings occur in programming languages in the form of *function abstractions*. A function abstraction implements a mapping in $S \to T$ by means of an algorithm, which takes any value in S (the *argument*) and computes its image in T (the *result*). The set S need not be finite.

Example 2.9
Consider the following Pascal function abstraction:

```
function even (n : Integer) : Boolean;
   begin
   even := (n mod 2 = 0)
   end
```

This function abstraction implements one particular mapping in Integer → Truth-Value, namely:

   {0 ↦ *true*, ±1 ↦ *false*, ±2 ↦ *true*, ±3 ↦ *false*, ...}

We could employ a different algorithm:

```
function even (n : Integer) : Boolean;
   begin
   n := abs (n);
   while n > 1 do   n := n - 2;
   even := (n = 0)
   end
```

but this function abstraction implements the same mapping as the one above.

The Pascal standard function `odd` implements a different mapping in Integer → Truth-Value, namely:

$$\{0 \mapsto \textit{false}, \pm1 \mapsto \textit{true}, \pm2 \mapsto \textit{false}, \pm3 \mapsto \textit{true}, \ldots\}$$

We can easily write function abstractions, such as `positive`, `prime`, and `composite`, that implement other mappings in Integer → Truth-Value.   □

A function abstraction is not the same thing as a mathematical function. It *implements* a function by means of a particular algorithm. Algorithms have properties (such as efficiency) that are not shared by mathematical functions. A more radical difference is that in many programming languages a function abstraction may access (and even update) values contained in nonlocal variables. For example, a function abstraction that returns a random number, or the current time of day, does not correspond to an ordinary mathematical function. For these reasons, when using the term 'function' in the context of programming languages, we must be clear whether we mean a mathematical function (mapping) or a function abstraction.

In most programming languages, a function abstraction may have *n* parameters, and will then be passed *n* arguments when called. We can easily fit such a function abstraction into our framework: we view it as receiving a single argument that happens to be an *n*-tuple.

Example 2.10
The following Pascal function abstraction:

```
function power (b : Real; n : Integer) : Real;
   ...
```

implements a particular mapping in Real × Integer → Real. Presumably, it maps the pair (2.5, 2) to 6.25, the pair (2.0, –2) to 0.25, etc.   □

It is noteworthy that both arrays and function abstractions may be understood in terms of mappings (and that both *n*-dimensional arrays and *n*-parameter function abstractions may be understood in terms of mappings from *n*-tuples). Indeed, programmers can sometimes use arrays and function abstractions interchangeably – see Exercise 2.4.

2.3.4   Powersets

The notion of a *set* is another one that crops up in various guises in programming languages. Consider a set of values S. We are interested in values that are themselves subsets of S. The set of all such subsets is called the ***powerset*** of S, and is written $\wp S$. Formally:

$$\wp S = \{ s \mid s \subseteq S \} \tag{2.14}$$

The basic operations on a set are the usual operations of set theory: membership test, inclusion test, union, and intersection.

Each value in S may be either a member or a nonmember of a particular set in $\wp S$. Therefore the cardinality of the powerset of S is given by:

$$\#(\wp S) = 2^{\#S} \tag{2.15}$$

Pascal is almost unique among programming languages in that it directly supports sets. A Pascal set type of the form:

set of *T*

has values that are sets in $\wp T$. All the basic set operations are provided by Pascal.

Example 2.11
Consider the Pascal set type defined as follows:

```
type Color = (red, green, blue);
     Hue   = set of Color
```

The set of values of this set type is Hue = $\wp$ Color, i.e., the set of all subsets of Color = {*red, green, blue*}. These values are the following eight sets:

{ }	{*red*}	{*green*}	{*red, green*}
{*blue*}	{*red, blue*}	{*green, blue*}	{*red, green, blue*}

□

Pascal permits only sets of discrete primitive values (i.e., sets of truth values, sets of characters, sets of enumerands, and sets of integers), because this restriction permits a very efficient implementation of sets. However, there are many programming problems that could be elegantly solved if sets of composite values (e.g., sets of strings, or of records) were permitted. Only a few sophisticated programming languages support such a generality of sets.

Take care not to be confused by the fact that $\wp S$ is a set of values that are themselves sets. Each of $S \times T$, $S + T$, $S \rightarrow T$, and $\wp S$ is a set of values. In the first three cases, the values are pairs, unions, and mappings, respectively. In the fourth case, $\wp S$, the values are themselves sets.

2.4   Recursive types

2.4.1   Lists

A *list* is a sequence of values. A list may have any number of components, including none. The number of components is called the *length* of the list. The unique list with no component is called the *empty list*.

A list is *l.omogeneous* if all its components are of the same type. Here we shall consider only homogeneous lists.

Suppose that we wish to define a type whose values are integer lists. We may define an integer list to be a value that is *either* empty *or* a pair consisting of an integer (its *head*) and a further integer list (its *tail*). This definition is recursive. It may be written as a set equation:

$$\text{Integer-List} = \text{Unit} + (\text{Integer} \times \text{Integer-List}) \tag{2.16}$$

or, in other words:

$$\text{Integer-List} = \{ \, nil \, () \, \}$$
$$\cup \, \{ \, cons \, (i, l) \mid i \in \text{Integer}, \, l \in \text{Integer-List} \, \} \tag{2.17}$$

where we have chosen *nil* and *cons* as tags. For brevity we will abbreviate *nil* () to *nil*.

Equations (2.16) and (2.17) are recursive, like our informal definition of integer lists. But what exactly do these equations mean? Consider the following set of values:

$$\{ \, nil \, \}$$
$$\cup \, \{ \, cons \, (i, nil) \mid i \in \text{Integer} \, \}$$
$$\cup \, \{ \, cons \, (i, cons \, (j, nil)) \mid i, j \in \text{Integer} \, \}$$
$$\cup \, \{ \, cons \, (i, cons \, (j, cons \, (k, nil))) \mid i, j, k \in \text{Integer} \, \}$$
$$\cup \, \dots$$

i.e., the set:

$$\{ \, cons \, (i_1, cons \, (\dots, cons \, (i_n, nil) \dots)) \mid$$
$$n \geq 0; \, i_1, \dots, i_n \in \text{Integer} \, \} \tag{2.18}$$

Set (2.18) corresponds to the set of all *finite* lists of integers. It is easy to show that this set is a solution of equation (2.17).

Set (2.18) is not, however, the only solution of (2.17). Another solution is the set of all *finite and infinite* lists of integers – a solution that is a superset of (2.18). It seems reasonable to discount this solution, however, since our interest is in values that can be computed, and no infinite list can be (completely) computed in a finite amount of time.

Generalizing from the above, the recursive set equation:

$$L = \text{Unit} + (S \times L) \tag{2.19}$$

has one *least* solution for L that corresponds to the set of all finite lists of values chosen from S. All other solutions are supersets of the least solution.

Lists (or sequences) are so widely useful that we introduce the notation $S*$ for the set of all finite lists of values chosen from S. Thus:

$$S* = \text{Unit} + (S \times S*) \tag{2.20}$$

In Pascal and Ada, recursive types must be defined in terms of pointers (for reasons that will be discussed in Section 3.4.2). Modern functional languages like ML, however, allow recursive types to be defined directly.

Example 2.12
The following ML declaration defines a type whose values are lists of integers:

```
datatype intlist =  nil
                  | cons of int * intlist
```

This corresponds to equation (2.16). Note that the phrase 'nil | cons of ...' is an abbreviation for 'nil of unit | cons of ...'.

Some values of type intlist, expressed in ML notation, are as follows:

```
nil
cons (11, nil)
cons(2, cons (3, cons (5, cons (7, nil))))
```

$\square$

In fact, ML has a whole family of list types, such as 'int list' (whose values are integer lists), 'bool list' (whose values are truth-value lists), 'int list list' (whose values are integer-list lists), and so on; list is a predefined type constructor. The basic operations on lists are test for emptiness, and selection of the head or tail of a (nonempty) list. These are predefined, as are further operations such as list concatenation and length measurement. (The latter operations could be defined explicitly in terms of the basic operations.)

2.4.2 Recursive types in general

A *recursive* type is one whose values are composed from values of the same type. A recursive type is defined in terms of itself. List types, discussed above, are recursive types.

In general, the set of values of a recursive type, T, will be defined by a recursive set equation of the form:

$$T = ... T ... \tag{2.21}$$

A recursive set equation may have many solutions. Fortunately, it may be shown that a recursive set equation always has a least solution that is a subset of every other solution. In computation, the least solution is the one in which we are interested.

The least solution to equation (2.21) can be determined iteratively as follows. Substitute the empty set for T in the right-hand side; this gives a first approximation for T. Then substitute this first approximation for T in the right-hand side; this gives a second and better approximation for T. Continue in this way, at each step substituting the latest approximation for T in the right-hand side. Then the successive approximations are larger and larger subsets of the least solution.

The cardinality of a recursive type is infinite. This is true even if every individual value of the type is finite. For example, the set of lists (2.18) is infinitely large, although every individual list in that set is finite. Therefore we can never enumerate *all* the values of a recursive type; but we can get as close as we like, by continuing the iteration long enough.

Example 2.13

The following ML declaration defines a recursive type inttree, whose values are binary trees containing integers at their leaves:

```
datatype inttree =  leaf of int
                   | branch of inttree * inttree
```

Some values of type inttree, expressed in ML notation, are as follows:

```
leaf 11
branch (leaf 11, leaf 5)
branch (branch (branch (leaf 5, leaf 7),
                leaf 9),
        branch (leaf 12, leaf 18))
```

The type definition corresponds to the following recursive set equation:

$$\text{Integer-Tree} = \text{Integer} + (\text{Integer-Tree} \times \text{Integer-Tree}) \tag{2.22}$$

Substituting the empty set for Integer-Tree in (2.22), we get our first approximation:

$$\{ \; leaf \, i \mid i \in \text{Integer} \; \}$$

which is in fact the set of all binary trees of depth 1. Substituting our first approximation for Integer-Tree in (2.22), we get our second approximation:

$$\{ \; leaf \, i \mid i \in \text{Integer} \; \}$$
$$\cup \{ \; branch \, (leaf \, i, leaf \, j) \mid i, j \in \text{Integer} \; \}$$

which is in fact the set of all binary trees of depth 2 or less. Substituting our second approximation for Integer-Tree in (2.22), we get:

$$\{ \; leaf \, i \mid i \in \text{Integer} \; \}$$
$$\cup \{ \; branch \, (leaf \, i, leaf \, j) \mid i, j \in \text{Integer} \; \}$$
$$\cup \{ \; branch \, (leaf \, i, branch \, (leaf \, j, leaf \, k)) \mid i, j, k \in \text{Integer} \; \}$$
$$\cup \{ \; branch \, (branch \, (leaf \, i, leaf \, j), leaf \, k) \mid i, j, k \in \text{Integer} \; \}$$
$$\cup \{ \; branch \, (branch \, (leaf \, i, leaf \, j), branch \, (leaf \, k, leaf \, l)) \mid$$
$$i, j, k, l \in \text{Integer} \; \}$$

which is in fact the set of all binary trees of depth 3 or less. Continuing in this way, we get closer and closer to the set of all finite binary trees. □

2.4.3 Strings

A *string* is a sequence of characters. Strings are supported by all modern programming languages, but no consensus has emerged among language designers on how strings should be classified. The issues are as follows. (a) Should strings be primitive or composite values? (b) What string operations should be provided? Typical string operations are equality test, concatenation, character or substring selection, and lexicographic ordering.

One possibility is to make String a primitive type, with values that are strings of any length. ML adopts this approach. Consequently, ML's string operations (equality test, concatenation, and decomposition into individual characters) are all built-in; they could not be defined in the language itself.

Another approach is to define a string to be an *array* of characters. Pascal and Ada adopt this approach, which makes all the usual array operations automatically applicable to strings. In particular, any character of a string can be selected, by array indexing. A consequence of the Pascal/Ada approach is that a given string variable (like any array variable) may contain only strings of a fixed length. That disadvantage is avoided in Algol-68, which defines a string to be a *flexible array* of characters, and thus a given string variable may contain a string of any length. (The properties of array variables will be discussed in Section 3.2.2.) String operations not provided for arrays in general, such as concatenation and lexicographic ordering, have to be provided specially.

Perhaps the most natural approach is to define a string to be a *list* of characters. Miranda and Prolog adopt this approach, which makes all the usual list operations automatically applicable to strings. In particular, the first character of a string can be selected, but the *n*th character cannot. Useful operations peculiar to strings, such as lexicographic ordering and substring selection, have to be provided in addition to the general list operations.

2.5 Type systems

2.5.1 Static and dynamic typing

Grouping values into types allows the programmer to describe data effectively. A type discipline also prevents programs from performing nonsensical operations, such as multiplying a character by a truth value. In this respect, high-level languages are clearly distinguished from low-level languages where the only 'type' is the byte or word.

To ensure that nonsensical operations are prevented, the language's implementation must provide prior *type checks* on operands. Before a multiplication is performed, for example, both operands must be checked to ensure that they are numbers. Similarly, before a logical operation is performed, both operands must be checked to ensure that they are truth values.

In the case of composite data, we must consider both the form of composition and the types of the individual components. For example, component selection in a record is different from indexing in an array. A type check is needed to ensure that a particular selection operation is applied to a suitable type of composite value.

Although the type check must be performed before the operation itself, there is still an important degree of freedom in the timing of the type check: it can be performed at compile-time or at run-time. This seemingly pragmatic issue in fact underlies an important classification of programming languages, into statically typed and dynamically typed languages.

In a *statically typed* language, every variable and parameter has a fixed type that is chosen by the programmer. Thus the type of each expression can be deduced, and each operation type-checked, at compile-time. Most high-level languages are statically typed.

In a *dynamically typed* language, only the *values* have fixed types. A variable or parameter has no designated type, but may take values of different types at different times. This implies that the operands must be type-checked *immediately* before performing an operation at run-time. Lisp and Smalltalk are examples of dynamically typed languages.

Example 2.14

Consider the following Pascal function definition:

```
function even (n : Integer) : Boolean;
   begin
   even := (n mod 2 = 0)
   end
```

Although we do not know what particular value n will take, we can assert that this value will always be an integer, since n is declared as such. From that assertion we can deduce that the operands of 'mod' will both be integers, and that its result will also be an integer. In turn, we can deduce that the operands of '=' will both be integers. Finally, we can deduce that the value ascribed to even will be a truth value, which is consistent with the declared result type, Boolean.

In each call of this function, e.g., 'even (i+1)', we can similarly check that the argument will indeed be an integer.   □

Example 2.15

Now consider a similar function definition, this time in a hypothetical dynamically typed language:

```
function even (n);
   begin
   even := n mod 2 = 0
   end
```

Now the type of n's value is not known in advance, so the operation 'mod' needs a run-time type check to ensure that its left operand is an integer.

This function could be called with arguments of different types, e.g., 'even (i+1)', or 'even (true)', or 'even (x)' where the type of x's value is itself not known in advance.   □

Example 2.16
The following procedure, also in a hypothetical dynamically typed language, illustrates that dynamic typing is sometimes genuinely useful:

```
procedure readliteral (var item);
    begin
    read a string of nonblanks;
    if the string constitutes an integer literal then
        item := numeric value of the string
    else
        item := the string itself
    end
```

The following commands might be used to read a date in the form '1983 2 23' *or* '1983 FEB 23', and manipulate it into a standard form:

```
read (y);  readliteral (m);  read (d);
if (m>=1) and (m<=12)  then  (* skip *)
else if m = "JAN"      then  m := 1
else if m = "FEB"      then  m := 2
else ...
```

Here the procedure call 'readliteral (m)' will read an integer or string literal, and assign the corresponding integer or string value to the variable m. Subsequently, the type of m's value influences the flow of control.   □

Dynamic typing implies that execution of the program is slowed down by implicit run-time type checks, and also implies that every value must be tagged to identify its type in order to make these type checks possible. These time and space overheads are avoided in a statically typed language, because all type checks are performed at compile-time. A more important advantage of static typing is *security*: type errors are guaranteed to be detected by the compiler, rather than being left to the vagaries of testing. (This is important because type errors account for a significant proportion of programming errors.) The advantage of dynamic typing is flexibility: a procedure such as readliteral would be awkward to program in a statically typed language, where the type discipline tends to 'get in the way'.

2.5.2   Type equivalence

Consider some operation that expects an operand of type T. Suppose that it is given instead an operand whose type turns out to be T'. Then we must check whether T is **equivalent** to T', written $T \equiv T'$. But what exactly does this mean? The answer depends on the programming language. (The following discussion assumes that the language is statically typed.)

One possible definition of type equivalence is as follows:

> *Structural equivalence:* $T \equiv T'$ if and only if T and T' have
> the same set of values.

Structural equivalence is so called because it may be checked by comparing the *structures* of the types T and T'. (It is unnecessary, and in general even impossible, to enumerate all their values!) Structural equivalence is adopted in Algol-68.

The following rules illustrate how we can decide whether types T and T', defined in terms of Cartesian products, disjoint unions, and mappings, are structurally equivalent or not. (We could similarly phrase the rules in terms of the types of a specific programming language.)

- If T and T' are both primitive, then $T \equiv T'$ if and only if T and T' are identical. For example, Integer $\equiv$ Integer.
- If $T = A \times B$ and $T' = A' \times B'$, then $T \equiv T'$ if and only if $A \equiv A'$ and $B \equiv B'$. For example, Integer $\times$ Character $\equiv$ Integer $\times$ Character.
- If $T = A + B$ and $T' = A' + B'$, then $T \equiv T'$ if and only if $A \equiv A'$ and $B \equiv B'$, *or* $A \equiv B'$ and $B \equiv A'$. For example, Integer + Character $\equiv$ Character + Integer.
- If $T = A \to B$ and $T' = A' \to B'$, then $T \equiv T'$ if and only if $A \equiv A'$ and $B \equiv B'$. For example, Integer $\to$ Character $\equiv$ Integer $\to$ Character.
- Otherwise, T is not equivalent to T'.

Although these rules are simple, it is not easy to see whether two *recursive* types are structurally equivalent. Consider the following:

$$T \ \ = \ \text{Unit} + (A \times T)$$
$$T' \ = \ \text{Unit} + (A \times T')$$

Intuitively, T and T' *are* structurally equivalent. However, the reasoning needed to decide whether two arbitrary recursive types are structurally equivalent makes type checking uncomfortably hard.

Another possible definition of type equivalence is as follows:

> *Name equivalence:* $T \equiv T'$ if and only if T and T' were defined
> in the same place.

The so-called name equivalence rule is adopted in Pascal and Ada. Consider the following Pascal declarations:

```
type  T1 = file of Integer;
      T2 = file of Integer;
var   f1 : T1;
      f2 : T2;
procedure p (var f : T1); ...
```

The procedure call 'p (f1)' would pass its type check, since the types of f and f1 are name-equivalent. However, the procedure call 'p (f2)' would fail its type check, since the types of f and f2 are not name-equivalent – T1 and T2 are defined in different declarations.

In this example, of course, the programmer could easily have declared f2 to be of type T1, but that solution is not always available. Consider the following two separate programs:

```
program p1 (f1);
    type T1 = file of Integer;
    var  f1 : T1;
    begin
    ...;  write (f1, ...);  ...
    end.

program p2 (f2);
    type T2 = file of Integer;
    var  f2 : T2;
    begin
    ...;  read (f2, ...);  ...
    end.
```

When program p1 is run, its parameter f1 will be associated with an external file that must be of type T1, and the program will write to that file. Similarly, when program p2 is run, its parameter f2 will be associated with an external file that must be of type T2, and the program will read from that file. But the file read by p2 cannot be the self-same file that was written by p1, since the types T1 and T2 are not name-equivalent. What is more, nothing can be done about this, because the types T1 and T2 are inevitably defined in different places.

In general, two Pascal programs cannot communicate legally through files (except though files of the predefined type Text)! This is clearly a language design error. In practice, the design error is masked by the fact that most Pascal implementations neglect to perform type checks on files, so program p2 could in fact read a file written by program p1. However, this negligence also allows p2 to read a character file as if it were an integer file, and so on, and generally subverts Pascal's type discipline.

2.5.3 The type completeness principle

In Section 2.1 we listed the various sorts of values found in Pascal. The list included procedure and function abstractions. We count them as values because they can be passed as arguments; but they cannot be evaluated, nor assigned, nor used as components of composite values. They are, in fact, *second-class values*. On the other hand, truth values, integers, records, arrays, etc., can be used in all these ways. These are *first-class values*.

This kind of class distinction is common in the major programming languages (such as Fortran, Algol-60, Pascal, and Ada). Nevertheless, some languages (such as ML, Miranda, and to some extent Algol-68) manage to avoid such class distinctions and to allow all values, including abstractions, to be manipulated in similar ways.

Even among the first-class values there may be finer class distinctions. For example, the result of a Pascal function abstraction must be a primitive value or a pointer; it may not be a string, set, or record. This irritating restriction forces programmers into circumlocution. For example, instead of a function with a string result, a procedure with a string variable parameter must be written instead. More modern languages such as Ada allow function results to be of any type.

Pascal's class distinctions are in fact very complicated (see Exercise 2.12). At the opposite extreme, some languages (mentioned above) manage to eliminate all class distinctions. We can characterize a language's class-consciousness in terms of its adherence to the following general principle:

> *The type completeness principle:* No operation should be *arbitrarily* restricted in the types of the values involved.

This is not meant to be dogma. It is merely a principle that language designers ought to bear in mind, because arbitrary restrictions tend to reduce the expressive power of a programming language. However, a restriction might be justified by other, conflicting, design considerations. For example, most imperative languages treat abstractions as second-class values in order to avoid certain important implementation problems (see Section 3.3). However, Pascal's restriction on function result types violates the type completeness principle, with very little justification.

2.6   Expressions

Having considered values and types, let us now examine expressions. An *expression* is a program phrase that will be *evaluated* to yield a value.

Expressions may be composed in various ways. Here we shall survey the fundamental kinds of expression:

* *literals*
* *aggregates*
* *function calls*
* *conditional expressions*
* *constant and variable accesses*

Two other kinds of expression will be discussed later: *command expressions* in Section 3.6.1, and *block expressions* in Section 4.5.2.

Our interest is not primarily in the syntactic details of expressions, but rather in their underlying concepts. It may reasonably be argued that a programming language is impoverished if it omits (or arbitrarily restricts) any of the above kinds of expression. Conversely, if a language provides additional kinds of expression, they might well be unnecessary accretions rather than genuine enhancements to the language's expressive power.

2.6.1 Literals

The simplest kind of expression is a *literal*, which denotes a fixed and manifest value of some type.

Example 2.17
Here are some examples of literals in Pascal:

```
365    3.1416    '%'    'QWERTY'
```

These denote an integer, a real number, a character, and a string, respectively. ☐

2.6.2 Aggregates

An *aggregate* is an expression that constructs a composite value from its component values. The component values are determined by evaluating subexpressions.

Example 2.18
The following ML tuple aggregate:

```
(a*2.0, b/2.0)
```

constructs a value of the tuple type `real * real`.
   The following ML record aggregate:

```
{y = thisyear+1, m = "Jan", d = 1}
```

constructs a value of the record type `{y: int, m: string, d: int}`. ☐

Example 2.19
The following ML list aggregate:

```
[31, if leap (thisyear) then 29 else 28,
 31, 30, 31, 30, 31, 31, 30, 31, 30, 31]
```

constructs a value of type `int list`.
   In the following Ada program fragment:

```
monthsize : array (Month) of Natural :=
    (31, 28, 31, 30, 31, 30, 31, 31, 30, 31, 30, 31);
...
if leap (thisyear) then
   monthsize(feb) := 29;
end if;
```

an array aggregate is used to construct a complete array value, which is used to initialize the variable `monthsize`. ☐

   As illustrated by Examples 2.18 and 2.19, ML provides aggregates for tuples, records, and lists. Ada provides aggregates for records and arrays. Pascal is deficient in that it provides no aggregates for records or arrays, but only for sets. To construct a record or array value, we must assign to its components one by one, e.g.:

```
newyearsday.y := thisyear+1;
newyearsday.m := jan;
newyearsday.d := 1
```

which is both tedious and error-prone. In Ada we would write:

```
newyearsday := (y => thisyear+1, m => jan, d => 1);
```

using a record aggregate that is quite similar to ML's.

2.6.3 Function calls

A *function call* computes a result by applying a function abstraction to an argument. The function call typically has the form 'F (AP)', where F determines the function abstraction to be applied, and the *actual parameter AP* (usually an expression) determines the argument to be passed to it.

In most languages (such as Pascal) F is just the identifier of a specific function abstraction. However, in those languages that treat function abstractions as first-class values (such as ML), F may be any expression yielding a function abstraction, e.g.:

```
(if ... then sin else cos) (x)
```

In the case of a function of n parameters, the function call typically has the form 'F $(AP_1, ..., AP_n)$'. We can view this function call as passing n distinct arguments; or we can view it as passing a single argument that is an n-tuple. We may adopt whichever view is more convenient.

Function abstractions and parameters will be discussed in greater detail in Sections 5.1.1 and 5.2.

An *operator* may be thought of as denoting a function. Applying a unary or binary operator to its operand(s) is essentially equivalent to a function call passing one or two arguments:

$$\oplus E \qquad \text{is essentially equivalent to} \quad \oplus (E)$$
$$E_1 \otimes E_2 \qquad \text{is essentially equivalent to} \quad \otimes (E_1, E_2)$$

For example, the conventional arithmetic expression:

```
a * b + c / d
```

is essentially equivalent to the composed function calls:

```
+ (*(a,b), /(c,d))
```

The convention by which we write a binary operator between its two operands is called the *infix notation*. Nearly all programming languages adopt the infix notation. Lisp is almost unique in that every function call must be expressed in the *prefix notation*, in which the operator is written before its operand(s).

Here are some examples of Pascal operators:

- The unary operator '**not**' denotes the function {*false* ↦ *true*, *true* ↦ *false*} in Truth-Value → Truth-Value.
- The binary operator '/' denotes a function in Real × Real → Real.
- The binary operator '*' denotes *three* functions simultaneously: one in Integer × Integer → Integer, one in Real × Real → Real, and one in Set × Set → Set. This is an example of *overloading* (see Section 7.2).

In Pascal there is only a rough analogy between operators and function abstractions. Overloading, for example, is peculiar to operators (and certain predefined procedures and functions) in Pascal.

Several modern languages (such as Ada and ML) explicitly recognize the analogy between operators and functions. '$E_1 \otimes E_2$' is then *exactly* equivalent to '$\otimes (E_1, E_2)$', and operators may be defined in *exactly* the same way as functions. Such languages tend to be easier to learn, since they avoid separate rules for operators and functions. At the same time such languages are notationally more convenient, since they allow the programmer to declare new operators.

2.6.4   Conditional expressions

A *conditional expression* has several subexpressions, from which exactly one is chosen to be evaluated. Choice is of course fundamental in computation. However, not all languages provide conditional expressions (as opposed to conditional *commands*).

Example 2.20
The following ML *if* expression yields the maximum of the values of x and y:

```
if x > y then x else y
```

□

Example 2.21
The following ML *case* expression yields the number of days in thismonth (which is of type string):

```
case thismonth of
   "Feb" => if leap (thisyear) then 29 else 28
 | "Apr" => 30
 | "Jun" => 30
 | "Sep" => 30
 | "Nov" => 30
 | _     => 31
```

If the value of thismonth is 'Feb', for example, the subexpression '**if** ... **else** 28' will be evaluated. In the last line, '_' matches any value of thismonth that is not explicitly listed.   □

Pascal and Ada are completely lacking in conditional expressions. Consequently, programmers are forced to resort to conditional *commands*, such as:

```
if x > y then max := x else max := y
```

All languages provide either conditional expressions or conditional commands, and the underlying concepts are similar. Conditionals will be discussed in more detail in Section 3.5.6.

2.6.5 Constant and variable accesses

One obvious kind of expression we have not yet discussed is an access to a named constant or variable. For example, within the scope of the Pascal declarations:

```
const pi = 3.1416;
var   r  : Real
```

consider the expression '2*pi*r'. Here 'pi' is a ***constant access***; it yields the value 3.1416 denoted by pi. On the other hand, 'r' is a ***variable access***; it yields the value currently *contained* in the variable denoted by r.

The value of an expression containing constant and variable identifiers thus depends on how these identifiers were declared, i.e., it depends on the *environment* of the expression. (See Section 4.1.)

A programming language should provide notation for accessing components of structured constants and variables. In Pascal, if V accesses a record variable, then '$V.I$' accesses a component of that record; and if V accesses an array variable, then '$V[E]$' accesses a component of that array. Inconsistently, Pascal does not provide similar notation for accessing components of structured constants. For example, within the scope of the declarations:

```
const classic = 'War and Peace    ';
var   title   : packed array [1..16] of Char
```

we can access title[1] but not classic[1]. Ada's notation for accessing record and array components is similar to Pascal's, but is consistent for both constants and variables.

2.7 Further reading

Composite types were first systematically treated, in terms of Cartesian products, disjoint unions, powersets, mappings, and recursive types, by Hoare (1972, 1975), based on earlier work by McCarthy (1963). A detailed and technical treatment may be found in Tennent (1981). Tennent shows that a simple treatment of types as sets of values needs to be refined when we consider recursive definitions involving function types.

Exercises 2

2.1   Show the set of values of each of the following Pascal types, using the notation of Cartesian products, disjoint unions, and mappings:

```
type Suit = (club, diamond, heart, spade);
     Rank = 2..14;
     Card = record s : Suit; r : Rank end;
     Hand = array [1..7] of Card;
     Turn = record
                case pass : Boolean of
                    false: (play : Card);
                    true:  ( )
            end
```

What is the cardinality of each type?

2.2*   Systematically analyse the types and expressions of your favorite programming language, in the same way as Pascal and ML have been analysed in this chapter. (a) What is the set of values of each primitive type? (b) How is the set of values of each composite type defined in terms of the sets of values of its component types? (c) Can recursive types be defined, and if so how? (d) Is your language statically or dynamically typed? (e) How is type equivalence defined in your language? (f) Compare the kinds of expression in your language with those discussed in Section 2.6. Are any relevant kinds missing? Are any exotic kinds provided, and are they essential?

2.3*   Analyse the following types of bulk data, in terms of Cartesian products, disjoint unions, mappings, powersets, and sequences: (a) *serial files*; (b) *direct files*; and (c) *relations* (as in relational databases).

2.4*   Explore the relationship between arrays and function abstractions. Use both a function abstraction and a (constant) array to implement each of the following: (a) the logical function `not`; (b) the factorial function over the first ten positive integers. In what ways are arrays and function abstractions fundamentally different? Try to answer this question in terms of the *essential* properties of arrays and function abstractions, neglecting any peculiarities they may have in your favorite programming language.

2.5   Imagine a language that allows an array to be indexed by a *record*, assuming that all the record's component types are themselves suitable index types. For example:

```
type Point = record
                x: 0..511; y: 0..255
            end;
```

$$\text{Screen} = \textbf{array} \ [\text{Point}] \ \textbf{of} \ 0..1$$

Compare this with the two-dimensional array type `Window` of Example 2.8, in terms of its set of values, and notation for accessing components. Can you think of an advantage that type `Screen` would have over type `Window`?

2.6   Explore the relationship between $S \rightarrow (T \rightarrow U)$ and $(S \times T) \rightarrow U$. (*Hint:* Compare the types '**array** $[S]$ **of array** $[T]$ **of** U' and '**array** $[S, T]$ **of** U' in Pascal; and also the corresponding types in Ada.)

2.7   Explore the relationship between $S \rightarrow$ Truth-Value and $\wp S$. (*Hint:* Compare Examples 2.7 and 2.11. Also, using the definition of `Card` in Exercise 2.1, consider whether a type like '**set of** `Card`' could sensibly be allowed in Pascal.)

2.8   Use the iterative method of Section 2.4.2 to determine the first four approximations to the least solution of the recursive set equation (2.19).

2.9*   Make a table showing the string operations provided by a language in which strings are primitive values (e.g., ML), a language in which strings are character arrays (e.g., Algol-68, Pascal, or Ada), and a language in which strings are character lists (e.g., Miranda or Prolog). In the latter two cases, which of the string operations are available for all arrays or lists, respectively? In all three cases, is any of the operations identified in Section 2.4.3 missing? Can each missing operation be defined in the language itself?

2.10*   If your favorite language is statically typed, find a program you have written that would have been simpler to write in a dynamically typed language. If your favorite language is dynamically typed, find a program you have written that could equally well have been written in a statically typed language.

2.11*   Recall the problem of the types of files, discussed at the end of Section 2.5.2. What is Ada's solution to this problem? Show that this solution implies runtime type checks on files.

2.12*   Make a table showing what types of value in Pascal may be (a) constants; (b) operands of operators; (c) results of operators; (d) arguments of functions and procedures; (e) results of functions; (f) array or record components. Do the same for your favorite programming language. How well does each language comply with the type completeness principle?

2.13**   Design the following extensions to Pascal: (a) record and array aggregates; (b) record and array constants. Look out for possible interactions between your extensions and other parts of the language.

CHAPTER THREE

Storage

'Once a programmer has understood the use of variables, he has understood the essence of programming.' This remark of Edsger Dijkstra might be considered an exaggeration now that functional and logic programming have become popular. Nevertheless, the imperative programming paradigm that is characterized by the use of variables and assignment still accounts for the overwhelming majority of programs, and will remain important for a long time to come.

In this chapter we study primitive and composite variables; a model of *storage* that allows us to understand variables; *lifetimes* of variables; the kinds of *command* that may be used in programs to update variables; and the possibility of *side effects* in expressions.

3.1 Variables and updating

In computing, a **variable** is an object that contains a value; this value may be *inspected* and *updated* as often as desired. Variables are used to model real-world objects that possess state, such as the population of the world, today's date, the current weather, or a country's economy.

Our definition of variables is quite general. In computing, variables occur in several guises. Most familiar to the programmer are the variables that are created and used within a particular program. Such variables are typically updated by *assignment*; and they are short-lived. However, files and databases are also variables. These are usually large and long-lived, they exist independently of any particular program, and usually they are updated only selectively.

The updatable variables we are discussing here are *not* analogous to mathematical variables. A mathematical variable stands for a fixed but unknown value; there is no implication of change over time, and therefore no analogy for the kind of updating illustrated by 'n := n+1' or 'write (f, x)' in a programming language. (The variables of a functional programming language *are*, however, analogous to mathematical variables.)

To understand what variables and updating *do* mean, we need some notion of **storage**. Real storage media (such as memories and disks) have properties that are irrelevant for present purposes (such as word size, capacity, and addressing conventions). Instead an abstract model of storage is perfectly adequate:

- A *store* is an collection of *cells* (or *locations*).
- Each cell has a current status, *allocated* or *unallocated*.
- Each allocated cell has a current *content*, which is either a *storable* value or *undefined*.

The term *storable* will be defined in Section 3.3.

Example 3.1
Consider a variable n in a Pascal program:

(1) The variable declaration '**var** n : Integer' causes some *unallocated* cell to have its status changed to *allocated*, and its content changed to *undefined*. Henceforth, n denotes that cell.
(2) The assignment 'n := 0' changes to zero the content of the cell denoted by n.
(3) The expression 'n+1' yields one more than the content of the cell denoted by n. The assignment 'n := n+1' adds one to the content of that cell.
(4) At the end of the block containing the declaration of n, the status of the cell denoted by n reverts to *unallocated*.

We can picture each allocated cell as a box, containing either a storable or '?' (*undefined*). Figure 3.1 pictures the cell denoted by n after steps (1) through (3).   □

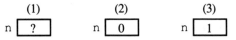

Figure 3.1 Storage for a primitive variable.

Strictly speaking, we should always say 'the content of the cell denoted by n'. We usually prefer to avoid such circumlocution by saying simply 'the value contained in n', or even 'the value of n'.

3.2   Composite variables

A value of a composite type consists of components that may be inspected selectively. Correspondingly, a variable of a composite type consists of components that are themselves variables, and the contents of these components can be inspected and updated selectively.

In Pascal, a variable of type *T* is defined to have the same structure as a value of type *T*. In particular, a record variable is a tuple of component variables, and an array variable is a mapping from an index set to a collection of component variables. A variable of a primitive type occupies a single cell, but a variable of a composite type may occupy several cells.

Example 3.2
Consider the following Pascal declarations and assignments:

```
type  Month = (jan, feb, mar, ..., oct, nov, dec);
      Date  = record
                   m : Month;   d : 1..31
              end;
var   today : Date;
...
today.d := 23;   today.m := feb
```

Each `Date` value is a pair consisting of a `Month` value and an integer value. Correspondingly, each `Date` variable is a pair consisting of a `Month` variable and an integer variable. Figure 3.2 shows the structure of the variable `today`, and the effect of the above assignments.

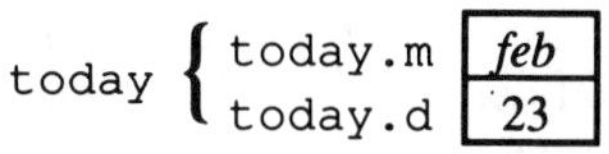

$$today \begin{cases} \texttt{today.m} & \boxed{\textit{feb}} \\ \texttt{today.d} & \boxed{23} \end{cases}$$

Figure 3.2 Storage for a record variable.

Now consider the following array variable:

```
var dates : array [1..3] of Date
```

Each value of this array type is a mapping from the index set {1, 2, 3} to three `Date` values. Correspondingly, the variable `dates` is a mapping from {1, 2, 3} to three distinct `Date` variables. Figure 3.3 shows the structure of the variable `dates`, and the effect of the following assignments:

```
dates[1].m := may;   dates[1].d := 5;
dates[2] := today
```

The last assignment copies the entire value of `today` (i.e., it updates the two cells of `dates[2]` with the contents of the two cells of `today`). □

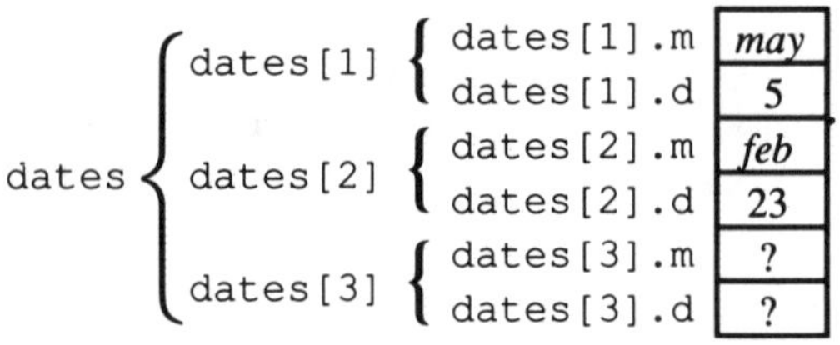

$$\text{dates} \begin{cases} \text{dates[1]} \begin{cases} \text{dates[1].m} & \boxed{may} \\ \text{dates[1].d} & \boxed{5} \end{cases} \\ \text{dates[2]} \begin{cases} \text{dates[2].m} & \boxed{feb} \\ \text{dates[2].d} & \boxed{23} \end{cases} \\ \text{dates[3]} \begin{cases} \text{dates[3].m} & \boxed{?} \\ \text{dates[3].d} & \boxed{?} \end{cases} \end{cases}$$

Figure 3.3 Storage for an array variable.

3.2.1 Total and selective updating

Consider the composite variable `today` of Example 3.2. The assignment 'today :=
dates[2]' updates the whole of `today` in a single step. This is an example of
total updating of a composite variable.

Now assume that the current value of `today` is the pair (*feb*, 23) before the
assignment 'today.d := 29' is executed. It is possible to view this as assigning to
`today` a complete new pair (*feb*, 29), which is equal to the old pair except that its
second component is 29. Similarly, it is possible to view the assignment 'dates[2]
:= today' as assigning to `dates` a complete new mapping, which is equal to the old
mapping except that 2 maps to the value of `today`.

In this view of things, an assignment to a component of V (a composite variable)
is just a shorthand for a total updating of V that happens to leave the other components of V containing the same values as before. However, a more intuitive view of
the assignment is that one component of V is updated, and the other components of
V are not involved at all. We call this *selective updating*.

Selective updating is not an essential feature of a language with composite
variables. ML, for example, treats variables rather differently from most imperative
languages. An object of the reference type 'T ref' acts as a variable to which we may
assign a value of type T. If T is a record type, we may assign a complete new record
value, but there is no notation for selective updating of one component of the record
variable – unless the component is itself declared to be of a reference type! A similar
point applies to constructions and lists. Inconsistently, however, ML arrays *are* always
selectively updatable, since the components of an object of type 'T array' are defined
to be of type 'T ref'.

Example 3.3
The following ML declarations:

```
datatype   month = jan | feb | mar | ... | dec
type       date  = month * int
val        today : date ref = ref (feb, 23)
```

declare and initialize a variable `today`, which contains a pair of type `date`. This
variable may be totally updated, e.g., by 'today := (feb, 29)', but it cannot be
selectively updated.

We could instead declare:

```
type datevar = month ref * int ref
val  today   : datevar = (ref feb, ref 23)
```

in which case either component of today may be selectively updated – but now today itself cannot be totally updated! □

3.2.2 Array variables

We can view an array variable as a mapping from an index set to a collection of component variables. We now consider how and when a given array variable's index set is actually determined. There are several possibilities:

- *static array* – the index set is fixed at compile-time
- *dynamic array* – the index set is fixed on creation of the array variable
- *flexible array* – the index set is not fixed at all

An array's index set is typically a range of consecutive values, and so is defined by a pair of *index bounds*. (In the case of an *n*-dimensional array, there will be *n* pairs of index bounds.)

A ***static array*** is an array variable whose index set is fixed at compile-time. Each index bound is determined by a literal or, more generally, by an expression that can be evaluated at compile-time.

Static arrays are illustrated by Pascal, in which an array's index set is in fact part of its type.

Example 3.4
Consider the following Pascal fragments:

```
const n      = 10;
type Vector = array [1..n] of Real;
var  a, b  : Vector;
procedure readvector (var v : Vector);   ...;
...
b := a;
readvector (a);   readvector (b)
```

Only a Vector value can be assigned to a Vector variable, and only a Vector argument can be passed to a procedure like readvector. Every Vector value and variable has index set {1, 2, ..., 10}. □

A ***dynamic array*** is an array variable whose index set is fixed at run-time, at the point when the variable is created. The index bounds are determined by expressions evaluated at that time. This implies that a dynamic array's index set cannot be part of its type.

In Ada, an array type incorporates the *type* of the index bounds but not their actual values.

Example 3.5

Consider the following pieces of Ada:

```
m : Integer := ...;
...

type Vector is array (Integer range <>) of Float;
a : Vector (1..10);
b : Vector (0..m);
procedure readvector (v : out Vector) is  ...;
...
a := b;
readvector (a);  readvector (b);
```

The type definition of Vector specifies that the index set is a subrange of the integers, but will be fixed only when a Vector variable is created. For example, b's upper bound is the value of m current when b is declared.

A Vector variable can be assigned any Vector value having the same number of components. For example, the assignment 'a := b;' will succeed only if b has exactly 10 components. But a procedure like readvector can be called with any Vector argument, regardless of its index set. Within the body of readvector, the actual bounds of v are taken from those of the argument array, and can be accessed using the notation v'first and v'last.   □

A *flexible array* is an array variable whose index set is not fixed at all. This allows the index bounds to be changed whenever a new array value is assigned to the array variable.

Example 3.6

Consider the following hypothetical extension to Ada:

```
type Vector is array (Integer range <>) of Float;
a : Vector := (1=>1.0, 2=>0.0, 3=>0.0);
...
a := (0=>0.0, 1=>0.1, 2=>0.2, 3=>0.3, 4=>0.4);
```

Here the Vector variable a is declared and initialized with index set {1, 2, 3}. Subsequently, however, it is assigned a new array value with index set {0, 1, 2, 3, 4}. In other words, a's index set may vary during a's lifetime.   □

A dynamic or flexible array must contain its own index bounds as well as a mapping from the index set to the component set. For example, the values of the Ada type Vector of Example 3.5 or Example 3.6 would be in the set:

Integer × Integer × (Integer → Real)

where it is to be understood that in the array value (l, u, m), l and u are the index bounds, and $m(i)$ is *undefined* unless $l \leq i \leq u$.

3.3 Storables

A composite variable occupies several cells, in general. Selective updating of a composite variable affects some but not all of its cells.

For each programming language we can list the sorts of value that can be stored in *single* cells, which cannot be selectively updated. These values are called the **storables** of the language.

Pascal's storables are the following:

- primitive values
- sets
- pointers

Note that sets are counted as storables, since set variables cannot be *selectively* updated in Pascal. Arrays, records, and files are not storables, since they can be selectively updated. Procedure and function abstractions are not storables, since they cannot be stored at all. References to variables cannot be stored either, except for pointers, a special case that will be discussed in Section 3.4.2.

ML's storables are the following:

- primitive values
- records, constructions, and lists
- function abstractions
- references to variables

Records, constructions, and lists are counted as storables, because they cannot be selectively updated (except for components that happen to be references). In fact, all ML values are storable except arrays – these can be selectively updated since their components are always references.

3.4 Lifetime

A property of every variable is that it is **created** (or *allocated*) at some definite time, and may be **deleted** (or *deallocated*) at some later time when it is no longer needed. The interval between creation and deletion is called the variable's **lifetime**.

The concept of lifetime is important for the pragmatic reason that a variable needs to occupy storage only while it is alive. After the variable is deleted, the storage cell(s) it formerly occupied may be reallocated for some other purpose. This allows storage to be used economically.

3.4.1 Local and global variables

A *local variable* is one that is declared within a block for use only within that block. (Here we are using the term *block* in its widest possible sense. Pascal procedure and function bodies, and ML *let* expressions, are examples of blocks. This will be explained more fully in Section 4.5.)

A *global variable* is one that is declared in the outermost block of a program. A global variable is also local in the sense that that it is declared for use only within a particular block. In this discussion of lifetime, therefore, *local* should always be understood to include *global*.

An *activation* of a block is a time interval during which that block is being executed. In the Algol-like languages, including Pascal and Ada, a lifetime of a local variable V corresponds exactly to an activation of the block containing V's declaration. In the special case where V is a global variable, V is alive throughout the program's execution time.

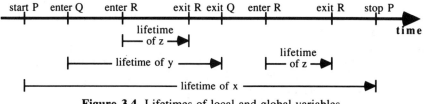

Figure 3.4 Lifetimes of local and global variables.

Example 3.7
Consider the following Pascal program skeleton:

```
program P;
   var x : ...;

   procedure Q;
      var y : ...;
      begin
      ... R ...
      end;

   procedure R;
      var z : ...;
      begin ...
      end;

   begin
   ... Q ... R ...
   end.
```

The blocks in this program are the main program P (the outermost block), and the procedures Q and R.

Suppose that P calls Q, which in turn calls R; and suppose that P later calls R directly. Then Figure 3.4 shows the lifetimes of the local variables x, y, and z. ☐

This example illustrates the general fact that the lifetimes of local variables are always nested, since the activations of blocks are themselves always nested. In Example 3.7, when block Q has activated block R, the activation of R must end before the activation of Q can end.

A local variable will have several lifetimes if the block in which it is declared is activated several times. In Example 3.7, since block R is activated on two separate occasions, the two lifetimes of z are disjoint. If block R were activated recursively, the lifetimes of z would be nested. This makes sense only if we understand that each lifetime of z is really a lifetime of a distinct variable, which is created at the beginning of the block activation (more precisely, when the declaration of z is elaborated), and deleted at the end of the block activation.

From the latter point it follows that a local variable cannot retain its content over successive activations of the block in which it is declared (contrary to a myth widely believed by Fortran programmers). In Pascal, a newly created variable always contains *undefined*. In Ada, a variable may be initialized as part of its declaration. In either case, the variable's previous lifetimes are irrelevant.

Some languages (such as PL/I and C) allow a variable to be declared as a *static variable*, which defines its lifetime to be the program's entire execution time even if the variable is declared inside an inner block. Static variables behave like global variables in respect of their lifetimes. Although this feature addresses a genuine need, there are better ways to achieve the same effect (see Section 6.3).

3.4.2 Heap variables

The pattern of nested lifetimes characteristic of local and global variables is adequate for many purposes, but not all. It is often necessary for variables to be created and deleted at will.

A *heap variable* is one that can be created, and deleted, at any time. Heap variables are quite distinct from the local variables discussed in the previous subsection. A heap variable is created by a command. It is anonymous, and is accessed through a *pointer*. (By contrast, a local variable is created by elaborating a declaration, and has an identifier.)

Pointers are first-class values, and thus may be assigned, incorporated in data structures, and so on. A program can build a complicated data structure (an arbitrary directed graph, in fact) in which connections between nodes are represented by pointers stored in the nodes. Such a structure can be selectively updated – to add a node, to remove a node, or to change a connection between nodes – by manipulation of pointers. (This is more radical than selective updating of a record or array variable, which affects the variable's contents but not its actual structure.)

Example 3.8

The following Pascal declarations illustrate a representation of integer lists:

```
type IntList = ^ IntNode;
     IntNode = record
                   head : Integer;
                   tail : IntList
               end;

var  odds, primes : IntList;

function cons (h : Integer; t : IntList) : IntList;
     (* returns a pointer to the list formed by prefixing h to the list t *)
     var l : IntList;
     begin
     new (l);
     l^.head := h;  l^.tail := t;
     cons := l
     end;
```

Now the commands:

```
odds   := cons (3, cons (5, cons (7, nil)));
primes := cons (2, odds)
```

leave the pointer variable primes pointing to a list containing the integers 2, 3, 5, and 7 (in that order), and odds pointing to the last three of these – see Figure 3.5. In the diagram, each arrow represents a pointer. There is a unique pointer value, *nil*, that points to nothing at all; this is used to signify the end of a list.

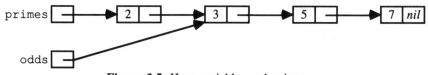

Figure 3.5 Heap variables and pointers.

Updating the pointer component of the 3-node to point to the 7-node would, in effect, remove the 5-node from both lists. Then the 5-node would become inaccessible, and could be deleted. On the other hand, if the pointer variable odds were updated to point to the 5-node (which in effect would remove the 3-node from the list that odds points to), then the 3-node would remain accessible from the list pointed to by primes, and so could not (yet) be deleted.

Suppose now that odds and primes are global variables in Example 3.7. Suppose further that program P calls procedure Q, which executes the above commands assigning to odds and primes; and then program P manipulates the pointers in order to remove the 5-node. Then the lifetimes of the variables would be as in Figure 3.6.

On the other hand, if `primes` and `odds` were local to Q, their own lifetimes would end on exit from Q, all the heap variables would become inaccessible at that point, and so they could be deleted too. □

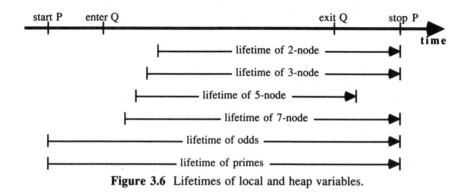

Figure 3.6 Lifetimes of local and heap variables.

This example illustrates the general fact that the lifetimes of heap variables follow no particular pattern.

Creation of a heap variable is requested by an operation called an ***allocator***, which returns a pointer to the newly created heap variable. The heap variable will remain accessible as long as at least one pointer is pointing to it. The heap variable's lifetime extends from its creation until it becomes inaccessible.

In Pascal the standard procedure `new` is an allocator. There is also a ***deallocator***, the standard procedure `dispose`, which forcibly deletes a given heap variable. This is dangerous, since any remaining pointers to the deleted heap variable become dangling references (see Section 3.4.4).

Pointers and heap variables can be used to *represent* recursive values such as lists and trees, but clearly the pointer is a low-level concept. Unless performed with care and discipline, manipulation of pointers is notoriously error-prone and obscure in its effects. Consider the pointer assignment 'p^.tail := q': we cannot tell by simple inspection which list is being selectively updated; its effect might even be to change the entire data structure, by introducing a cycle!

Nevertheless, nearly all imperative languages provide pointers rather than supporting recursive types directly. The reasons for this are the semantics and implementation of assignment.

Consider the Pascal assignment 'primes := odds'. This assigns a *pointer*, thus causing `primes` to point to the same list as `odds`. The list is now ***shared*** by the two pointer variables. Any selective update to the list pointed to by `odds` also affects the list pointed to by `primes`, because they are one and the same list.

Suppose that Pascal were extended to support list types directly, e.g.:

var primes, odds : **list of** Integer

Then how would we expect the assignment 'primes := odds' to be interpreted?

There are two possibilities:

(a) One possible interpretation of the assignment would be to place in `primes` a *reference* to the list referred to by `odds`. This interpretation would again involve sharing, and would amount to using pointers in disguise. It would be inconsistent with the assignment of a record or array in Pascal, which causes the record or array to be *copied* rather than shared. The advantage of this interpretation would be ease of implementation.

(b) Another possible interpretation of the assignment would be to place in `primes` a complete copy of the list contained in `odds`. Any subsequent update to either `odds` or `primes` would have no effect on the other. This would be consistent with assignment of arrays and records in Pascal, and is surely the more natural interpretation. However, copying of lists is expensive.

A possible compromise would be simply to prohibit selective updating of lists. Then assignment could be *implemented* by sharing, but the *effect* would be similar to copying.

Similar points apply to other recursive types in imperative languages.

3.4.3 Persistent variables

Files are composite variables, according to our definition in Section 3.1. For example, a *serial file* is a sequence of components; and a *direct file* is an array of components. Files are typically (but not exclusively) used to contain large bodies of long-lived data.

Most programming languages severely restrict the ways in which files may be inspected and updated, for efficiency reasons. In Pascal, for example: (a) a file may be inspected only by reading components one at a time, in order, starting at the beginning of the file; (b) a file may be updated only by emptying it and then appending components one at a time; (c) assignment of a complete file is forbidden. Languages that support direct files typically allow a designated component to be read and written at any time, but also forbid assignment of a complete file.

Here we are concerned principally with the lifetimes of files. What distinguishes files from ordinary variables in this respect is that they are typically persistent. A *persistent variable* is one whose lifetime transcends an activation of any particular program. By contrast, a *transient variable* is one whose lifetime is bounded by the activation of the program that created it. Local and heap variables are transient.

In Pascal, a *program parameter* denotes a persistent variable that is already alive when activation of the program starts, and continues to live after the activation has ended. Any file variable other than a program parameter is an ordinary local variable in that its lifetime is an activation of the block within which it is declared.

Pascal provides no means for creation or deletion of files. Ada does provide such means, by calls to procedures in a standard input–output package. This allows a program to create a file at any time, and also allows the file can be deleted at any later time, either during the same program activation or during a future activation of the same program or a different program.

There are certain analogies between persistent variables and transient variables. Persistent variables usually have arbitrary lifetimes, like heap variables, but some systems also allow them to have nested lifetimes, like local variables. Just as transient variables reside in a store, persistent variables reside in a *filestore*, which has the same (abstract) properties as an ordinary store (see Section 3.1).

Despite these analogies, most programming languages provide different types for persistent variables and transient variables. In Pascal, a transient variable may be of any type (including a file type), but a persistent variable must be of file type. Why not allow persistent variables to be of primitive, record, or array type? For example, a persistent variable of array type would be a *direct file*. (In fact, the lack of direct files in Pascal is a serious omission.) Most languages are worse than Pascal, in that their persistent data types and transient data types are completely disjoint.

The type completeness principle suggests that all the types of the programming language should be allowed for both transient variables and persistent variables. A language applying this principle would be simplified by having no special types, commands, or procedures for input–output. The programmer would be spared the unprofitable effort of converting data from a persistent data type to a transient data type on input, and *vice versa* on output.

Example 3.9

The Pascal program outlined below has a parameter statsfile, which will denote a persistent file variable when the program is run. The program reads records from this file into the transient array variable stats, and then proceeds to analyse them.

```
program StatisticsAnalysis (statsfile);

type Country    = (B,D,DK,E,F,GB,GR,I,IRL,L,NL,P);
     Statistics = record
                      population : 0..100000000;  ...
                  end;
var  stats      : array [Country] of Statistics;
     statsfile  : file of Statistics;

procedure readstats;
   var cy : Country;
   begin
   reset (statsfile);
   for cy := B to P do read (statsfile, stats[cy])
   end;

procedure analysestats;
   var cy : Country;
   begin
   ... stats[cy].population ...
   end;

begin
readstats;
```

```
analysestats
end.
```

If a Pascal program parameter could denote a persistent *array* variable, we could simplify the program as follows. We make `stats` itself a parameter, which will denote a persistent array variable when the program is run. The program will analyse records in `stats` directly. (It assumes that these records have previously been written by some other program.)

```
program StatisticsAnalysis (stats);

type Country   = (B,D,DK,E,F,GB,GR,I,IRL,L,NL,P);
     Statistics = record
                     population : 0..100000000;  ...
                end;
var  stats      : array [Country] of Statistics;

procedure analysestats;
   var cy : Country;
   begin
   ... stats[cy].population ...
   end;

begin
analysestats
end.
```

The program has no input operations, and is much simplified as a result.   □

3.4.4 Dangling references

References to heap variables (i.e., pointers) are always first-class values, but references to local variables are usually second-class values. The reason for this distinction is illustrated by the following example.

Example 3.10
Consider a hypothetical extension to Pascal allowing assignment of references to local variables:

```
var r : ^ Integer;

procedure P;
   var v : Integer;
   begin
   r := &v
   end;

begin
P;
```

```
r^ := 1
end
```

The command 'r := &v' in P is supposed to assign to r a *reference* to the local variable v. After exit from P, the command 'r^ := 1' attempts to access the variable to which r currently refers, i.e., v. But v's lifetime ended on exit from P!

Note that if r were declared inside P, using r^ to access v would always be safe, since then v would be alive throughout r's own lifetime. □

An (attempted) reference to a variable that is no longer alive is called a ***dangling reference***. Example 3.10 shows that a dangling reference can arise when a reference to a local variable is assigned to a variable with a longer lifetime.

Pascal avoids this particular problem by making references to local variables not storable at all. A reference to a local variable may be passed as an argument, and will then be bound to a formal (variable) parameter, but no dangling reference can arise because the lifetime of the formal parameter is always nested within the lifetime of the argument variable.

Assignment of a reference to a heap variable should never give rise to a dangling reference, since by definition a heap variable is alive as long as any reference to it exists. This, however, assumes that the programming language has no deallocator. Pascal's dispose procedure is such a deallocator; it forcibly deletes a heap variable, and thus makes all existing references to that variable into dangling references.

Treating procedure and function abstractions as first-class values is another potential cause of dangling references.

Example 3.11
Consider a hypothetical extension to Pascal allowing assignment of function abstractions:

```
var fv : Integer -> Boolean;

procedure P;
   var v : ...;

   function f (n : Integer) : Boolean;
      begin
      ... v ...
      end;

   begin
   fv := &f
   end;

begin
P;
... fv(0) ...
end
```

P assigns the local function abstraction f to the global variable fv. After exit from P, 'fv(0)' calls f indirectly, since that function abstraction is the current value of fv.

Now f accesses the variable v, which by this time is no longer alive.   □

Dangling references arise not only through assignment of references and abstractions, but also through returning such values as function results. This is particularly important in the functional programming languages (such as ML and Miranda). In such languages function abstractions are first-class values and are frequently returned as results of other functions.

A partial solution to the problem of dangling references is adopted by Algol-68. Assignment of references is allowed, but with the restriction that a reference to a local variable may not be assigned to a variable with a longer lifetime. There is a corresponding restriction on assignment of abstractions. These restrictions are just sufficient to avoid dangling references, but in general they require run-time checks. Moreover, they sometimes awkwardly restrict the programmer.

The solution adopted by the functional languages is to treat *all* variables as heap variables. This implies that, at the end of a block activation, each variable declared within it continues to live as long as a (direct or indirect) reference to it still exists. Consequently, storage allocation is less efficient than in those languages (such as Algol, Pascal, and Ada) in which local variables have nested lifetimes.

3.5   Commands

Having considered variables and storage, let us now examine commands. A ***command*** is a program phrase that will be ***executed*** in order to update variables.

Commands are a characteristic feature of the *imperative* programming languages (such as Fortran, Cobol, Algol, PL/I, Pascal, Ada, and many others). Commands are often called *statements*, but we shall avoid using that term because it means something entirely different in logic (and in English).

There are various kinds of command. Some commands are primitive; others are composed from simpler commands. The following kinds of command are fundamental:

- *skips*
- *assignments*
- *procedure calls*
- *sequential commands*
- *collateral commands*
- *conditional commands*
- *iterative commands*

Another kind of command will be discussed in Section 4.5.1: *block commands*.

Our interest is not primarily in the syntactic details of commands, but rather in their underlying concepts. It may reasonably be argued that an imperative language is impoverished if it omits (or arbitrarily restricts) any of the above kinds of command. Conversely, if a language provides additional kinds of command, they might well be unnecessary accretions rather than genuine improvements to the language's expressive power. For example, special input–output commands (as in Cobol, Fortran, and PL/I) might be replaced by procedure calls (as in Pascal and Ada), or might even be eliminated altogether (see Section 3.4.3).

All the above commands exhibit *single-entry single-exit* control flow. This pattern of control flow is adequate for most practical purposes, but occasionally is too restrictive. Nearly all imperative languages provide *sequencers* such as jumps, exits, and exceptions, which allow *single-entry multi-exit* control flows (at least) to be programmed. These will be covered in Chapter 8.

3.5.1   Skips

The simplest possible kind of command is the ***skip*** (or *dummy*) command, which has no effect whatsoever. Skips are particularly useful as components of conditional commands. For example, in many languages '`if` E `then` C' is an abbreviation for '`if` E `then` C `else skip`'.

3.5.2   Assignments

The concept of ***assignment*** has been extensively discussed in Sections 3.1 and 3.2. The assignment command typically has the form '$V := E$ '. Here V is a *variable access*, a kind of expression that is evaluated to yield a reference to a variable. The assignment command updates this variable to contain the value yielded by E. (Note that this variable could be a component of a composite variable, in which case the effect would be selective updating of that composite variable.)

In those languages in which references to variables are first-class values (such as ML and Algol-68), V is just an ordinary expression of reference type. For example, if we have declared m and n to be of type `int ref` in ML, then we can write not only 'm := 7' but also:

```
(if ... then m else n) := 7
```

More general kinds of assignment are possible. A *multiple assignment*, typically written in the form '$V_1 := ... := V_n := E$', causes the same value to be assigned to several variables. For example, the following multiple assignment zeros two variables, m and n:

```
m := n := 0
```

A *simultaneous assignment*, typically written in the form '$V_1, ..., V_n : = E_1, ..., E_n$', causes the values yielded by n expressions to be assigned simultaneously to n variables. For example, the following simultaneous assignment swaps the contents of two variables, m and n, without using an auxiliary variable:

```
m, n := n, m
```

Some languages (such as Algol-68 and C) allow certain binary operators to be combined with assignment. For example, the following command increments the value of the variable n:

```
n +:= 1
```

which is equivalent to 'n := n+1'. This kind of command can be traced back as far as Cobol, in which it would be written rather less concisely as 'ADD 1 TO n'.

Before we leave assignments, let us study *variable accesses* in a little more detail. Consider the following commands:

```
read (n);   n := n + 1;   write (n)
```

Two of these occurrences of the variable access n yield the current *content* of the variable. The other two occurrences yield a *reference* to the variable (i.e., the cell that it occupies), not the value contained in it. (Which ones are which?)

More generally, what is the 'meaning' of a variable access? We could think of a variable access as yielding a reference to a variable in some contexts, and the current content of that variable in other contexts. An alternative point of view is that a variable access *always* yields a reference to a variable, but in certain contexts there is an implicit operation that replaces a reference to a variable by the current content of that variable. This operation is called ***dereferencing***. Here are the above commands with the dereferencing operation made explicit:

```
read (n);   n := content(n) + 1;   write (content(n))
```

In a few languages, dereferencing *is* made explicit. In ML we would write 'n := !n + 1', where '!' denotes the dereferencing function.

3.5.3   Procedure calls

A ***procedure call*** achieves its effect by applying a procedure abstraction to some arguments. The procedure call typically has the form 'P $(AP_1, ..., AP_n)$', where P determines the procedure abstraction to be applied, and the *actual parameters* AP_1, ..., and AP_n determine the arguments to be passed to it.

An actual parameter may be an expression, in which case the argument will be a value. Alternatively, an actual parameter may be a variable access, in which case the argument will be a reference to a variable.

The net effect of a procedure call, like any command, is to update variables. One way in which the procedure can achieve this effect is by updating variables passed as arguments. The other way is by updating variables declared outside the procedure. (Updating the procedure's own local variables will have no *net* effect, because such variables are alive only during the procedure's activation.)

Procedure abstractions and parameters will be discussed in greater detail in Sections 5.1.2 and 5.2.

3.5.4 Sequential commands

Since commands update variables, the order in which commands are executed is important. Much of the programming effort in an imperative language is concerned with *control flow*, i.e., ensuring that the commands will be executed in a suitable order. This and the following three subsections are concerned with ways of composing commands to achieve different control flows.

The commonest control flow is **sequential** composition of two (or more) commands. This is usually written '$C_1; C_2$'. Command C_1 is executed before command C_2. Sequential composition is available in every imperative language, and is so familiar that it needs no further discussion here.

3.5.5 Collateral commands

Less common is **collateral** composition of commands, sometimes written 'C_1, C_2'. Both C_1 and C_2 are executed, but in no particular order. Here is an example:

```
m := 7,  n := n + 1
```

where the variables m and n are updated independently, and the order of execution is irrelevant.

An unwise use of collateral composition would be:

```
n := 7,  n := n + 1
```

The net effect of this collateral command depends on the order of execution. Suppose that n initially contains 0.

- If 'n := 7' is executed first, n will end up containing 8.
- If 'n := 7' is executed second, n will end up containing 7.
- If 'n := 7' is executed between evaluation of 'n+1' and assignment of its value to n, n will end up containing 1.

A computation is **deterministic** if we can predict in advance exactly which sequence of steps will be followed. Otherwise the computation is **nondeterministic**. Collateral commands are nondeterministic.

A given nondeterministic computation might have a predictable net effect, although the sequence of steps by which it gets there is unpredictable. We call such a computation *effectively deterministic*. A collateral command is effectively deterministic if neither subcommand inspects a variable updated by the other.

3.5.6 Conditional commands

A **conditional command** has a number of subcommands, from which exactly one is chosen to be executed.

The most elementary kind of conditional command is the *if* command. This is found in every imperative language, and typically has the form:

$$\textbf{if } E \textbf{ then } C_1 \textbf{ else } C_2$$

Here the choice is between the two subcommands, C_1 and C_2, and is based on the value yielded by the truth-valued expression E.

The *if* command can be used to allow choice among several subcommands:

```
if        E₁ then  C₁
else if E₂ then  C₂
...
else if Eₙ then  Cₙ
else             C₀
```

Here the truth-valued expressions $E_1, E_2, ..., E_n$ are evaluated *sequentially*, and the first E_i that yields *true* causes the corresponding subcommand C_i to be chosen. If no E_i yields *true*, C_0 is chosen instead.

The above conditional commands are deterministic – in each case it is predictable which subcommand will be chosen. A *nondeterministic* conditional command is also sometimes useful, and might be written in the form:

```
if E₁ then  C₁
 | E₂ then  C₂
...
 | Eₙ then  Cₙ
end if
```

Here the truth-valued expressions $E_1, E_2, ..., E_n$ are evaluated *collaterally*, and *any* E_i that yields *true* causes the corresponding subcommand C_i to be chosen. If no E_i evaluates to *true*, the command fails.

Example 3.12
Compare the following Pascal *if* command:

```
if x >= y then max := x else max := y
```

with the following hypothetical nondeterministic conditional command:

```
if x >= y then max := x
 | x <= y then max := y
end if
```

The latter has the advantage of making explicit the condition under which 'max := y' may be executed; it also emphasizes that it does not matter which subcommand is chosen in the case that x and y have equal values. (This particular command is effectively deterministic.)   □

Nondeterministic conditional commands tend to be available only in concurrent programming languages (such as Ada), where nondeterminism is present anyway, but their advantages are not restricted to such languages.

Choice based on values other than truth values is also possible. Pascal's *case* command has the form:

```
case E of
    L₁ : C₁
    ...
    Lₙ : Cₙ
end
```

Here the value yielded by the expression E must equal the value of one of the literals L_i, and then the corresponding subcommand C_i is chosen. If the value yielded by E equals none of the L_i, the command fails. (The L_i must all be distinct, so the choice is deterministic.)

Example 3.13
In the following Pascal *case* command, choice is based on a value of the enumeration type Month (Example 3.2):

```
var   today : Date;
      name  : packed array [1..3] of Char;
...
case today.m of
    jan: name := 'JAN';
    feb: name := 'FEB';
    ...
    dec: name := 'DEC'
end
```

□

In Pascal and Ada, choice must be based on values of a discrete primitive type, e.g., characters, enumerands, or integers. In principle, however, choice in a *case* command may be based on values of *any* type for which an equality relation is defined. ML's *case* expression (see Example 2.21) does have the maximum generality: choice may be based on strings, records, constructions, etc. – in fact any values except functions.

3.5.7 Iterative commands

Procedure calls have their counterparts as function calls, and conditional commands have their counterparts as conditional expressions, but iteration is peculiar to the world of commands. An *iterative command* (commonly known as a *loop*) has a subcommand (the *loop body*) that is to be executed repeatedly, and usually some kind of phrase that determines when iteration will cease.

We can classify iterative commands according to whether the number of iterations is determined in advance, or not. Thus we have:

- *indefinite iteration*
- *definite iteration*

First let us examine ***indefinite iteration***. This concerns loops where the number of iterations is not determined in advance.

Indefinite iteration is typically provided by the *while* command, which consists of a loop body C and a truth-valued expression E (the *loop condition*) that controls whether iteration is to continue:

```
while E do C
```

This command is exactly equivalent to:

```
if E then
   begin
   C;
   while E do C
   end
```

Note that this definition is recursive. In fact iteration is just a special form of recursion.

As this definition makes clear, the loop condition in a *while* command is tested *before* each iteration of the loop body. Pascal also has a *repeat* command in which the loop condition is tested *after* each iteration:

```
repeat C until E
```

A form of loop in which the loop condition may be tested *anywhere* within the loop body has often been advocated. This might be written:

```
repeat C₁ while E do C₂
```

This form can be specialized to the *while* command (if C_1 is a skip), or to Pascal's *repeat* command (if C_2 is a skip). The case for including such a form of loop in a programming language is undermined by experience which suggests that it is still not general enough! In practice, the *while* command is perfectly adequate in the great majority of cases, but occasionally the programmer needs a loop with several loop conditions in different parts of the loop body. That need is best served by some kind of escape sequencer (see Section 8.2).

Example 3.14

The following Pascal loop writes every character from a character file f:

```
while not eof (f) do
   begin read (f, ch);  write (ch) end
```

The following Pascal loop does likewise, but assumes that the characters are terminated by the character '*':

```
read (f, ch);
while ch <> '*' do
   begin write (ch);  read (f, ch) end
```

Note the duplication of code. This could be avoided using our hypothetical loop with an exit in the middle:

```
repeat
    read (f, ch)
while ch <> '*' do
    write (ch)
```

☐

Now let us consider *definite iteration*. This concerns loops where the number of iterations is determined in advance. Definite iteration is characterized by the use of a *control variable*. The loop body is executed with the control variable taking each of a predetermined sequence of values. We shall call this sequence of values the *control sequence*.

The Pascal *for* command illustrates definite iteration:

for $V := E_1$ **to** E_2 **do** C

Here the control variable is V, and the control sequence consists of the consecutive values $v_1, succ(v_1), ..., v_2$, where v_1 and v_2 are the values yielded by E_1 and E_2, respectively. These values, and the control variable, may be of any discrete primitive type.

Some languages (such as Algol and PL/I) allow the control sequence to be an arbitrary arithmetic progression, e.g.:

for $V := E_1$ **to** E_2 **by** E_3 **do** C

Here the control sequence is the longest sequence $v_1, v_1+v_3, v_1+2v_3, ...$ that does not properly encompass v_2, where v_1, v_2, and v_3 are the values yielded by E_1, E_2, and E_3, respectively.

There is no fundamental reason why the control sequence should be restricted to an arithmetic progression, nor even why it should consist of primitive values. A more general kind of *for* command would be iteration over an arbitrary *list*, as follows:

for V **in** E **do** C

Here E would be a list expression, which is evaluated to determine the control sequence. (A phrase like 'E_1 **to** E_2' could be regarded as a form of list expression. Then the Pascal *for* command would just be a special case of the more general list-oriented *for* command.)

Iteration over a *set* is also possible. In this case the control sequence would consist of all elements of the set, but in no particular order. A set-oriented *for* command would be nondeterministic.

Example 3.15
The following Pascal *for* command writes all the uppercase letters in turn:

for ch := 'A' **to** 'Z' **do** write (ch)

where ch is a Char variable.

If Pascal allowed iteration over a file (its nearest equivalent to a list), the following *for* command would write every character in the character file f:

```
for ch in f do write (ch)
```

(Compare with Example 3.14.)

If Pascal allowed iteration over a set, the following *for* command would write an unpredictable permutation of the uppercase and lowercase letters:

```
for ch in ['A'..'Z', 'a'..'z'] do write (ch)
```

This would be nondeterministic. The following computation would, however, be effectively deterministic:

```
f := 1;   for i in [2..n] do f := f * i
```

(Why?)   □

The status of the control variable itself varies from language to language. In some languages (such as Fortran, Algol-60, PL/I, Pascal), it is an ordinary variable that must be declared in the usual way. This interpretation of '**for** V ... **do** C' is as follows:

> *determine the control sequence;*
> V := *first value of the control sequence; C;*
> ...
> V := *last value of the control sequence; C*

which leads to such awkward questions as the following:

(a) What is the control variable's value after termination of the loop?
(b) What is the control variable's value after a jump out of the loop?
(c) What happens if the loop body causes an assignment to the control variable?

In other languages (such as Algol-68 and Ada), the *for* command itself constitutes a declaration of the control variable; moreover, it is held constant within the loop body. This interpretation of '**for** V ... **do** C' is as follows (in Pascal-like notation):

> *determine the control sequence;*
> **const** V = *first value of the control sequence;* **begin** C **end;**
> ...
> **const** V = *last value of the control sequence;* **begin** C **end**

which makes the *for* command completely self-contained, and neatly answers all the above questions:

(a) The control variable has no value outside the loop – it is inaccessible.
(b) Ditto.
(c) The loop body cannot cause an assignment to the control variable – it is in fact a constant!

3.6 Expressions with side effects

The primary purpose of evaluating an expression is to yield a value. In some imperative languages, however, it is possible that evaluating an expression has the *side effect* of updating variables. Here we consider expressions with this property.

3.6.1 Command expressions

Suppose that we are required to write an *expression* to evaluate the polynomial:

$$a_n x^n + ... + a_2 x^2 + a_1 x + a_0$$

There are two possible solutions: recursion or iteration. The former solution would imply defining and calling a recursive function, which we might prefer to avoid. Since iteration is found in commands but not expressions, the latter solution is possible only if the programming language includes some kind of *command expression*.

Example 3.16
The following hypothetical command expression would evaluate our polynomial:

```
var p : Real; i : Integer;
begin
p := a[n];
for i := n-1 downto 0 do p := p * x + a[i];
yield p
end
```

Here we are assuming a command expression quite similar in form to a Pascal block. The subexpression after **yield** is evaluated after the preceding commands have been executed, and determines the value yielded by the command expression.   □

In Pascal and Ada, the body of a function abstraction is, in effect, a command expression. This allows the full power of assignment and iteration to be used in computing function results, but also introduces the danger of side effects in a function body.

In fact, any kind of command expression introduces the possibility of side effects. In Example 3.16 there were actually no side effects, since all the assignments were to *local* variables. But now consider the following example.

Example 3.17
Suppose that we have a function abstraction getchar, which reads a character from a given file and returns that character. The function call 'getchar(f)' has a side effect on the file variable f. In consequence, the following program fragment:

```
if getchar(f) = 'F' then
    gender := female
```

```
else if getchar(f) = 'M' then
   gender := male
else ...
```

is misleading: *two different characters* are read and compared with 'F' and 'M'.   □

Side effects introduce nondeterminism into expression evaluation. This is evident in an expression of the form '$E_1 \otimes E_2$', where E_1 has a side effect that affects the evaluation of E_2, and/or *vice versa*. Indeed it is evident in any expression with sub-expressions that are to be evaluated collaterally. Curiously, the imperative languages Pascal and Ada do allow collateral evaluation of subexpressions, but the functional language ML (which we might expect to be less concerned with evaluation order) avoids this problem by prescribing left-to-right evaluation of subexpressions!

In summary, side effects tend to make programs hard to understand, and are widely held to be bad programming practice.

3.6.2   Expression-oriented languages

An *expression-oriented language* is an imperative language in which all distinctions between expressions and commands are eliminated. Evaluating an expression both yields a value and (in general) has the side effect of updating variables. Algol-68 and ML (and C, to some extent) are examples of expression-oriented languages.

One consequence of this design is to avoid duplications between analogous kinds of expression and command. An expression-oriented language does not need both function and procedure abstractions. Nor does it need both conditional expressions and conditional commands.

The assignment '$V := E$' could be defined to yield the value of E, together with the side effect of assigning that value to the variable determined by V. Since the assignment is itself an expression, we can also write '$V' := (V := E)$', and so on. In other words, we get multiple assignment free. (However, some expression-oriented languages define their assignment differently. For example, an ML assignment expression actually yields the 0-tuple ().)

There is no such obvious result for a skip or loop. Typically an expression-oriented language defines them to yield a neutral value such as 0 or ().

Thus expression-oriented languages achieve a certain simplicity and uniformity by eliminating the distinction between expressions and commands. So why do languages like Pascal and Ada still retain this distinction? The justification is an issue of programming style. Although expressions may have side effects in these languages, the use of side effects by programmers is informally deprecated. (Indeed the designers of both languages initially attempted, unsuccessfully, to prohibit side effects.) On the other hand, expression-oriented languages positively encourage the use of side effects, leading to a cryptic programming style, e.g.:

```
while (ch := getchar (f)) <> '*' do
   write (ch)
```

3.7 Further reading

The notion that distinctions between persistent and transient data types should be avoided is receiving much attention at the time of writing. For a survey of research in this area, see Atkinson and Buneman (1987).

The nondeterministic conditional command discussed in Section 3.5.6, and a corresponding nondeterministic iterative command, were designed by Dijkstra (1976) to support the particular programming discipline that he advocates.

The design of loops with multiple exits attracted much attention in the 1970s, e.g., see Zahn (1974).

Exercises 3

3.1* Systematically analyse the variables and commands of your favorite programming language. (a) What forms of composite variable are supported, and how are they selectively updated? Can they also be totally updated? (b) Are static, dynamic, or flexible arrays provided? (c) Which values are storable? (c) How is the lifetime of each variable defined? (d) Can dangling references arise, and (if so) how? (e) Compare the kinds of command in your language with those discussed in Section 3.5. Are any relevant kinds missing? Are any exotic kinds provided, and are they essential?

3.2* In many programming languages strings are defined to be arrays of characters. Compare the consequences of this when a string variable is: (a) a static array, as in Pascal; (b) a dynamic array, as in Ada; (c) a flexible array, as in Algol-68. Consider string operations such as assignment, comparison, and concatenation. Can comparison and concatenation be defined in the language itself?

3.3 Make a diagram showing the lifetimes of the variables in the following Pascal program:

```
program P;
   var m : Integer;
   procedure R (n : Integer);
      begin
      if n > 0 then R (n-1)
      end;
   begin
   R (2)
   end.
```

Note that R will be activated three times, recursively. Note also that n is, in effect, a local variable of R.

3.4   Complete the following program in Pascal (or your own favorite language, if appropriate):

```
program P;
    type IntList = ^ IntNode;
         IntNode = ...;    (* as in Example 3.8 *)
    var  bag : IntList;

    procedure ins (i : Integer);
        ... (* inserts a node containing i into list bag,
                keeping the list in ascending order *)

    procedure out (i : Integer);
        ... (* removes the node containing i from list bag *)

begin
bag := nil;
ins (6);  ins (2);  ins (9);  ins (5);
out (9);  out (6)
end.
```

Make a diagram showing the lifetimes of the heap variables and bag.

3.5**   Design a modification to Pascal (or your own favorite language, if appropriate) that would add list types to the language (e.g., '**var** odds : **list of** Integer'). Lists are not to be selectively updatable. Provide suitable list aggregates, including one for generating arithmetic progressions. Replace the existing *for* command by one where the control sequence is specified by a list, as suggested in Section 3.5.7.

3.6*   Design a modification to Pascal (or your own favorite language, if appropriate) that would abolish pointer types, and instead would allow recursive types to be defined directly by the programmer. Consider carefully the sharing and copying interpretations of assignment discussed in Section 3.4.2.

3.7   Make a summary of your favorite language's transient data types and persistent data types. What overlap is there between them, if any?

3.8**   Redesign your favorite language to eliminate all specific input–output features. Instead, allow the programmer to create persistent variables (of *any* type) in much the same way as heap variables. What types would be suitable replacements for your language's existing persistent data types? Choose an existing program in your language – one with a large proportion of (nontext) input–output – and rewrite it in your redesigned language.

3.9*   We can gain insight into the nature of commands by writing down equivalences between different commands, e.g.:

$$C; \textbf{skip} \quad \equiv \quad C$$
$$C_1, C_2 \quad \equiv \quad C_2, C_1$$

but, of course, 'C_1; C_2' is *not* equivalent to 'C_2; C_1'. Write down as many such equivalences as you can discover.

3.10 Recursively define the Pascal command '**repeat** C **until** E', and the hypothetical command '**repeat** C_1 **while** E **do** C_2', in a similar manner to that in which the *while* command was defined in Section 3.5.7.

3.11* Consider the questions (a), (b), and (c), posed in Section 3.5.7, concerning the interpretation of '**for** V ... **do** C' where V is an ordinary variable. Find out how Pascal answers these questions.

3.12* Some programmers assert that side effects in expressions are a useful feature of a programming language. Develop arguments for and against this assertion.

3.13* Formulate restrictions on Pascal functions that would eliminate side effects. Bear in mind that any such restrictions ought to be easily enforceable at compile-time (or, failing that, at run-time). Do your restrictions seriously reduce the language's expressive power?

CHAPTER FOUR

Bindings

A concept common to all programming languages is the programmer's ability to *bind* identifiers to entities such as constants, variables, procedures, functions, and types. This concept is enormously important in all programming paradigms. Well-chosen identifiers help to make a program easier to understand. More profoundly, binding an identifier to an entity in one place, and subsequently using that identifier to denote the entity in many other places, helps to make the program flexible: if the entity's implementation is to be changed, the change affects the single place where the entity is bound, not the many places where the entity is used.

In this chapter we study *bindings*, *scope*, and *visibility*; the various kinds of *declaration* that bind identifiers to entities; and *blocks*, program phrases that influence the scopes of declarations.

4.1 Bindings and environments

Consider expressions such as 'n+1' and 'f(x)', and commands such as 'x := 0'. They cannot be interpreted in isolation. Their interpretation depends on what the identifiers within them denote, i.e., on how these identifiers were declared.

Most programming languages allow the further complication that a given identifier such as x can be declared in several parts of the program, possibly denoting different entities. Thus the interpretation of an expression or command containing an occurrence of x may depend on where the expression or command appears in the program.

Example 4.1
Consider the Pascal expression 'n+1'. In the scope of the following declaration:

    const n = 7

n denotes the integer seven, so the expression 'n+1' is evaluated by adding one to seven.

On the other hand, in the scope of the following declaration:

```
var n : Integer
```

n denotes a variable, so the expression 'n+1' is evaluated by adding one to the current value of that variable (i.e., the value last assigned to it). □

We can understand the effects of declarations by invoking the concepts of bindings and environments. We say that a declaration produces an association or **binding** between the declared identifier and the entity that it will denote. The constant definition in Example 4.1 would bind n to the integer 7, i.e., it makes n denote that integer. The variable declaration in the same example would bind n to a newly created variable.

An **environment** is a set of bindings. Each expression and command is interpreted in a particular environment, and all identifiers occurring in the expression or command must have bindings in that environment. Expressions and commands in different parts of the program may be interpreted in different environments.

Usually at most one binding per identifier is allowed in any environment. An environment is then a partial mapping from identifiers to the entities that they denote.

Example 4.2
Consider the following Pascal program skeleton:

```
program p;
   const z = 0;
   var   c : Char;

   procedure q;
      const c = 3.0e6;
      var   b : Boolean;
      begin
②  ...
      end;

   begin
①  ...
   end.
```

The environment at point ① is:

> { c ↦ a character variable,
>   q ↦ a procedure abstraction,
>   z ↦ the integer 0 }

The environment at point ② is:

> { b ↦ a variable that will contain a truth value,
>   c ↦ the real number 3000000.0,
>   q ↦ a procedure abstraction,
>   z ↦ the integer 0 }

□

4.2   Bindables

One characteristic of a programming language is which sorts of entity may be bound to identifiers. These entities are called the **bindables** of the language. (They are also called *denotables* – entities that may be denoted by identifiers.)

The bindables of Pascal, and the kinds of declaration in which they may be bound, are as follows:

- primitive values and strings   (in constant definitions)
- references to variables   (in variable declarations)
- procedure and function abstractions   (in procedure and function definitions)
- (identities of) types   (in type definitions)

Note that only certain types of value are bindable in Pascal constant definitions. For example, we cannot bind an identifier to a record value, nor to an array value (other than a string), nor to a set. (The best we can do is to bind an identifier to a variable that may *contain* a record, array, or set value.) This irregularity in the language is a source of real irritation to Pascal programmers.

The bindables of ML are:

- primitive values, composite values,
  function abstractions, references to variables   (in value definitions)
- types   (in type and 'datatype' declarations)
- exceptions   (in exception declarations)

Note that every type of value is bindable in an ML value definition. In this respect ML is more regular than Pascal.

4.3   Scope

Only in a very simple language does each declaration affect the environment of the whole program. In general, each declaration has a certain *scope*, which is the portion of the program text over which the declaration is effective. In order that we can discuss scope issues without getting into the details of a particular language, we first introduce the concept of *block structure*.

4.3.1   Block structure

A **block** is any program phrase that delimits the scope of any declarations that it may contain. In Section 4.5 we shall look at blocks in detail. Here we are concerned only with the language's **block structure**, i.e., the textual relationship between blocks. In particular, we are interested in whether blocks can be nested within one another.

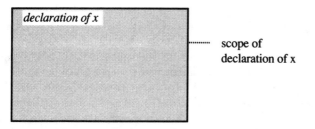

Figure 4.1 Monolithic block structure.

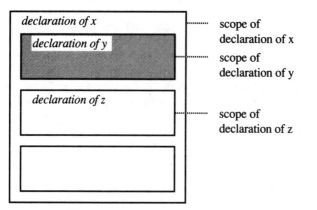

Figure 4.2 Flat block structure.

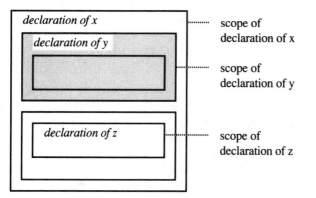

Figure 4.3 Nested block structure.

Figures 4.1, 4.2, and 4.3 contrast three kinds of block structure. Each block is represented by a box. The scopes of some declarations are indicated by shading.

The simplest possible block structure is the monolithic block structure (Figure 4.1), in which the entire program is a single block. This is exemplified by (older versions of) Cobol. The scope of every declaration is the whole program. This block structure is far too crude, particularly for writing large programs. All declarations must be grouped in the same place, even if the declared identifiers are used in different parts of the program. It is awkward for several programmers to work on the same program, since they must take ensure that all declared entities have distinct identifiers.

An obvious improvement is the flat block structure (Figure 4.2), in which the program is partitioned into distinct blocks. This is exemplified by Fortran, in which all subprograms (procedure and function abstractions) are separate, and each acts as a block. A variable can be declared inside a particular subprogram, and is then local to that subprogram. The scope of the subprogram identifiers themselves is the whole program. Likewise, the scope of global variables is the whole program. One disadvantage of the flat block structure is that all subprograms and global variables must have distinct identifiers. Another disadvantage is that any variable that cannot be local to a particular subprogram is forced to be global, and thus have the whole program as its scope, even if it is accessed by only a couple of subprograms.

A further improvement (and much the most popular) is the nested block structure, in which each block may be nested inside any other block (Figure 4.3). This is exemplified by the Algol-like languages. A block can be located wherever convenient, and identifiers can then be declared inside it. The nested block structure is not ideal, however, and we shall explore its disadvantages in Chapter 6.

4.3.2   Scope and visibility

Identifiers occur in two different contexts. We shall use the term *binding occurrence* for an occurrence of an identifier at the point where it is declared, i.e., bound to some entity; and we shall use the term *applied occurrence* for each occurrence of the identifier at which it denotes that entity. For example, the occurrence of n in 'const n = 7' is a binding occurrence, at which n is bound to 7; and the subsequent occurrences of n in the expression 'n * (n-1)' are applied occurrences, at which n denotes 7.

When a program contains more than one block, it is possible for the same identifier *I* to be declared in different blocks. In general, *I* will denote a different entity in each block. This freedom allows the programmer to declare and use identifiers within a given block, without worrying about whether the same identifiers might have been declared and used in other blocks.

But what happens if the same identifier is declared in two nested blocks (Figure 4.4)? Most languages with nested block structure do permit this. Suppose that a block *B* lies within the scope of a declaration of identifier *I*. If *B* contains no declaration of *I*, then applied occurrences of *I* both inside and outside *B* correspond to the same declaration of *I*. If *B* does contain a declaration of *I*, on the other hand, then all applied occurrences of *I* inside *B* correspond to the inner, not the outer, declaration of *I*; the outer declaration of *I* is said to be *invisible* within *B*, or to be *hidden* by the inner declaration of *I*.

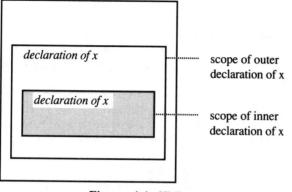

Figure 4.4 Hiding.

Recall Example 4.2. The constant definition of c inside the procedure hides the variable declaration of c in the main program. All the other declarations in the main program, however, are visible inside the procedure.

In this subsection we have made certain simplifying assumptions, which will later be examined in detail:

- that the language has static binding (see Section 4.3.3)
- that the scope of each declaration is the entire enclosing block (see Section 4.4.7)
- that there is no overloading (see Section 7.2)

4.3.3 Static and dynamic binding

Consider the following program outline:

```
const s = 2;

function scaled (d : Integer);
   begin
   scaled := d * s
   end;

procedure ...;
   const s = 3;
   begin
②  ... scaled (h) ...
   end

begin
①  ... scaled (h) ...
end
```

The result of 'scaled (h)' depends on how we interpret the occurrence of s in the body of function scaled.

The most common interpretation is called ***static binding*** (or *static scopes*). The function body is evaluated in the environment of the function *definition*. At that point s denotes 2, so 'scaled (h)' always returns the value of h doubled – regardless of where the function is called from.

The alternative interpretation is called ***dynamic binding*** (or *dynamic scopes*). The function body is evaluated in the environment of the function *call*. Thus the function call 'scaled (h)' at point ① returns the value of h doubled, since s denotes 2 at that point. On the other hand, the function call 'scaled (h)' at point ② returns the value of h trebled, since s denotes 3 at that point!

The terminology of static and dynamic binding is based on when we can determine which binding occurrence of an identifier *I* corresponds to a given applied occurrence of *I*. With static binding we can do this at compile-time; with dynamic binding we must delay this until run-time.

With static binding, we can determine which binding occurrence of *I* corresponds to a given applied occurrence of *I*, just by examining the program text. We find the smallest block containing the applied occurrence of *I* that also contains a binding occurrence of *I*; the latter is the binding occurrence we seek. Note that the association between applied occurrences and binding occurrences is fixed. In our example, therefore, we could safely replace the applied occurrence of s in the body of scaled by the literal 2.

With dynamic binding, the binding occurrence of *I* corresponding to a given applied occurrence of *I* depends on the program's dynamic flow of control. Whenever the entity denoted by *I* is needed, we find the most recently elaborated declaration of *I* that is inside a currently active block.

It should be evident that dynamic binding does not fit with static typing. In the example, suppose that the global definition of s were replaced by '**const** s = 0.5'. With static binding, the type error in 'scaled := d*s' would be detected by static type checking. With dynamic binding, the function call 'scaled (h)' at point ② would be unaffected, but the function call 'scaled (h)' at point ① would result in a type error. Static type checking could predict this type error only if the program's flow of control were predictable – which is not the case, in general.

For this reason, languages with dynamic binding (such as Lisp and Smalltalk) also have dynamic typing. The mismatch with static typing illustrates a more general problem with dynamic binding, namely the fact that it tends to make procedure and function abstractions harder to understand. If a procedure *P* accesses a nonlocal constant or variable, or calls a nonlocal function or procedure, the effect will depend on where *P* was called. Indeed, *P* might be used in ways never anticipated by its programmer.

Nearly all programming languages (including Fortran, Algol, Pascal, Ada, and ML) opt for static binding. In this book we shall usually assume static binding, unless dynamic binding is explicitly referred to.

An applied occurrence of an identifier *I* is said to be *free* in a program phrase *P* if there is no corresponding binding occurrence of *I* in *P*. For example, the applied occurrences of x and y are free in the expression 'x+y'; and the applied occurrences of x and z (but *not* y) are free in the ML expression '**let val** y = z+1 **in** x+y'.

4.4 Declarations

Having considered bindings, block structure, and visibility, let us now examine declarations. A **declaration** is a program phrase that will be **elaborated** to produce bindings.

The following kinds of declaration are fundamental:

- *definitions*
- *collateral declarations*
- *sequential declarations*
- *recursive declarations*

We also consider two particular kinds of declaration that do more than just produce bindings: a *type declaration* may create a new type, and a *variable declaration* may create a new variable. As usual, our interest is not primarily in the syntactic details of declarations, but rather in their underlying concepts.

4.4.1 Definitions

Recall that a declaration is elaborated primarily to produce bindings. We define a **definition** to be a simple declaration whose *only* effect is to produce bindings. Simple as this concept may be, the definition is an important part of the programmer's toolkit because it allows an entity (such as a constant, type, procedure, or function) to be defined once, and subsequently used wherever required simply by using the identifier that denotes it.

Pascal's *constant definition* binds an identifier to a value that is determined at compile-time. It has the form '**const** $I = E$', and when elaborated it binds the identifier I to the value of the expression E. The latter expression is very restricted: it can only be a literal, an identifier denoting a constant, or unary '+' or '−' applied to one of these; and it must yield a primitive value or string. These restrictions ensure that E can be evaluated at compile-time; but they could easily be relaxed.

Example 4.3
The following illustrates the full generality of the Pascal constant definition!

```
const minint = -maxint
```

The following illustrate what a Pascal programmer *cannot* define:

```
const letters = ['a'..'z', 'A'..'Z'];
      minchar = chr (0);
      halfpi  = 0.5 * pi
```

although in every case the expression on the right-hand side could still be evaluated at compile-time. □

Some other languages (such as Algol-68, Ada, and ML) avoid such restrictions, allowing any value of any type to be bound. Moreover, the value is obtained by evaluating an ordinary expression, which need not be evaluated at compile-time. For example, ML's *value definition* has the form '**val** $I = E$', where E is any expression.

Example 4.4
Consider the following ML value definitions:

```
fun aftertax (income: real) =
      let
          val taxable = income - 4000.00;
          val tax      = if taxable <= 0.0⁾
                         then 0.00
                         else 0.25 * taxable
      in
          income - tax
      end
```

Note that the value of income, and therefore the values of taxable and tax, are unknown at compile-time.   □

Pascal's *procedure definition* binds an identifier to a procedure abstraction, and similarly a *function definition* binds an identifier to a function abstraction.

Example 4.5
The following Pascal function definition:

```
function even (n : Integer) : Boolean;
   begin
   odd := (n mod 2 = 0)
   end
```

binds the identifier even to an appropriate function abstraction.   □

In ML function abstractions are first-class values, so they can be bound in ordinary value definitions.

Example 4.6
Consider the following ML value definition:

```
val even =
      fn (n: int) => (n mod 2 = 0)
```

The right-hand side is an expression whose value is a function of type Integer $\rightarrow$ Truth-Value – a function whose formal parameter is n and whose body is '(n mod 2 = 0)'. The value definition binds the identifier odd to that function.

ML also has a special function definition:

```
fun even (n: int) = (n mod 2 = 0)
```

but this is merely a syntactic shorthand for the above value definition.

However, ML value definitions are more general than function definitions, since the right-hand side of a value definition can be *any* function-valued expression:

```
fun naturallogarithm (x: real) = ...;
val ln = naturallogarithm

val wave = if ... then sin else cos

val odd = not o even
```

(The binary operator o composes two functions.) □

The possibilities illustrated at the end of Example 4.6 are ruled out by languages like Pascal in which the conventional procedure or function definition is the only form of definition that binds an identifier to a procedure or function abstraction.

In a programming language that is regular and self-consistent, we would expect all entities to be bindable, including types and (references to) variables. So we would expect the language to provide a definition that binds an identifier to an existing type, and a definition that binds an identifier to an existing variable. For convenience, we discuss type definitions in Section 4.4.2, and variable definitions in Section 4.4.3.

4.4.2 Type declarations

A *type definition* serves only to bind an identifier to an existing type. Type definitions in this strict sense can be found only in languages with structural equivalence of types (see Section 2.5.2).

An alternative kind of type declaration is one that creates a new and distinct type: a *new-type declaration*. This kind of type declaration fits well with name equivalence of types (see Section 2.5.2).

Example 4.7
Consider the following ML type definitions:

```
type book   = string * int;
type author = string * int
```

The intention is to represent a book by a pair consisting of its title and edition number, and to represent an author by his/her name and age. Whatever the programmer's intentions, book and author denote exactly the same type. Thus book and author values may be confused; in fact they are indistinguishable.

However, ML also has a new-type declaration, the so-called *datatype declaration*:

```
datatype book   = bk of string * int;
datatype author = au of string * int
```

which was discussed (in a different context) in Section 2.3.2. Here, each book value has a tag *bk*, and each author value has a tag *au*. The types are distinct, so no confusion of values is possible. □

Pascal adopts a different approach. Each occurrence of a type constructor (e.g., '**record** ... **end**' or '**array** [...] **of** ...') creates a new and distinct type. The type definition itself merely binds an identifier to a type.

Example 4.8
When the following Pascal type definition is elaborated:

```
type Person =
        record
            name    : packed array [1..20] of Char;
            age     : Integer;
            height  : Real
        end
```

a new array type and a new record type are created. The new array type remains anonymous; the new record type has the identifier Person bound to it by the type definition. When the following type definition is elaborated:

```
type Title = packed array [1..20] of Char
```

another new array type is created. This type is distinct from the type of name.   □

4.4.3   Variable declarations

A *variable definition* serves only to bind an identifier to an *existing* variable. Not many languages provide variable definitions. One disadvantage is that they establish *aliases*, and the existence of aliases tends to make programs harder to understand and to reason about. (See Section 5.2.2.)

A *new-variable declaration* creates a new and distinct variable. This kind of variable declaration is far more common – some means of creating new variables is essential in any imperative language.

Example 4.9
The following Pascal new-variable declaration:

```
var count : Integer
```

creates a new Integer variable, and binds the identifier count to it. The following Ada new-variable declaration:

```
count : Integer := 0;
```

does likewise, and additionally initializes the variable to zero.

Ada also has a variable definition (called a *renaming declaration*), e.g.:

```
pop : Integer renames population(state);
```

This binds the identifier pop to an *existing* Integer variable, namely a particular component of an array variable population (the one whose index is the current value of state). Subsequently, and as often as desired, pop can be used to access this component variable concisely and efficiently, e.g.:

```
pop := pop + 1;
```

☐

In ML references to variables are first-class values, and the language has no special variable declaration. Instead we use an allocator to create a variable; and independently we may use a value definition to bind an identifier to a variable (whether newly created or not).

Example 4.10
When the following ML value definition is elaborated:

```
val count = ref 0
```

the allocator 'ref 0' creates a new integer variable, initialized to zero. The identifier count is then bound to (a reference to) that variable. The following value definition:

```
val pop = population sub state
```

binds pop to an existing variable, namely a component of the array population. Compare Example 4.9. ☐

4.4.4 Collateral declarations

We now consider how declarations may be composed. The choice is between *collateral* composition, which is discussed here, and *sequential* composition, which is discussed in the next subsection.

A *collateral declaration* might be written in the form 'D_1 **and** D_2'. Its effect is to elaborate the subdeclarations D_1 and D_2 independently of each other, and then to combine the bindings they produced. Neither subdeclaration can use an identifier declared in the other subdeclaration.

Collateral declarations are not very common; for example, they are not found in either Pascal or Ada. In ML, however, a group of declarations of the same kind (value, type, etc.) may be elaborated collaterally.

Example 4.11
The following ML collateral value definition:

```
val pi  = 3.14159
and sin = fn (x: real) => ...
and cos = fn (x: real) => ...
```

combines independent definitions of the identifiers pi, sin, and cos. It would be *illegal* to add:

```
and tan = fn (x: real) => sin (x) / cos (x)
```

since this definition is dependent on the others. ☐

4.4.5   Sequential declarations

The most common way of composing declarations is sequentially. Typically a *sequential declaration* is written in the form 'D_1; D_2'. Its effect is to elaborate the subdeclaration D_1 folowed by the subdeclaration D_2, allowing the bindings produced by D_1 to be used in D_2.

Example 4.12
In the following Pascal sequential declaration:

```
var count : Integer;
procedure bump;
   begin
   count := count + 1
   end
```

the identifier count is declared in the first subdeclaration and used in the second.   □

ML has sequential declarations too. The problem mentioned in Example 4.11 can easily be solved by a sequential declaration in which the collateral declaration of pi, sin, and cos is followed by a declaration of tan.

4.4.6   Recursive declarations

A *recursive declaration* is one that uses the very bindings that it produces itself. Some elderly languages (such as Fortran and Cobol) do not support recursion at all, and are seriously weakened as a consequence. The more modern programming languages do support recursion, usually restricting it to type, procedure, and function definitions. These are in fact the most useful kinds of recursion.

In Pascal, a sequence of type definitions is automatically treated as recursive, allowing definitions of recursive types like intlist in Example 3.8. (A syntactic constraint ensures that Pascal recursive types always involve pointers.) A sequence of procedure and function definitions is also treated as recursive in Pascal. Constant definitions and variable declarations are always nonrecursive.

Example 4.13
The following Pascal procedure definitions are mutually recursive:

```
procedure parseExpression;   forward;

procedure parsePrimary;
   begin
   if acceptable ('(') then
      begin parseExpression; accept (')') end
   else
```

```
        parseVariable
    end;

procedure parseExpression;
    begin
    parsePrimary;
    while acceptable ('+') do
        parsePrimary
    end
```

(Here forward is merely a compiler directive, and does not affect the *meaning* of the procedure definitions.) □

There are disadvantages in treating declarations as *automatically* recursive. The old argument, that recursion is inefficient, is not the most important, as an example will show.

Example 4.14

Suppose that an existing Pascal program uses the standard eof function to detect the end of a text file. It is now required to treat the character '*' as marking the end of a text file. To minimize modifications to the existing program, we might try to redefine eof as follows, in terms of the standard eof:

```
function eof (var f : Text) : Boolean;
    begin
    eof := eof (f) or (f^ = '*')
    end
```

However, the function call 'eof (f)' here does *not* call the standard function – it calls the newly defined function recursively!

If the programmer were enabled to distinguish between recursive and nonrecursive declarations, the function eof here could be declared as nonrecursive, and would then work as intended. □

ML and some other languages allow the programmer to state explicitly whether a declaration is to be recursive.

Example 4.15

Consider the following ML recursive value definition:

```
val rec power =
        fn (x: real, n: int) =>
            if n = 0 then 1.0
            else if n < 0 then 1.0 / power (x, -n)
            else x * power (x, n-1)
```

If this definition were not recursive, the two applied occurrences of power would correspond to some declaration of power elsewhere (if any existed). □

4.4.7 Scopes of declarations

Simple, collateral, sequential, and recursive declarations differ in their influence on scope. This point is illustrated most clearly by ML value definitions, which come in all these forms – see Figure 4.5.

The scope of a simple declaration in ML (in the absence of recursion) extends from the end of the declaration to the end of the enclosing block. With a collateral declaration, the scopes of the subdeclarations extend from the end of the collateral declaration to the end of the block. A sequential declaration is similar, except that the scope of the first subdeclaration includes the second subdeclaration.

All this is changed if the declaration is recursive: then the scope of the declaration includes itself.

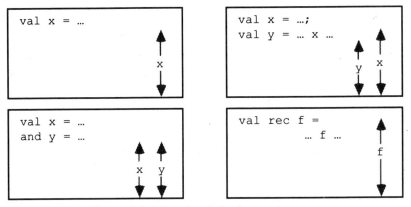

Figure 4.5 ML value definitions and scopes.

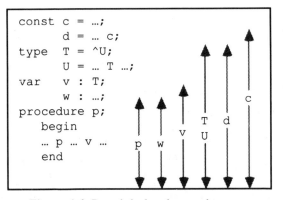

Figure 4.6 Pascal declarations and scopes.

Pascal declarations are less flexible in several respects: (a) there are no collateral declarations; (b) type, procedure, and function definitions are always recursive; (c) constant definitions and variable declarations are always nonrecursive. The consequences are illustrated in Figure 4.6. The scope of each constant definition extends from the end of the definition; the scope of each type definition extends from the *beginning* of the group of type definitions; the scope of each variable declaration extends from the end of the declaration; the scope of each procedure and function definition extends from the *beginning* of the group of procedure and function definitions.

4.5 Blocks

In Section 4.3 we loosely defined a ***block*** to be a program phrase that delimits the scope of any declarations that it might contain. Now let us examine blocks in more detail.

It makes sense to allow declarations to be local to the execution of a command, giving us a *block command*. Equally it makes sense to allow declarations to be local to the evaluation of an expression, giving us a *block expression*. There are other possibilities too.

4.5.1 Block commands

A ***block command*** is a command containing a declaration, the bindings produced by which are used only for executing that command.

In Pascal, a block command has the form '*D* **begin** *C* **end**'. The command *C* is executed in an environment in which the bindings produced by *D* override the bindings of the outside environment.

The only net effect of executing a block command is to update variables. (The elaboration of *D* has only a localized effect.) Thus a block command behaves like any other command. Nevertheless, a Pascal block command cannot be placed with the same freedom as ordinary commands; it can occur only as a program body or procedure body. This is an irregularity in the language. Its practical consequence is that the programmer cannot place declarations just where they are needed.

Example 4.16
Suppose that m and n are Integer variables, and their contents are to be sorted such that m contains the smaller integer. In Pascal we would write:

```
if m > n then
    begin t := m; m := n; n := t end
```

but the auxiliary variable t must be declared somewhere else, perhaps at the head of the enclosing program, procedure, or function body. Thus the declaration of t might be widely separated from its use.

If Pascal counted a block command as an ordinary command, we could declare t locally:

```
if m > n then
    var t : Integer;
    begin t := m; m := n; n := t end
```

Such localization tends to make programs easier to understand and to modify.   □

The omission of a block command from Pascal was in fact a retrograde step. Its predecessor Algol-60 had a block command, of the form '**begin** *D*; *C* **end**'.

4.5.2   Block expressions

A *block expression* is an expression containing a declaration, the bindings produced by which are used only for evaluating that expression.

In Pascal the closest equivalent to a block expression is a function body. The net effect of executing a function body is to yield a value (the function result), and possibly to cause side effects. This is just like evaluating an ordinary expression. (See Exercise 4.6.)

ML has a block expression, of the form '**let** *D* **in** *E* **end**', that may be placed wherever any other expression may be placed. The subexpression *E* is evaluated in an environment in which the bindings produced by *D* override the bindings of the outside environment.

Example 4.17
Suppose that a, b, and c denote the lengths of the sides of a triangle. The following ML block expression yields the area of that triangle:

```
let val s = (a + b + c) * 0.5
in  sqrt (s * (s-a) * (s-b) * (s-c))
end
```

□

4.5.3   The qualification principle

We may summarize the preceding subsections as follows:

- A *block expression* is one containing a local declaration, the bindings produced by which are used only for *evaluating* the *block expression*.
- A *block command* is one containing a local declaration, the bindings produced by which are used only for *executing* the *block command*.

Note the analogy between block expressions and block commands. Can we take this analogy further? In other words, are there other kinds of phrase that we can sensibly make into blocks? In principle, we can take the analogy further:

The qualification principle: It is possible to include a block in any syntactic class, provided that the phrases of that class specify some kind of computation.

One very useful example of this is a ***block declaration***:

* A *block declaration* is one containing a local declaration, the bindings produced by which are used only for *elaborating* the *block declaration*.

This construct is found in ML and (in a disguised form) in Ada. It supports the concept of *encapsulation*, which is important enough to merit a chapter to itself (Chapter 6). For the present a simple example of a block declaration must suffice.

Example 4.18
The following ML block declaration declares a function `leap`, using an auxiliary function `multiple`:

```
local
    fun multiple (n: int, d: int) =
            (n mod d = 0)
in
    fun leap (y: int) =
            (multiple(y,4)
                andalso not multiple(y,100))
                orelse multiple(y,400)
end
```

When elaborated this block declaration produces just one binding, for `leap`. The scope of the definition of `multiple` is restricted to the block declaration itself. □

Example 4.18 is too small to be entirely realistic. A large module might declare numerous entities (say A, B, C, D, ..., Y, Z), but only a few of them (say A, B, C) are to be exported, i.e., made visible outside the module, the rest being auxiliary declarations. Use of a block declaration allows the module's interface to be kept narrow by limiting the number of bindings visible outside the module:

```
local
    declarations of D, ..., Y, Z
in
    declarations of A, B, C
end
```

4.6 Further reading

The qualification principle is stated and explained in Tennent (1981).

Exercises 4

4.1* Systematically analyse the declarations and blocks of your favorite programming language. (a) What is your language's block structure? (b) What are its bindables? (c) Compare the various kinds of declaration in your language with those discussed in Section 4.4. Are any relevant kinds missing? Are any exotic kinds provided, and are they essential? (d) What are your language's scope and visibility rules? (e) What kind(s) of blocks are provided?

4.2 What is the environment at each numbered point in the following Pascal program?

```
program p;
   const x = 999;
①  type Nat = 0..x;
②  var   m, n : Nat;

③  function f (n : Nat) : Nat;
       begin
④      ...
       end;

⑤  procedure w (i : Nat);
⑥     const n = 6;
       begin
⑦      ...
       end;

   begin
⑧   ...
   end.
```

4.3 What is the environment at each numbered point in the following ML program?

```
let
    val pi  = 3.14159
    and sin = fn (x: real) =>
                 ①  ...
    and cos = fn (x: real) =>
                 ②  ...;

③  val tan = fn (x: real) =>
                 ④  sin (x) / cos (x);

⑤  val rec f = fn (n: int) =>
                 ⑥  ...
in
```

⑦   ...
end

(Note that, in the function abstraction '**fn** (*I*: *T*) => *E* ', the scope of the formal parameter *I* is the function body *E*.)

4.4   Consider the following program outline, which shows binding occurrences (*declaration of I*) and applied occurrences (... *I* ...) of some identifiers. Assume that the language has static bindings. Which of the applied occurrences are legal, and which are their associated binding occurrences? What is the exact scope of each declaration? Take the programming language to be: (a) Pascal; (b) ML; (c) your favorite language.

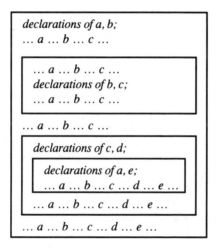

4.5*   As well as ordinary function definitions (similar to Pascal's), Ada also has special renaming declarations for functions, e.g.:

```
function matrix_inversion (m : Matrix)
                  return Matrix is
    ...;    -- function body

function inv (m : Matrix) return Matrix
            renames matrix_inversion;
```

Show how Ada's function definitions might be generalized to make function renaming declarations redundant. (*Hint:* Compare Example 4.6.)

4.6*   The Pascal procedure body could easily be made into a block command in its existing form – see Example 4.16. However, the Pascal function body could not be made into a block expression in its existing form. Why not? Redesign the Pascal function body so that it could be used as a block expression as well. (*Hint:* Consider the Ada function body.)

4.7   The ML recursive value definition '**val rec** x = ... x ...' is legal only if the value being bound is a function abstraction. Why do you think this is so? (*Hint:* Consider '**val rec** x = x + 1'.)

4.8*   A directory or catalog in a filestore may be regarded as a kind of environment, being a set of bindings of filenames to filestore locations. The files themselves are composite variables held at these locations.

A hypothetical programming language assumes that each file is a sequence of components, all of the same type, and has the file input–output operations illustrated here:

```
var   f : file of Employee;
      e : Employee;
begin
reset (f, 'EMPS');
read (f, e);
...
end
```

The variable f will contain a pointer to some file component of type Employee. The command 'reset (f, 'EMPS')' opens the file named EMPS, and makes f point to the first component of that file. The command 'read (f, e)' assigns to e the file component that f currently points to, and updates f to point to the next component of the same file. There are analogous operations for writing to files.

Show that in this language the file 'environment' is quite distinct from the ordinary environment. Show further that the language has dynamic binding with respect to the file 'environment' (even if the language has static binding with respect to the ordinary environment).

Most programming languages are essentially similar to the hypothetical language in this respect. Analyse your favorite language's file input–output from this point of view.

Abstraction

Abstraction is a mode of thought by which we concentrate on general ideas rather than on specific manifestations of these ideas. Abstraction is the whole basis of philosophy and mathematics, and is also fruitful in many other disciplines, including all branches of computer science.

In systems analysis, abstraction is the discipline by which we concentrate on essential aspects of the problem on hand, and ignore all extraneous aspects. For example, in air traffic control there are numerous details, such as the color and external markings of each aircraft, the names of the crew and passengers, etc., that are irrelevant to the working of the system; in designing a system we abstract away from these details, and concentrate on the essentials, namely each aircraft's type and call sign.

In programming, abstraction alludes to the distinction we make between (a) *what* a piece of program does and (b) *how* it is implemented. A programming language itself consists of constructs that are (ultimately) abstractions of machine code. But this is not the end of the story; we exploit abstraction whenever we introduce a procedure (or function). When we call a procedure we should be concerned only with *what* the procedure does; only when we write a procedure are we concerned with *how* it is implemented. By implementing higher-level procedures in terms of lower-level procedures, programmers can introduce as many new levels of abstraction as desired. This kind of hierarchy is an essential tool in building large programs.

We also use the term *abstraction* for a programming language construct that supports the concept of abstraction. In this chapter we study various kinds of abstraction, such as procedures and functions; parameterization of abstractions with respect to values on which they depend; and the relationship between parameters and binding.

5.1 Kinds of abstraction

We define an ***abstraction*** to be an entity that embodies a computation. For example, a *function abstraction* embodies an expression to be evaluated; and a *procedure abstraction* embodies a command to be executed. The embodied computation is to be performed whenever the abstraction is called.

Abstractions support the separation of concerns mentioned in the introduction: only the programmer who implements an abstraction is concerned with *how* the embodied computation is performed; the programmers who subsequently use the abstraction by calling it need be concerned only with *what* that computation does.

The effectiveness of abstraction is enhanced by parameterization. The examples in this section will have parameters, but we shall defer detailed discussion of parameters until Section 5.2.

5.1.1   Function abstractions

A *function abstraction* embodies an expression to be evaluated, and when called will yield a result value. The user of the function abstraction observes only this result, not the steps by which it was evaluated.

In Pascal, a function abstraction is constructed in a function definition. This has the form:

$$\textbf{function } I \ (FP_1; \ ...; \ FP_n) \ : \ T; \quad B$$

where the FP_i are formal parameters, and where B is a block that contains at least one command of the form '$I := E$'. The function abstraction will be called by an expression of the form '$I \ (AP_1, \ ..., \ AP_n)$'. This function call causes B to be executed, during which the last command of the form '$I := E$' executed determines the result value.

Example 5.1
The following Pascal function definition:

```
function power (x : Real; n : Integer) : Real;
   begin    (* assume that n > 0 *)
   if n = 1 then
      power := x
   else
      power := x * power (x, n-1)
   end
```

binds `power` to a function abstraction. The function call 'power (b, 10)' will compute the tenth power of the value of b.   □

Pascal's notation for function abstractions is very untidy. The function body always contains commands, which invite the programmer to introduce side effects. The result is defined by assignment to a pseudo-variable, as in 'power := ...'. It is quite possible for the end of a function body to be reached without executing such an assignment – an error that is all too easy to make. The function identifier denotes two different things over the same scope. Consider the assignment 'power := x * power (x, n-1)': the applied occurrence of power on the left-hand side denotes the pseudo-variable where the result is to be placed; the other applied occurrence denotes the function abstraction itself (implying a recursive call).

A Pascal function body is syntactically a command, but semantically a (strange) kind of expression, since it yields a value. It is more natural for a function body to be an ordinary expression. This is the case in ML.

Example 5.2
The ML function abstraction defined here is equivalent to the Pascal one of Example 5.1:

```
fun power (x: real, n: int) =
   if n = 1
   then x
   else x * power (x, n-1)
```

☐

This form of function abstraction is much easier to understand. Moreover, there need be no loss of expressive power – if the programmer really wants to use commands and variables to compute the result, a command expression (Section 3.6.1) can be employed as the function body.

Let us consider carefully what is meant by a function definition like:

function I $(FP_1; \ldots; FP_n)$ **is** E

This binds the identifier I to a certain function abstraction, which is an entity possessing the property that it will yield a result whenever called with appropriate arguments.

Consider the function call 'I $(AP_1, \ldots, AP_n)$', where the actual parameters $AP_1, \ldots, AP_n$ will determine the arguments. The *user's* view of this function call is that it will map the arguments to a result. Only this mapping is of concern to the user. The *implementor's* view of this same function call is that it will evaluate the function body E, having previously bound the formal parameters to the corresponding arguments. The *algorithm* encoded in E is the implementor's concern.

Example 5.3
Consider the function abstraction of Example 5.2. The user's view of this function abstraction is that it maps each real–integer pair (x, n) to x^n. The implementor's view is that it computes its result by repeated multiplication.

Now consider the following alternative version:

```
fun power (x: real, n: int) =
   if n = 1
   then x
   else if even (n)
            then power (sqr (x), n div 2)
            else power (sqr (x), n div 2) * x
```

The user's view of this version is that it maps each real–integer pair (x, n) to x^n, i.e., the same mapping as before. The implementor's view, however, is that it computes its result by repeated squaring and multiplication, i.e., a faster algorithm than before.   □

Although function abstractions are most commonly constructed in function definitions (and in many languages this is the *only* way to construct them), it is perfectly possible for a language to separate the distinct concepts of abstraction and binding. In ML:

> **fn** $(I: T) \Rightarrow E$

is an *expression* that yields a function abstraction. Its formal parameter is I (of type T), and its body is E.

Example 5.4
The following ML expression:

> **fn** (x: real) => x * x * x

yields a function abstraction that implements the cube function. The conventional function definition:

> **fun** cube (x: real) = x * x * x

is just an abbreviation for the value definition:

> **val** cube =
>   **fn** (x: real) => x * x * x

in which the value bound to cube happens to be a function abstraction.
    Consider the following integration function, which has a formal parameter f that is the function to be integrated:

> **fun** integral (a: real, b: real, f: real->real) =
>   ...   (* *returns the direct integral of* f(x) *over the interval* [a..b] *)

When we call integral, the actual parameter corresponding to f can be any function-valued expression, e.g.:

> ... integral (0.0, 1.0, cube) ...
> ... integral (0.0, 1.0, **fn** (x: real) => x*x*x) ...

□

The function integral could also be programmed in Pascal. However, the actual parameter corresponding to f would have to be an *identifier* denoting a function, such as cube, since Pascal has no function-valued expressions.

5.1.2   Procedure abstractions

A *procedure abstraction* embodies a command to be executed, and when called will update variables. The user of the procedure abstraction observes only these updates, not the steps by which they were effected.

In Pascal, a procedure abstraction is constructed in a procedure definition. This has the form:

procedure *I* (*FP*₁; ...; *FP*ₙ); *B*

where the FP_i are formal parameters, and where *B* is a block. The procedure abstraction will be called by a command of the form '*I* (*AP*₁, ..., *AP*ₙ)'. This procedure call causes *B* to be executed.

Example 5.5
Consider the following Pascal procedure definition:

```
type WordSequence = array [...] of Word;
procedure sort (var words : WordSequence);
    ...
```

This binds the identifier `sort` to a procedure abstraction. The body of the procedure might, for instance, be an implementation of the insertion-sort algorithm. This is the implementor's view. The user's view is that a command like 'sort (dict)', calling this procedure abstraction, would have the net effect of ordering the values contained in the array variable `dict`.

If the implementation were improved, for instance by using the Quicksort algorithm, the procedure might execute more efficiently, but the user would observe exactly the same net effect. □

Let us consider carefully what is meant by a procedure definition like:

procedure *I* (*FP*₁; ...; *FP*ₙ) **is** *C*

This binds the identifier *I* to a certain procedure abstraction, which is an entity possessing the property that it will update variables whenever called with appropriate arguments.

Consider the procedure call '*I* (*AP*₁, ..., *AP*ₙ)', where the actual parameters *AP*₁, ..., *AP*ₙ will determine the arguments. The *user's* view of this procedure call is that it will update variables in a manner influenced by the arguments. Only this updating is of concern to the user. The *implementor's* view of this same procedure call is that it will execute the procedure body *C*, having previously bound the formal parameters to the corresponding arguments. The *algorithm* encoded in *C* is the implementor's concern.

5.1.3   The abstraction principle

We may summarize the preceding subsections as follows:

- A *function abstraction* is an abstraction over an *expression*. That is to say, a *function abstraction* has a body that is an *expression*, and a *function call* is an *expression* that will *yield a value* by evaluating the *function abstraction's* body.

- A *procedure abstraction* is an abstraction over a *command*. That is to say, a *procedure abstraction* has a body that is a *command*, and a *procedure call* is a *command* that will *update variables* by executing the *procedure abstraction's* body.

Thus there is a clear analogy between function and procedure abstractions. Can we extend this analogy to construct other kinds of abstraction? In principle, we can:

The abstraction principle: It is possible to construct abstractions over any syntactic class, provided only that the phrases of that class specify some kind of computation.

For instance, Pascal has a syntactic class of variable accesses. A variable access yields a reference to a variable. We could imagine extending Pascal by designing an abstraction over variable accesses, a kind of abstraction that when called returns a reference to a variable. Such an abstraction has in fact been proposed, and is called a **selector abstraction**:

- A *selector abstraction* is an abstraction over a *variable access*. That is to say, a *selector abstraction* has a body that is a *variable access*, and a *selector call* is a *variable access* that will *yield a reference to a variable* by evaluating the *selector abstraction's* body.

Example 5.6
Consider the Pascal definitions outlined here:

```
type Queue = ...;    (* queues of integers *)

function first (q : Queue) : Integer;
    ...    (* returns the first integer in q *)
```

Now a function call allows the first integer of a queue to be *fetched*, e.g., by 'i := first (queueA)'. But there is no corresponding way to *update* the first integer of a queue, e.g., by 'first (queueA) := 0'. (Why not?)

But now suppose that Pascal were extended with selector abstractions. Then we could define first to be a selector rather than a function:

```
selector first (var q : Queue) : Integer is
    ...    (* returns a reference to the first integer in q *)
```

This would allow the following calls to be written:

```
i := first (queueA);
first (queueA) := first (queueA) - 1
```

because a selector call would yield a *reference* to a variable, not its current value. Dereferencing can then be done where necessary (e.g., on the right-hand sides above).

One possible implementation of our selector abstraction would be:

```
type Queue = record
                item : array [1..max] of Integer;
                front, rear, count : 0..max
             end;
```

```
selector first (var q : Queue) : Integer is
    q.item[q.front]
```

Note that the variable access 'q.item[q.front]' is used to define the result of
first. The selector call 'first (queueA)' would yield a reference to the variable
queueA.item[queueA.front].

An alternative implementation would be:

```
type Queue = ^ QNode;
     QNode = record
                 head : Integer;
                 tail : Queue
             end;
selector first (var q : Queue) : Integer is
    q^.head
```

Here the variable access 'q^.head' is used to define the result of first. The selector
call 'first (queueA)' would yield a reference to the variable queueA^.head. □

Like most imperative languages, Pascal has built-in selectors ('*V.I*' for records,
'*V[E]*' for arrays, and '*V^*' for files), but no way to use abstraction to add to this
repertoire. By contrast, function abstractions can be used to add to the repertoire of
operators and standard functions. This comparison illustrates how the abstraction principle helps to identify ways of making a language both more regular and more
expressive.

Another example of using the abstraction principle is to consider whether we can
abstract over *declarations*. This is a much more radical idea, but it has been adopted in
some modern languages such as Ada and ML. We get something called a *generic
abstraction*:

• A *generic abstraction* is an abstraction over a *declaration*. That is to say, a *generic
  abstraction* has a body that is a *declaration*, and a *generic instantiation* is a
  declaration that will *produce bindings* by elaborating the *generic abstraction's*
  body.

This is a very powerful concept. We shall study it in Section 6.4.

5.2 Parameters

If we simply make an expression into a function, or a command into a procedure, we
construct an abstraction that will always perform (more or less) the same computation
whenever called. (But see Exercise 5.3.) To realize the full power of the abstraction
concept, we need to *parameterize* abstractions with respect to values on which they
operate.

Example 5.7

Consider the following (parameterless) ML function abstraction:

```
val pi = 3.1416;
val r  = 1.0;
fun circum () = 2 * pi * r.
```

The function call 'circum()' returns the circumference of a circle of unit radius. In other words, a call to this function abstraction always performs the same computation, since the free identifier r is always bound to the same value. (This assumes static binding.)

We can make the function abstraction more useful by parameterizing it with respect to r:

```
fun circum (r: real) = 2 * pi * r
```

Now we can write function calls, such as 'circum(1.0)' and 'circum(a+b)', to compute the circumferences of different circles. How each function call works is that r is bound to the argument (such as 1.0, or the value yielded by a+b) before the body of circum is evaluated.   □

An identifier used within an abstraction to denote an argument is called a *formal parameter* (e.g., r above). An expression (or other phrase) that yields an argument is called an *actual parameter* (e.g., '1.0' and 'a+b' above).

An *argument* is a value that may be passed to an abstraction. What sorts of values may be used as arguments depends on the programming language.

In Pascal, the following sorts of value can be used as arguments:

- primitive values
- composite values (except files)
- pointers
- references to variables
- procedure and function abstractions

i.e., all Pascal values except files. (See Exercise 5.4.)

In ML, the following sorts of value can be used as arguments:

- primitive values
- composite values
- function abstractions
- references to variables

i.e., *all* ML values.

When an abstraction is called, each formal parameter will become associated, in some sense, with the corresponding argument. We now study in detail the possible associations between formal and actual parameters, the so-called *parameter mechanisms*.

Different languages provide a bewildering variety of parameter mechanisms, e.g., value parameters, result parameters, constant parameters, variable parameters, name parameters, procedural parameters, and functional parameters. Fortunately, these parameter mechanisms can all be understood in terms of a small number of distinct concepts. In the following subsections we examine these concepts.

5.2.1 Copy mechanisms

A *copy mechanism* allows for values to be copied into and/or out of an abstraction when it is called. The formal parameter X denotes a local variable of the abstraction. A value is copied into X on entry to the abstraction, and/or is copied out of X (to a nonlocal variable) on exit from the abstraction. Because it is a local variable, X is created on entry to the abstraction, and deleted on exit.

The so-called *value parameter* of Algol-60 and Pascal is well known. On entry to the abstraction, the local variable X is created and assigned the argument value. Thereafter X behaves like any local variable: its value may be inspected and even updated. Since it is a local variable, however, any updating of X has no effect on any nonlocal variable.

The mirror-image of the value parameter is the *result parameter*. In this case the argument must be (a reference to) a variable. Again the local variable X is created, but its initial value is undefined. On exit from the abstraction, the final value of X is assigned to the argument variable.

These two mechanisms may be combined to give the *value-result parameter*. The argument again is (a reference to) a variable. On entry to the abstraction, the local variable X is created and assigned the argument variable's current value. On exit, the final value of X is assigned back to the argument variable.

Example 5.8
The following pseudo-Pascal procedure abstractions illustrate copy parameters:

```
type Vector = array [1..n] of Real;

procedure add (value v, w : Vector;
                    result sum : Vector);
① var i : 1..n;
   begin
   for i := 1 to n do  sum[i] := v[i] + w[i]
② end;

procedure normalize (value result u : Vector);
③ var i : 1..n;  s : Real;
   begin
   s := 0.0;
   for i := 1 to n do  s := s + sqr (u[i]);
   s := sqrt (s);
   for i := 1 to n do  u[i] := u[i] / s
④ end
```

Suppose that a, b, and c are Vector variables. The procedure call 'add (a, b, c)' has the following effect. At point ①, local variables v and w are created and assigned the values of a and b, respectively; and local variable sum is created but not initialized. The body of add then assigns values to (the components of) sum. At point ②, the final value of sum is assigned to c.

The procedure call 'normalize (c)' has the following effect. At point ③, local variable u is created and assigned the value of c. The body of normalize then updates (the components of) u. At point ④, the final value of u is assigned to c.   □

The copy mechanisms display a pleasing symmetry, as shown in Table 5.1 (where X stands for the formal parameter). Since they are based on the concept of assignment, however, the copy mechanisms are unsuitable for types that lack assignment (e.g., file types in Pascal). Another disadvantage is that copying of large composite values is expensive.

Table 5.1 Summary of copy mechanisms.

Mechanism	*Argument*	*Effect on entry*	*Effect on exit*
Value parameter	a first-class value	$X := argument$	—
Result parameter	a variable	—	$argument := X$
Value-result parameter	a variable	$X := argument$	$argument := X$

5.2.2   Definitional mechanisms

A ***definitional mechanism*** allows for the formal parameter X to be bound directly to the argument. This gives rise to a simple uniform semantics of parameter passing, suitable for all values in the programming language (not just first-class values). Definitional mechanisms appear under several guises in programming languages.

In the case of a *constant parameter*, the argument is a (first-class) value. X is bound to the argument value during the activation of the called abstraction.

In the case of a *variable* (or *reference*) *parameter*, the argument is a reference to a variable. X is bound to the argument variable during the activation of the called abstraction. Thus any inspection (or updating) of X is actually an indirect inspection (or updating) of the argument variable.

In the case of a *procedural parameter*, the argument is a procedure abstraction. X is bound to the argument procedure during the activation of the called abstraction. Thus any call to X is actually an indirect call to the argument procedure.

In the case of a *functional parameter*, the argument is a function abstraction. X is bound to the argument function during the activation of the called abstraction. Thus any call to X is actually an indirect call to the argument function.

It is important to observe that these are not really distinct parameter mechanisms. In every case, the effect is as if the abstraction body were surrounded by a block, in which there is a definition that binds X to the argument – hence our terminology *definitional mechanism*.

The definitional mechanism is the *only* one in ML – a language in which all values (including function abstractions and references to variables) are first-class values. A very early version of Pascal relied consistently on the definitional mechanism, with constant, variable, procedural, and functional parameters; however, a subsequent revision replaced constant parameters by value parameters.

Example 5.9

The following pseudo-Pascal procedure abstractions, similar to those of Example 5.8, illustrate definitional parameters:

```
type Vector = array [1..n] of Real;

procedure add (const v, w : Vector;
                     var sum : Vector);
①   var i : 1..n;
    begin
    for i := 1 to n do   sum[i] := v[i] + w[i]
②   end;

procedure normalize (var u : Vector);
③   var i : 1..n;   s : Real;
    begin
    s := 0.0;
    for i := 1 to n do   s := s + sqr (u[i]);
    s := sqrt (s);
    for i := 1 to n do   u[i] := u[i] / s
④   end
```

The procedure call 'add (a, b, c)' has the following effect. At point ①, v and w are bound to the values of a and b, respectively; and sum is bound to the variable c. The body of add thus indirectly inspects (the components of) a and b, and indirectly updates (the components of) c.

The procedure call 'normalize (c)' has the following effect. At point ③, u is is bound to the variable c. The body of normalize thus indirectly inspects and updates (the components of) c.

Notice that nothing happens at points ② and ④. Notice also that no copying is needed, even to implement constant parameters. Since the formal parameters v and w are constants, there can be no assignment to them; therefore the corresponding arguments a and b cannot be indirectly updated, even if these parameters are implemented by passing *references* to a and b.   □

Examples 5.8 and 5.9 illustrate the fact that constant and variable parameters together provide similar expressive power to the copy mechanisms, i.e., the ability to pass values into and out of an abstraction. The choice between definitional and copy mechanisms is an important decision for the language designer.

The definitional mechanism has simpler semantics, and is suitable for all types of value (not just types for which assignment is available). The definitional mechanism relies on indirect access to argument data, which is usually more efficient than copying of the data. (In a distributed implementation, however, the abstraction body might be running on a processor remote from the argument data; in these circumstances, indirect access might actually be *less* efficient than copying of the data followed by local access.)

A disadvantage of variable parameters is the possibility of ***aliasing***. This occurs when two or more identifiers are simultaneously bound to the same variable (or to a composite variable and one of its components). Aliasing tends to make programs harder to understand and harder to reason about.

Example 5.10
Consider the following Pascal procedure abstraction:

```
procedure confuse (var m, n : Integer);
   begin
   n := 1;   n := m + n
   end
```

If the variable i currently has value 4, we might expect the procedure call 'confuse (i, i)' to update i to 5 – and so it would if m were a value parameter. But the actual effect is to update i to 2! This is because both m and n are aliases of i, and hence of each other.

Why do we expect i to be updated to 5? It is because we are accustomed to reason (perhaps unconsciously) that 'n := 1; n := m+n' is equivalent to 'n := m+1'. But this is correct only if m and n denote distinct variables!   □

Aliasing can arise from variable (renaming) definitions (Section 4.4.1), but more commonly arises from variable parameters. When the programming language has such features, the onus is on the programmer to avoid harmful aliasing. No compiler can accurately detect aliasing in general. The aliasing in 'confuse (i, i)' is obvious. In the procedure call 'confuse (a[i], a[j])', however, the existence of aliasing depends on the (possibly unknown) values of i and j.

5.2.3   The correspondence principle

The perceptive reader might have noticed a correspondence between certain parameter mechanisms and certain kinds of declaration. For example:

- A constant parameter corresponds to a constant definition. In each case, an identifier is bound to a (first-class) value.
- A variable parameter corresponds to a variable (renaming) definition. In each case, an identifier is bound to an existing variable.
- A value parameter corresponds to a new-variable declaration with initialization. In each case, a new variable is created and initialized, and an identifier is bound to that variable.

The essential difference between declarations and parameter mechanisms is obvious. A declaration specifies both the identifier and the entity to which it will be bound. A formal parameter specification specifies only the identifier (and perhaps its type); the argument comes from elsewhere (i.e., from an actual parameter). For example, compare the following in a Pascal-like language:

> **const** $X = E$ **procedure** P (**const** $X : T$); ...;
>
>   ...
>
> P (E)

In each case, X is bound to the value of the expression E. In the first case, E is part of the constant definition. In the second case, E is the actual parameter in a particular procedure call.

In the interests of simplicity and regularity, a language designer might wish to eliminate all *inessential* differences between declarations and parameter mechanisms. In principle, this is feasible:

> **The correspondence principle:** For each form of declaration there exists a corresponding parameter mechanism, and *vice versa*.

ML complies with the correspondence principle, if we consider only first-class values. It has a single parameter mechanism, which corresponds directly to its value definition. (Recall that function abstractions and references to variables are first-class values, and so need no special forms of declaration or parameter mechanisms.)

On the other hand, Pascal does not come close to complying with the correspondence principle, even if we restrict our attention to first-class values and variables. There is no constant parameter mechanism to correspond to the constant definition. The new-variable declaration corresponds only partly to the value parameter mechanism, because the former lacks initialization. Finally, there is no variable (renaming) definition to correspond to the variable parameter mechanism. (Do not be misled by the fact that a new-variable declaration and a variable parameter specification both look like '**var** I : T' in Pascal; they do not correspond to each other at all, since the former creates a new variable but the latter merely aliases an existing variable.)

Table 5.2 A redesign of some of Pascal's declarations and parameter mechanisms.

Declaration	*Formal parameter*	*Actual parameter*
const $I = E$ (constant definition)	**const** $I : T$ (constant parameter)	an expression E of type T
var $I := E$ (new-variable declaration)	$I : T$ (value parameter)	an expression E of type T
var $I = V$ (variable definition)	**var** $I : T$ (variable parameter)	a variable access V of type T

It is instructive to redesign Pascal to comply with the correspondence principle: see Table 5.2. Note that the redesign would make the language not only more regular but also more expressive, particularly in its repertoire of declarations: the constant definition would be generalized to allow any expression of any type on its right-hand side; the new-variable declaration would be generalized to include initialization; and a variable (renaming) definition would be added to the language.

5.3 Evaluation order

In this section we shall study an important issue neglected in the previous section: exactly *when* is each actual parameter evaluated when an abstraction is called? The basic choice is: (a) to evaluate the actual parameter at the point of call, or (b) to delay its evaluation until the argument is actually used.

For the moment, we shall concentrate on the purely functional subset of ML (i.e., excluding variables and side effects). Consider the function defined below:

```
fun sqr (n: int) = n * n
```

and the function call 'sqr (p+q)'. Suppose that p's value is 2 and q's value is 5. Here are two different ways in which we could evaluate this function call:

- First we evaluate 'p+q', yielding 7. Then we bind the formal parameter n to 7. Finally we evaluate 'n * n', yielding $7 \times 7 = 49$.
- First we bind the formal parameter n to the expression 'p+q' itself. Then, each time the value of n is required during the evaluation of 'n * n', we (re)evaluate the expression to which n is bound; thus the computation is $(2+5) \times (2+5) = 49$.

The first evaluation order is called *eager evaluation* (or *applicative-order evaluation*). We evaluate the actual parameter once, and (in effect) substitute its value for each occurrence of the formal parameter.

The second evaluation order is called *normal-order evaluation*. We do not immediately evaluate the actual parameter, but (in effect) substitute the actual parameter itself for each occurrence of the formal parameter. (This is an over-simplification – see Exercise 5.12.)

In the case of the sqr function, both evaluation orders yield the same result (although eager evaluation is the more efficient). However, the behavior of certain other functions does depend on the evaluation order. Consider the function defined below:

```
fun cand (b1: bool, b2: bool) =
    if b1 then b2 else false
```

and the function call 'cand (n>0, t/n>0.5)'. First suppose that n's value is 2 and t's value is 0.8:

- With eager evaluation, 'n>0' evaluates to *true* and 't/n>0.5' evaluates to *false*; therefore the function call also evaluates to *false*.

- With normal-order evaluation, in effect we evaluate '`if` n>0 `then` t/n>0.5 `else` false', which also yields *false*.

But now suppose that n's value is 0:

- With eager evaluation, 'n>0' evaluates to *false* but evaluation of 't/n>0.5' fails (due to division by zero); therefore the function call itself fails.
- With normal-order evaluation, in effect we evaluate '`if` n>0 `then` t/n>0.5 `else` false', which yields *false*.

The essential difference between the sqr and cand functions is in whether their argument values are actually needed. The sqr function is said to be **strict**, which means that a call to this function can be evaluated only if its argument can be evaluated. The cand function is said to be **nonstrict** in its second argument, which means that a call to this function can sometimes be evaluated even if its second argument cannot. (The cand function is, however, strict in its first argument.)

These examples demonstrate that the purely functional subset of ML possesses the following important property:

The Church–Rosser property: If an expression can be evaluated at all, it can be evaluated by consistently using normal-order evaluation. If an expression can be evaluated in several different orders (mixing normal-order and applicative-order evaluation), then all of these evaluation orders yield the same result.

Any language that allows side effects (such as Pascal or ML proper) does *not* possess the Church–Rosser property. In a function call '$F(E)$' where evaluating E has side effects, it certainly makes a difference when and how often E is evaluated – even if we neglect the possibility that E cannot be evaluated at all!

For example, suppose that 'getint (f)' reads an integer from the file variable f (a side effect) and yields that integer. Consider the function sqr defined above, and the function call 'sqr (getint (f))'. With eager evaluation, it would cause one integer to be read, and would yield the square of that integer. With normal-order evaluation, it would cause *two* integers to be read, and would yield their product!

Normal-order evaluation is clearly inefficient when it causes the same argument to be evaluated several times. If the argument value will always be the same, time can be saved if the argument value is stored as soon as it is first evaluated, and the stored value is used whenever the argument value is needed again. This is called *lazy evaluation* – the argument is evaluated only when it is first needed (which might be never, if the function is nonstrict). If a language possesses the Church–Rosser property, lazy evaluation always yields exactly the same result as normal-order evaluation.

We have presented normal-order, eager, and lazy evaluation as implementation strategies, but they are always incorporated into the semantics of the programming language. Algol-60 allows the programmer to choose between eager evaluation (value parameters) and normal-order evaluation (so-called *name parameters*). The combination of name parameters and side effects gives rise to bizarre effects, such as the one illustrated above. Miranda adopts lazy evaluation, which supports a novel style of programming (see Chapter 13), but is difficult to implement efficiently. A large majority of languages provide only eager evaluation, including Algol-68, Pascal, Ada, Lisp, and ML.

5.4 Further reading

The abstraction and correspondence principles were formulated by Tennent (1977), who also applied them to Pascal. The principles were based on earlier work by Landin (1966) and Strachey (1967).

The Church–Rosser property is based on a theorem about the lambda-calculus, an account of which may be found in Rosser (1982). (The lambda-calculus is an extremely simple functional language, much used as an object of study in the theory of computation.)

Exercises 5

5.1*   Consider redesigning Pascal function abstractions so that a function body is an expression, rather than a block. Show that this change, in isolation, would reduce the expressive power of Pascal function abstractions. What other changes to Pascal would be needed to compensate? (*Hint:* Compare Pascal's expressions with the kinds discussed in Sections 2.6 and 4.5.2.)

5.2   Would it make sense to apply the abstraction principle to: (a) literals; (b) types?

5.3   Find at least one example of a parameterless abstraction that does not perform exactly the same computation every time it is called. Under what circumstances, in general, will a parameterless abstraction behave like this?

5.4   What restriction in Pascal prevents file *values* from being passed as arguments?

5.5*   Make a list of all the values that can be passed as arguments in your favorite programming language, as was done for Pascal and ML in Section 5.2. Also make a list of any values that *cannot* be passed as arguments. Why are the latter values excluded?

5.6   Consider the following Pascal procedure:

```
procedure multiply (var m, n : Integer);
   begin
```

```
m := m * n;
writeln (m, n)
end
```

Suppose that i contains 2, and j contains 3. Show what is written during the procedure calls:

(a) `multiply (i, j)`
(b) `multiply (i, i)`

Now suppose that the variable parameters could be replaced by value-result parameters. Repeat the above exercise. Explain the different effect.

5.7   Show that, with normal-order or lazy evaluation, we can write a function `if_then_else` such that '`if_then_else` (E_1, E_2, E_3)' has *exactly* the same effect as '**if** E_1 **then** E_2 **else** E_3'. Why can we not write such a function using eager evaluation alone?

5.8   In ML and Ada, 'E_1 **andthen** E_2' yields *true* if and only if both E_1 and E_2 yield *true*; moreover, evaluation of E_2 is short-circuited if E_1 happens to yield *false*. Show that this operator cannot be defined as an ordinary function (unlike other operators in these languages).

5.9*   Show how to obtain the *effect* of the following in ML: (a) a value parameter; (b) a result parameter; (c) a value-result parameter; (d) a variable parameter; (e) normal-order evaluation; (f) lazy evaluation. (Parts (e) and (f) are strictly for ML experts!)

5.10*   Ada is deliberately unspecific about its parameter mechanisms. Consider the following procedure:

$$\textbf{procedure } P \ (X_1 \ : \ \textbf{in } T_1; \ X_2 \ : \ \textbf{out } T_2) \ ;$$

The implementation is free to use either the constant parameter mechanism or the value parameter mechanism for X_1 if T_1 is a composite type (but must use the value parameter mechanism if T_1 is a primitive type). Likewise the implementation is free to use either the variable parameter mechanism or the result parameter mechanism for X_2 if T_2 is a composite type (but must use the result parameter mechanism if T_2 is a primitive type). What is the advantage, if any, of allowing the implementation such freedom? Under what circumstances will the procedure's behavior be affected by the implementation?

5.11   In Pascal, would it make sense to apply the correspondence principle to: (a) types; (b) record fields; (c) labels?

5.12*   Consider the function definition '**fun** $F \ (X: T \ ) \ = E$ ' and the function call '$F \ (E' \ )$'. Normal-order evaluation might be characterized by:

$$F \ (E' \ ) \ \equiv \ subst \ (E, X, E' \ )$$

where *subst* (E, X, E') is the expression obtained by substituting E' for all free occurrences of X in E.

(a) Characterize eager evaluation in an analogous fashion.

(b) Show that *subst* has to be defined carefully, because of the possibility of confusing the scopes of an identifier with more than one declaration. Consider, e.g.:

```
let
    val n = 2;
    fun f (x: int) =
            let val n = 7 in n * x end
in
    f (n+1)
end
```

CHAPTER SIX

Encapsulation

The concepts covered in Chapters 2–5 underlie what is sometimes called *programming in the small*. Language designed using only these concepts (such as Pascal) are suitable for program construction on a small scale, where the largest program units are procedures and functions.

Since the 1970s language design has focused more on supporting *programming in the large*. This is about construction of large programs from modules. A *module* is any named program unit that can be implemented as a (more or less) independent entity. A well-designed module has a single purpose, and presents a narrow interface to other modules. Such a module is likely to be reusable, i.e., able to be incorporated in many programs, and modifiable, i.e., able to be revised without forcing major changes to other modules.

The key to modularity is abstraction. We can ask the following questions about a module:

- *What* is the module's purpose?
- *How* does it achieves that purpose?

Only the *what* is of concern to the user of the module. The *how* is of concern only to the implementor of the module. Of course, the user and implementor might well be different people.

A module could be a single procedure or function, as discussed in Chapter 5. More typically, however, a module is a group of several components declared for a common purpose. These components could be types, constants, variables, procedures, functions, and so on. A module is said to *encapsulate* its components.

To achieve a narrow interface to other modules, a module typically makes only a few components visible outside. Such components are said to be *exported* by the module. There may be other components that remain *hidden* inside the module, being used only to assist the implementation of the exported components.

In this chapter we study several important concepts that support modularity. A *package* is simply a named group of declared components. Packages are especially useful in conjunction with the ability to hide components. This makes packages quite general, and they can be used to program more specialized kinds of module such as the following. An *abstract type* is a type defined indirectly by its operations (constants, functions, procedures, etc.), rather than defined directly by its set of values. An *object* is a hidden variable together with a group of exported operations (functions, procedures, etc.) that access it. We also examine *classes* of objects. Finally we study *generics*, modules that are parameterized with respect to values and types on which they depend.

6.1 Packages

6.1.1 Simple packages

A *package* is a group of declared components. In general, the declared components can be any bindables of the programming language, such as types, constants, variables, procedure, functions, and even (sub)packages.

A package may be viewed as an encapsulated set of bindings. We shall illustrate this by looking at two simple packages, expressed in Ada.

Example 6.1
The following Ada package groups together some physical constants:

```
package physics is
    c : constant Float := 3.0e+8;
    G : constant Float := 6.7e-11;
    h : constant Float := 6.6e-34;
end physics;
```

The effect of this package declaration is to bind physics to the encapsulated set of bindings $\{c \mapsto 3.0{\times}10^8, G \mapsto 6.7{\times}10^{-11}, h \mapsto 6.6{\times}10^{-34}\}$. All the components of this package are constants (first-class values). Outside the package they may be accessed by physics.c, physics.G, and physics.h.

Example 6.2
The following Ada package groups together some types, constants, and variables:

```
package Earth is
    type Continent is
                (Africa, Antarctica, Asia, Australia,
                 Europe, NorthAmerica, SouthAmerica);
    radius : constant Float := 6.4e6;          -- km
    area   : constant array (Continent) of Float :=
             (30.3e9, 13.0e9, 43.3e9, 7.7e9,
              10.4e9, 24.9e9, 17.8e9);          -- km2
    population : array (Continent) of Integer;
end Earth;
```

The effect of this package declaration is to bind Earth to the following encapsulated set of bindings:

{ Continent ↦ the type {*Africa, Antarctica, ..., SouthAmerica*},
      radius ↦ 6.4×10⁶,
        area ↦ {*Africa* ↦ 30.3×10⁹, ..., *SouthAmerica* ↦ 17.8×10⁹},
  population ↦ an integer array variable }

The following code uses some of the components of this package:

```
for cont in Earth.Continent loop
    put (Earth.population(cont) / Earth.area(cont));
end loop;
```

□

Simple package declarations in Ada have the form:

```
package I is
    D
end I;
```

where *D* is a (sequential) declaration. The package declaration is elaborated as follows. First *D* is elaborated to produce some bindings; then a package encapsulating these bindings is formed; then the identifier *I* is bound to that package.

In ML, the equivalent of a package is the so-called *structure*. A structure declaration, similar in effect to the Ada simple package declaration, would look like this:

```
structure I =
    struct
        D
    end
```

6.1.2 Information hiding

The packages of Examples 6.1 and 6.2 are not typical. All their components are exported; there are no hidden implementation details. More commonly, a package contains declarations of both exported and hidden components, the latter serving only to support the implementation of the exported components.

In Ada, the exported and hidden components are distinguished by splitting the package into two parts. The *package declaration* declares (only) the exported components; the *package body* contains declarations of any hidden components. If any procedure or function is exported, its *body* is placed in the package body. Thus the package declaration generally contains no implementation details at all.

Example 6.3
Here is an Ada trigonometric function package. It exports a pair of functions named sin and cos, each being of type Real → Real. The package declaration specifies that fact, and nothing else:

```
package trig is
    function sin (x : Float) return Float;
    function cos (x : Float) return Float;
end trig;
```

The corresponding package body fills in the necessary implementation details:

```
package body trig is
    pi : constant Float := 3.1416;

    function norm (x : Float) return Float is
        ...;    -- return x modulo 2*pi

    function sin (x : Float) return Float is
        ...;    -- return the sine of norm(x)

    function cos (x : Float) return Float is
        ...;    -- return the cosine of norm(x)

end trig;
```

It is the package body that actually defines the function abstractions to which `sin` and `cos` are bound. The package body also declares a constant `pi` and a function `norm`, to assist in the implementation of `sin` and `cos`. Since `pi` and `norm` are not declared in the package declaration, they are hidden components of the package.

The effect of elaborating the above package declaration and body together is to bind `trig` to the following encapsulated set of bindings:

{ `sin` ↦ a function abstraction approximating the sine function,
  `cos` ↦ a function abstraction approximating the cosine function }

The hidden components are excluded, since they are not visible to the user of the package.

The exported functions can be called in the usual way, e.g.:

```
... trig.cos (theta/2.0) ...
```

Note that the package declaration contains just enough information for the user of the package to write such calls and have them type-checked by the compiler.   □

If the language has a *block declaration* (see Section 4.5.3), it can be used to achieve information hiding within a package. This possibility is illustrated by ML, whose block declaration has the form '**local** D_1 **in** D_2 **end**'. (Elaborating this declaration produces only the bindings produced by D_2; the bindings produced by D_1 are available only in D_2.)

Example 6.4
Here is an ML trigonometric function package. Like the Ada package of Example 6.3, it exports a pair of functions named `sin` and `cos`, each being of type Real → Real.

```
structure trig =
   struct
      local
         val pi = 3.1416;

         fun norm (x: real) =
                 ...   (* compute and return x modulo 2*pi *)

      in

         fun sin (x: real) =
                 ...   (* compute and return sine of norm(x) *)

         and cos (x: real) =
                 ...   (* compute and return cosine of norm(x) *)

      end
   end
```

The effect of elaborating this structure declaration is to bind trig to the same encapsulated set of bindings as in Example 6.3. Again, the exported functions can be called in the usual way:

```
... trig.cos (theta/2.0) ...
```

Note that it is the block declaration, and not the structure declaration itself, that enforces the information hiding.   □

Packages with information hiding can also be used to define abstract types and objects. These important kinds of module are examined in the the next two sections.

6.2 Abstract types

In Chapter 2 we viewed a type in terms of a set of values. This view is reasonable for most purposes, but it can lead to problems when we define a new type in terms of existing ones. For then we must choose a *representation* for values of the new type, and it is quite likely that the representation will have unwanted properties.

Example 6.5
Suppose that we wish to define a type whose values will be rational numbers, with arithmetic operations (such as addition) that are *exact*. In ML we could write the following declarations:

```
datatype rational = rat of (int * int);

val zero = rat (0, 1)
and one  = rat (1, 1);
```

```
fun op ++ (rat(m1,n1): rational,
           rat(m2,n2): rational) =
    rat (m1*n2 + m2*n1, n1*n2)
```

Here each rational number is represented by a tagged pair of integers, of which the first is assumed to be the numerator and the second to be the denominator. Thus $3/2$ can be represented by the tagged pair *rat* (3, 2). But it can also be represented by *rat* (6, 4), *rat* (9, 6), *rat* (–3, –2), etc. The rational numbers these tagged pairs are supposed to represent are mathematically equal, but the tagged pairs themselves are all distinct.

Now consider the effect of the following comparison:

```
if one ++ h = rat (6, 4) then ... else ...
```

when h is equal to *rat* (1, 2). The subexpression 'one ++ h' will yield *rat* (3, 2), which is *not* equal to *rat* (6, 4). This is clearly an unwanted property of the representation. Another unwanted property is that there is nothing to prevent a tagged pair such as *rat* (0, 0) or *rat* (1, 0) from being constructed, although it does not correspond to any rational number.

The set of values of the type defined above is:

$$\text{Rational} = \{ \; rat\,(m, n) \mid m, n \in \text{Integer} \; \} \tag{6.1}$$

Ideally we would like to define the following set of values:

$$\{ \; rat\,(m, n) \mid \quad m, n \in \text{Integer}; \; n > 0; \\ m \text{ and } n \text{ have no common factor} \; \} \tag{6.2}$$

but ML has no type with this set of values. Therefore simply defining `rational` in terms of an existing type is unsatisfactory.

Notice that using a *type definition* for `rational`, e.g.:

```
type rational = int * int;
val zero = (0, 1)
    ...
```

is even less satisfactory. Now we can confuse `rational` values with values of other types that happen to have the same representation. Suppose that we define the following type to represent positions on a grid:

```
type position = int * int
```

Then what is the type of the expression '(0,1)'? Both `rational` and `position` are correct answers (as well as simply `int*int`). In fact, `rational` and `position` are exactly the same type, although we presumably intend them to be distinct. If we inadvertently compare a rational number and a position, this will not be detected as a type error.   □

Types as complicated as (6.2) cannot in fact be defined in any (existing) programming language. If they were, type checking would be extremely complicated, and would have to be dynamic. Consider the expression 'rat (m, n) '. The necessary type check would be to ensure that the value of n is positive and that the values of m and n have no common factor. Such a check would have to be done at run-time, when the values of m and n are known.

Here is a summary of the difficulties that may arise, in general, when we represent a desired type by another type (the *representation type*):

- The representation type might have values that do not correspond to any values of the desired type.
- The representation type might have several values that correspond to the same value of the desired type. Comparisons would then yield incorrect results.
- Unless we use a new-type declaration, values of the desired type can be confused with values of the representation type.

These difficulties prompt us to seek an alternative way of defining a new type, in such a way that undesirable properties of the representation type can be suppressed.

An **abstract type** is a type defined by a group of operations. The operations are typically constants, functions, and procedures. The set of values of the type is defined only indirectly; it consists of all values that can be generated by successive applications of the operations, starting with the constants.

The concept of abstract type gives rise to an important kind of module, which is supported directly by ML and some other modern languages. Typically the programmer chooses a representation for the values of the abstract type, and implements the operations in terms of this chosen representation. The key point is that the representation is *hidden*; the module exports only the abstract type itself and its operations. We illustrate this by reworking Example 6.5.

Example 6.6
We could declare rational as an abstract type in ML as follows:

```
abstype rational = rat of (int * int)
with
    val zero = rat (0, 1)
    and one  = rat (1, 1);

    fun op // (m: int, n: int) =
            if n <> 0
            then rat (m, n)
            else ...   (* invalid rational number *)

    and op ++ (rat(m1,n1): rational,
               rat(m2,n2): rational) =
            rat (m1*n2 + m2*n1, n1*n2)

    and op == (rat(m1,n1): rational,
               rat(m2,n2): rational) =
            (m1*n2 = m2*n1)

end
```

Now the following code will work as it should:

```
val h = 1//2
```

...
if one ++ h == 6//4 **then** ... **else** ...

The abstract type declaration produces the following set of bindings:

{ rational ↦ an abstract type,
    zero ↦ the rational number equal to 0,
    one ↦ the rational number equal to 1,
    // ↦ a function abstraction that constructs a rational,
    ++ ↦ a function abstraction that adds two rationals,
    == ↦ a function abstraction that tests two rationals for equality }

The *user* of the module sees it as exporting just the above. Informally, '*m*//*n*' yields the rational number mathematically equal to *m/n* (unless *n* is zero); '*r* ++ *s*' yields the sum of the rational numbers *r* and *s*; and '*r* == *s*' yields *true* if and only if the rational numbers *r* and *s* are mathematically equal. The representation chosen for values of the new type is hidden from the user, along with the implementation of the functions.

The *implementor* of the module sees it as representing each rational number by a tagged pair *rat* (*m*, *n*). All the operations are implemented in such a way that the second component *n* is always nonzero.

The only way for the user to generate values of type rational is by evaluating expressions involving the constants zero and one, and the functions '//' and '++'. Values of type rational can be compared only by calling the function '=='. A particular rational number might be represented in several ways (e.g., $3/2$ by *rat* (3, 2), *rat* (6, 4), etc.), depending on the way it was computed. But this is hidden from the user, since the function '==' correctly implements mathematical equality.   □

An abstract type can also be defined using an Ada package, although not so concisely as in ML. (See Example 6.9 in the next section.)

With an abstract type it does not matter that a given value of the type has several possible representations, because the representations are hidden from the user. What is important is that only desired properties of the values are *observable* using the operations associated with the abstract type. In Example 6.6, the difference between representations such as *rat* (3, 2) and *rat* (6, 4) is not observable, because the function '==' treats them as equal.

An abstract type's representation can always be changed (e.g., to improve the efficiency of the operations), without forcing any changes outside the module. In Example 6.6, we might decide to represent each rational number in reduced form (e.g., *rat* (3, 2) but not *rat* (6, 4), *rat* (−3, −2), etc.). This would require operations that construct new rational numbers (i.e., '++' and '//') to eliminate common factors. The benefit would be to make the implementation of '==' trivial. (See Exercise 6.5.)

Defining an abstract type does involve extra work, precisely because the representation is hidden from the user of the type. This implies that the abstract type must generally be provided with *constructor* operations, to compose values of the abstract type, and *destructor* operations, to decompose such values.

In Example 6.6, the function '`//`' is needed to allow values of type `rational` to be composed, e.g., by '`3//2`'. (The user cannot simply write '`rat(3,2)`', because the representation as a tagged pair is hidden.) The function '`//`' is an example of a constructor operation. The constants `zero` and `one` are also constructor operations.

In Example 6.6 there were no destructor operations. However, if we added the following function, it would be a destructor operation:

```
fun float (rat(m,n): rational) =
      m / n
```

Abstract types are similar to built-in types such as Truth-Value and Integer. The values of a built-in type themselves have a representation (in terms of bits, bytes, and words), but this is hidden from the programmer. With the operations provided, the programmer can observe only the desired properties of the values. For example, a particular implementation of Truth-Value might represent *false* by a zero byte and *true* by a nonzero byte, but with the usual Truth-Value operations the programmer would be able to observe only the usual mathematical properties of truth values.

6.3 Objects and classes

6.3.1 Single objects

Another special and important kind of module is one that consists of a hidden variable together with a group of exported operations on that variable. The variable is typically a data structure such as a table or database. Being hidden, the variable can be accessed only through the exported operations. This has the advantage that the variable's representation can be changed (e.g., to improve the efficiency of the operations), without forcing any changes outside the module. Furthermore, the module can control the *order* of accesses to the hidden variable, e.g., to prevent extraction of data before any have been put in.

The term **object** is often used for the hidden variable in a module (or for the module itself). Objects are supported by a number of programming languages. We illustrate the concept here using Ada packages.

Example 6.7
The following Ada package encapsulates a telephone directory, with procedures `insert` and `lookup` that operate on it. The variable representing the directory is hidden; only the two procedures are exported.

The package declaration simply specifies the two procedures:

```
package directory_object is
    procedure insert (newname   : in Name;
                      newnumber : in Number);
```

```
procedure lookup (oldname    : in Name;
                  oldnumber : out Number;
                  found      : out Boolean);
end directory_object;
```

The package body contains all the implementation details. Here we choose to represent the directory by an ordered binary tree, with the variable root containing a pointer to the tree's root node. The package body declares this hidden variable and its type, and also defines the exported procedures. The command just before the end of the package body specifies how the directory is to be initialized. (Some details have been omitted for space reasons.)

```
package body directory_object is
    type DirNode;
    type DirPtr is access DirNode;
    type DirNode is record
                        entryname    : Name;
                        entrynumber : Number;
                        left, right  : DirPtr;
                    end record;
    root : DirPtr;

    procedure insert (newname    : in Name;
                      newnumber : in Number) is
        ...;    -- add a new entry for newname with newnumber
                -- to the directory

    procedure lookup (oldname    : in Name;
                      oldnumber : out Number;
                      found      : out Boolean) is
        ...;    -- try to find an entry for oldname in the directory

begin
    ...;    -- initialize the directory
end directory_object;
```

Elaboration of this package creates a single object, denoted by directory_object. This object may be accessed (only) by calls to the exported procedures:

```
directory_object.insert (me, 6041);
...
directory_object.lookup (me, mynumber, ok);
```

The compiler prevents any attempt to access the hidden variable root directly from outside the package.

Since the directory representation is hidden, it could easily be changed (e.g., to a hash table) by revising only the package body. Other modules would be unaffected, since they can access the directory only by calling the exported procedures.   □

Since an object has a variable component, it has a lifetime. In Ada, the lifetime of an object such as `directory_object` is an activation of the smallest block enclosing the package. In other words, the object has the same lifetime as an ordinary local variable declared at the same place as the package.

6.3.2 Object classes

So far we have considered only single objects. It is also important to be able to create a whole *class* of similar objects. In Ada, a package that specifies and implements a single object can easily be made into a *generic package*, which then defines an object class.

Example 6.8
Suppose that we wish to be able to create and access several telephone directories. We can make the package of Example 6.7 generic:

```
generic package directory_class is
   procedure insert (newname    : in Name;
                     newnumber  : in Number);
   procedure lookup (oldname    : in Name;
                     oldnumber  : out Number;
                     found      : out Boolean);
end directory_class;

package body directory_class is
   ...   -- exactly as in Example 6.7
end directory_class;
```

Elaboration of this generic package simply binds `directory_class` to an object class. It does not actually create any object.

To create individual objects, we must *instantiate* the generic package:

```
package homedir is new directory_class;
package workdir is new directory_class;
```

These declarations create two similar but distinct objects, denoted by `homedir` and `workdir` respectively. We can now access these objects in the usual way:

```
workdir.insert (me, 6041);
homedir.insert (me, 8715);
workdir.lookup (me, mynumber, ok);
```

The above command will store 6041 (not 8715) in `mynumber`, since the objects `homedir` and `workdir` are distinct.   □

The concepts of abstract type and object class have much in common. Each allows us to create several variables of a type whose representation is hidden, and to access these variables (only) by operations provided for the purpose. However, the two concepts are subtly different, as we can see if we rework Example 6.8 as an abstract type.

Example 6.9

The following Ada package declaration exports an abstract (*limited private*) type
`Directory`, together with procedures `insert` and `lookup`. The representation of
the type is hidden.

```
package directory_type is
   type Directory is limited private;
   procedure insert (dir        : in out Directory;
                     newname    : in Name;
                     newnumber  : in Number);
   procedure lookup (dir        : in Directory;
                     oldname    : in Name;
                     oldnumber  : out Number;
                     found      : out Boolean);
private
   type DirNode;
   type Directory is access DirNode;
   type DirNode   is record ... end record;
end directory_type;
```

The part of the package declaration between **private** and **end** defines the
representation of the abstract type `Directory`. (It would be more logical to define the
representation in the package body, along with the other implementation details. This
anomaly will be explained in Section 10.3.6.)

The corresponding package body would look like this:

```
package body directory_type is

   procedure insert (dir        : in out Directory;
                     newname    : in Name;
                     newnumber  : in Number) is
      ...;    -- add a new entry newname with newnumber to dir

   procedure lookup (dir        : in Directory;
                     oldname    : in Name;
                     oldnumber  : out Number;
                     found      : out Boolean) is
      ...;    -- try to find an entry for oldname in dir
end directory_type;
```

Elaboration of this package does not create any variable. It simply binds
`directory_type` to the following encapsulated set of bindings:

{ `Directory` ↦ an abstract type,
  `insert` ↦ a procedure abstraction that updates a given directory,
  `lookup` ↦ a procedure abstraction that looks up a given directory }

However, the abstract type may subsequently be used to declare several variables, each
of which will represent a distinct directory:

```
use directory_type;    -- allows us to abbreviate the dot notation
homedir : Directory;
workdir : Directory;
...
insert (workdir, me, 6041);
insert (homedir, me, 8715);
lookup (workdir, me, mynumber, ok);
```

Again, the last command will store 6041 in `mynumber`.   □

(The *use clause* '**use** *P* ; ', where *P* is a package name, allows us to name exported components of *P* more concisely. Throughout the scope of this *use* clause, we can abbreviate *P . I* to *I*.)

Examples 6.8 and 6.9 illustrate the similarities and also the differences between the object class and abstract type concepts. Consider the insertion procedure in each case. In the abstract type case, `insert` has a parameter of the abstract type `Directory`. Only one procedure `insert` is defined, regardless of how many variables of type `Directory` are created. In the object class case, several instantiations define several distinct procedures (e.g., `homedir.insert` and `workdir.insert`), each of which accesses a distinct object (`homedir` and `workdir`, respectively).

We can examine the difference from another point of view by comparing corresponding procedure calls. In the abstract type case, we might write '`insert (workdir, me, 6041)`'. Here, obviously, the particular directory to be accessed is an argument to the procedure. In the object class case, we would write '`workdir. insert (me, 6041)`'. Here the particular directory to be accessed is a kind of implicit argument, but it is an argument fixed when the object is created, not when the procedure is called.

The abstract type concept has certain advantages over the object class concept:

• Abstract types are similar to built-in types, and defining a new abstract type smoothly extends the variety of types available to the programmer. In most languages (including Ada and ML), the values of an abstract type are first-class values, but objects are not. (In Example 6.9, `workdir` and `homedir` are ordinary variables and can be passed as arguments; in Example 6.8, `workdir` and `homedir` are objects and cannot be passed as arguments.)

• The notation for calling an operation of an abstract type is surely more natural, since values and variables of the abstract type are explicit arguments. (See the illustration above, and see also Exercise 6.9.)

• Abstract types are useful in all programming paradigms. Objects, being updatable variables, fit only into an imperative style of programming. (Compare Example 6.6 and Exercise 6.9.)

Nevertheless, the object concept is the whole basis of the important paradigm of *object-oriented programming*. Object-oriented languages (such as Smalltalk) are based squarely on this single concept, allowing entire software systems to be constructed in a modular fashion from objects and object classes. See Chapter 12 for a more thorough discussion of the object-oriented paradigm.

6.4   Generics

6.4.1   Generic abstractions

We have seen that functions are abstractions over expressions, and that procedures are abstractions over commands. The abstraction principle (Section 5.1.3) suggests that we can extend this analogy to give us abstractions over declarations. And indeed this is possible:

• A *generic abstraction* is an abstraction over a *declaration*. That is to say, a *generic abstraction* has a body that is a *declaration*, and a *generic instantiation* is a *declaration* that will *produce bindings* by elaborating the *generic abstraction's* body.

In Ada, this concept appears most importantly in the form of the *generic package*. We have already seen parameterless generic packages used to define object classes, such as directory_class in Example 6.8. Each generic instantiation like:

```
package homedir is new directory_class;
```

is a declaration, and is elaborated as follows. First, the declaration and body of directory_class are elaborated, and the resulting set of bindings encapsulated in a package. Then homedir is made to denote that package.

Generic packages can be parameterized, like any other useful abstractions.

Example 6.10
The following Ada generic package encapsulates a bounded queue of characters. The package is parameterized with respect to the capacity of the queue (which must be a positive integer).

```
generic
    capacity : in Positive;
package queue_class is
    procedure append (newitem : in Character);
    procedure remove (olditem : out Character);
end queue_class;

package body queue_class is
    items : array (1..capacity) of Character;
    size, front, rear : Integer range 0..capacity;

    procedure append (newitem : in Character) is
        ...;   -- add newitem to the rear of the queue

    procedure remove (olditem : out Character) is
        ...;   -- remove olditem from the front of the queue

begin
    ...;   -- empty the queue
```

```
    end queue_class;
```

The formal parameter of this generic package is capacity, and there are corresponding applied occurrences of capacity in the generic package's body.

We can now write an instantiation of this generic package such as:

```
    package line_buffer is new queue_class (120);
```

This declaration is elaborated as follows. First, the formal parameter capacity is bound to the argument, 120. Next, the package declaration and body are elaborated, producing a package that encapsulates a queue with space for 120 characters. Finally, line_buffer is made to denote that package.

Here is another instantiation:

```
    package terminal_buffer is new queue_class (80);
```

Here terminal_buffer is made to denote a package that encapsulates a queue with space for 80 characters. □

6.4.2 Type parameters

A declaration can make use of previously defined values. As we have seen, it can also be made into a generic abstraction and parameterized with respect to such values.

Now, a declaration can also make use of previously defined *types*. Can it also be parameterized with respect to such types? The correspondence principle (see Section 5.2.3) suggests that it can. Thus we have a completely new kind of parameter, a *type parameter*. In Ada, generic packages can have type parameters.

Example 6.11
The queue_class package of Example 6.10 contains free occurrences of the identifier capacity, denoting a (constant) integer, and we chose to parameterize the package with respect to capacity. But the package also contains free occurrences of the identifier Character, denoting the type of the items held in the queue. Since the package does not actually depend on the fact that these items are characters, we can generalize it further, by parameterizing it with respect to the type of these items:

```
    generic
        capacity : in Positive;
        type Item is private;
    package queue_class is
        procedure append (newitem : in Item);
        procedure remove (olditem : out Item);
    end queue_class;

    package body queue_class is
        items : array (1..capacity) of Item;
        size, front, rear : Integer range 0..capacity;

        procedure append (newitem : in Item) is
```

```
begin
   ...;  items(rear) := newitem;  ...;
end;

procedure remove (olditem : out Item) is
begin
   ...;  olditem := items(front);  ...;
end;

begin
   front := 1;  rear := 0;
end queue_class;
```

The formal parameters of this generic package are `capacity` (denoting a value) and `Item` (denoting a type).

In the following:

```
package line_buffer is
        new queue_class (120, Character);
...
line_buffer.append ('*');
```

the generic instantiation is elaborated as follows. First, the generic package's formal parameter `capacity` is bound to the first argument, the value 120; and its formal parameter `Item` is bound to the second argument, the type denoted by `Character`. Then the package declaration and body are elaborated, producing a package that encapsulates a queue with space for 120 characters. Finally `line_buffer` is made to denote that package. Thereafter `line_buffer` can be used like any ordinary package.

In the following:

```
type Transaction is record ... end record;
package audit_trail is
        new queue_class (100, Transaction);
```

the generic instantiation is elaborated similarly. Here `audit_trail` is made to denote a package that encapsulates a queue with space for 100 transactions.   □

If an abstraction is parameterized with respect to a value, it can use the argument value, even if nothing is known about that value except its type. Similarly, if an abstraction is parameterized with respect to a variable, it can inspect and update the argument variable, even if nothing is known about that variable except its type.

Type parameters are fundamentally different, however. A type parameter denotes an unknown argument type. But nothing useful can be done with the type parameter unless *something* is known about the argument type – in particular, what operations are applicable to values of the argument type.

In Example 6.11, the phrase '`type Item is private`' is Ada's way of stating that assignment must be a valid operation for the actual type denoted by `Item`, although the actual type is unknown. Inside the generic package body, therefore, we find assignments like '`items(rear) := newitem`', where both sides are of type `Item`.

The following example illustrates a type parameter about which rather more has to be known.

Example 6.12

Languages suitable for serious numerical computations (such as Fortran and Ada) have two or more types of floating-point numbers (e.g., Float and Long_Float). A numerical algorithms package should be parameterized with respect to the type of the floating-point numbers involved:

```
generic
   type Real is digits <>;
package numerical is
   function sqrt (x : Real) return Real;
      ...
end numerical;
```

The phrase 'type Real is digits <>' is Ada's way of stating that the actual type denoted by Real must be a floating-point type. Inside the generic package body, we can now apply the usual floating-point operations (e.g., '>', '+', '*', '/', '**') to operands of type Real:

```
package body numerical is

   function sqrt (x : Real) return Real is
      root : Real := x / 2.0;
   begin
      while abs (x - root**2)
            > 2.0 * x * Real'epsilon loop
         root := (root + x/root) / 2.0;
      end loop;
      return root;
   end;

   ...
end numerical;
```

This generic package can be instantiated with different floating-point types as arguments:

```
package single_precision is
        new numerical (Float);
package double_precision is
        new numerical (Long_Float);
...
a, b : Float;
...
... single_precision.sqrt (a**2 + b**2) ...
```

In each instantiation of numerical, the compiler checks that the argument type is indeed a floating-point type.   □

More generally, if a generic abstraction is to have a type parameter *T*, we specify it by a phrase of this form:

type *T* **is** *specification of operations applicable to type T;*

The compiler checks each generic instantiation to ensure that:

operations applicable to the argument type
$\supseteq$ *operations specified as applicable to T*   (6.3)

and checks the generic abstraction itself to ensure that:

operations specified as applicable to T
$\supseteq$ *operations used for T in the generic abstraction*   (6.4)

Together, (6.3) and (6.4) guarantee that every operation used for *T* in the generic abstraction is indeed applicable to the argument type.

Type parameters have another peculiar property: they allow formal parameters to be mutually dependent. It is possible for one formal parameter to have a type that is itself a (type) parameter. Or one type parameter may depend on another. These possibilities are illustrated by the following example.

Example 6.13
The following is a generic sorting package in Ada. It is parameterized with respect to the type Item of the items to be sorted, and with respect to the type Sequence of arrays of such items. Thus the type parameter Sequence is dependent on the type parameter Item. Furthermore, the generic is parameterized with respect to a function that tests whether one value of type Item should precede another in the sorted sequence.

```
generic
   type Item is private;
   type Sequence is
             array (Integer range <>) of Item;
   with function precedes (x, y : Item)
                                  return Boolean;
package sorting is
   procedure sort   (seq : in out Sequence);
   procedure merge (seq1, seq2 : in Sequence;
                    seq : out Sequence);
end sorting;
```

The formal parameters of this generic package are the type Item, the type Sequence, and the function precedes. As in Example 6.11, the specification of type parameter Item tells us that values of this type can be assigned. The specification of type parameter Sequence tells us that values of this type are arrays and can be indexed by integers. This information can be exploited in the generic package body:

```
package body sorting is

   procedure sort (seq : in out Sequence) is
```

```
begin
    ...
    if precedes (seq(j), seq(i)) then ...
    ...
end;

procedure merge (seq1, seq2 : in Sequence;
                 seq : out Sequence) is
    ...

end sorting;
```

Since the parameters are mutually dependent, the arguments supplied in each instantiation of sorting must be consistent with these dependencies:

```
type FloatSequence is
        array (Integer range <>) of Float;
package ascending is
        new sorting (Float, FloatSequence, "<=");
package descending is
        new sorting (Float, FloatSequence, ">=");
...
readings : FloatSequence;
...
ascending.sort (readings);
```

Here is another possible instantiation:

```
type Transaction is record ... end record;
type TransSequence is
        array (Integer range <>) of Transaction;

function earlier (t1, t2 : Transaction)
                        return Boolean is
    ...;   -- return true iff t1 has an earlier timestamp than t2

package transaction_sorting is
        new sorting (Transaction,
                        TransSequence, earlier);
```

☐

It is interesting to summarize what entities may be used as arguments in Ada: see Table 6.1. Note the omissions:

(a) It is an anomaly that an Ada procedure or function abstraction cannot be parameterized with respect to another procedure or function abstraction. Many simpler languages allow this (see Example 5.4), including even Fortran!

(b) It is normal that procedure and function abstractions cannot have type parameters. No major language allows this.

Table 6.1 Arguments in Ada.

Sort of argument	Procedure/function abstraction	Generic abstraction
first-class value	•	•
(reference to a) variable	•	•
procedure/function abstraction	(a)	•
type	(b)	•

6.5 Further reading

The importance of encapsulation in the design of large programs was first clearly recognized by Parnas (1972). He advocated that access to each global data structure should be restricted to procedures provided for the purpose, on the grounds that this discipline would tend to make the modules of a large program independent of one another. A data structure hidden in this way is just what we now call an object.

The concept of an object class can be traced back to Simula-67, described in Dahl *et al.* (1970). However, no component of a Simula-67 object could be hidden. Furthermore, Simula-67 confuses the concept of object with the independent concepts of *reference* and *coroutine*. Simula-67 also introduced the idea that an object class can *inherit* operations from another object class. (Inheritance will be covered in Section 7.6.)

The concept of abstract types was introduced by Liskov and Zilles (1974). This concept has proved to be extremely valuable for structuring large programs. Abstract types are amenable to formal specification, and much research has focused on the properties of such specifications, and in particular on exploring exactly what set of values are defined by such a specification.

The activities of programming in the small and programming in the large were first distinguished by DeRemer and Kron (1976). They argued that a special *module interconnection language* should be used for programming in the large, and that an ordinary programming language should be used only for programming in the small. However, modern programming languages like Ada and ML are powerful enough for specifying module interconnections as well as programming the individual modules.

Programming is just one aspect of software engineering, and the programming language is just one of the tools in the software engineer's kit. A thorough exploration of the relationship between programming languages and the wider aspects of software engineering may be found in Ghezzi and Jazayeri (1987).

A discussion of encapsulation in general, and a rationale for the design of Ada packages and generics in particular, may be found in Chapter 8 of Ichbiah (1979).

Exercises 6

6.1 Which programming activities are peculiar to programming in the small? Which ones are peculiar to programming in the large?

6.2 (a) Given that Pascal lacks packages, how would Example 6.3 be reprogrammed in Pascal? What are the disadvantages of Pascal's lack of packages? (b) Repeat, assuming that Pascal is extended with a block declaration, similar to ML's. (See Example 6.4.)

6.3* Choose a programming language that has *ad hoc* text input–output features (e.g., Fortran or Pascal). Design a package that provides equivalent functionality. The user of the package should be able to achieve all the usual input–output effects without resorting to *ad hoc* language features. (See Ichbiah (1983) for an example of such a package.)

6.4 Design each of the following as an abstract type: (a) Complex; (b) Money; (c) Date; (d) Fuzzy (with values *yes*, *no*, and *unknown*, and logical operations such as *and* and *or*). Give at least one possible representation in each case.

6.5 (a) Enrich the rational numbers abstract type of Example 6.6 with further operations, e.g., subtraction, multiplication, division, and magnitude comparison. (b) Reimplement the abstract type, representing each rational number in reduced form (i.e., by a pair of integers with no common factor).

6.6 (a) Implement an object `counter` in a suitable language The object's user may zero the counter, increment it, or inspect its current value. No other operations are permitted. (b) Generalize your answer to implement a *class* of counters.

6.7 When an object is implemented in Ada or Smalltalk, we may include commands that automatically initialize the object. What are the advantages and disadvantages of automatic initialization of an object? (The alternative is for the object to export an explicit initialization procedure.)

6.8* Most text editors use a *text buffer*, held in main store, that contains the text being edited. Sketch the design and implementation of such a text buffer, with operations to load a given file into it, to save its contents to a file, to insert or remove given text at a given place, etc. The text buffer should be an object.

6.9 (a) Reimplement the rational numbers abstract type of Example 6.6 in Ada (or another suitable language). (b) Program the same example as an *object class*. In each case, write some code that declares a few rational number variables, assigns values to them, adds them, etc.

6.10   Complete the generic packages of Examples 6.10 and 6.11.

6.11*   Design and implement in Ada (or another suitable language) a generic package that implements sets, along the following lines:

```
generic
   type Item is ...;
package set_type is
   type Set is ...;    -- sets of values of type Item
   empty : constant Set := ...;
   function single (anitem : Item)
                          return Set;
   function union   (set1, set2 : Set)
                          return Set;
   function member (anitem : Item;
                     aset : Set)
                          return Boolean;
      ...
   end set_type;
```

(a) Assume as little as possible about the argument type. What assumption are you absolutely forced to make?

(b) Now assume that the argument type will always be a primitive discrete type. Exploit this to make the package more efficient. What price will the package *user* pay for this improved efficiency?

6.12*   Modify the generic packages of Exercise 6.11 to implement mappings from type Item to a second type Data, both these types being parameters. Assume as little as possible about the actual type denoted by Data.

CHAPTER SEVEN

Type Systems

Classical programming languages such as Pascal have very simple type systems. Every constant, variable, function result, and formal parameter must be declared with a specific type. A type system like this is called *monomorphic*, and makes type checking straightforward.

Unfortunately, experience quickly shows that a purely monomorphic type system is unsatisfactory, especially for writing reusable software. Many standard algorithms (such as sorting algorithms) are inherently *generic*, in the sense that they depend only loosely, or not at all, on the type of the values being manipulated. Yet whenever we attempt to program such an algorithm as a procedure, a monomorphic language forces us to declare a specific type for these values. Many standard data structures (such as homogeneous lists and trees) are also generic, but a monomorphic language provides no way to define them generically.

These and other problems have prompted development of more powerful type systems, which have appeared in several modern languages such as Ada and ML. The most important of these type systems are studied in this chapter. The relevant concepts are *overloading*, which is the ability of a single identifier or operator to denote several abstractions simultaneously; *polymorphism*, which is concerned with abstractions that operate uniformly on values of different types; and *inheritance*, which is concerned with subtypes and supertypes, in particular the ability of subtypes to inherit operations from their supertypes.

7.1 Monomorphism

In previous chapters we have assumed, for simplicity, that the programming language has a very simple type system. In fact, we have been assuming that each constant, variable, parameter, and function result has a unique type. A type system that has this property is called **monomorphic**. (This word literally means 'single-shaped'). The Pascal type system is basically monomorphic.

Example 7.1

Consider the following Pascal function:

```
type CharSet = set of Char;

function disjoint (s1, s2 : CharSet) : Boolean;
   begin
   disjoint := (s1 * s2 = [])
   end
```

The type of this function is $\wp$ Character $\times$ $\wp$ Character $\rightarrow$ Truth-Value. As such it can be applied to a pair of arguments, each of type $\wp$ Character:

```
var chars : CharSet;
...
if disjoint (chars, ['a','e','i','o','u']) then ...
```

This tests whether the set in `chars` is disjoint from the set { 'a', 'e', 'i', 'o', 'u' }.

This function's body uses set operations, but no operations that are peculiar to characters. Nevertheless, the function is monomorphic, and it cannot be applied to arguments of type $\wp$ Integer, nor $\wp$ Color, nor any other set type other than $\wp$ Character.   □

Pascal forces us to specify the exact type of every formal parameter and function result. As a consequence, every explicitly defined function and procedure in Pascal is monomorphic.

Nevertheless, neither Pascal nor any major programming language is strictly monomorphic. For example, many of Pascal's *built-in* functions and procedures have types that cannot be expressed in Pascal's own type system. This is possible only because these built-in entities are treated as special cases by the compiler.

Consider the Pascal built-in procedure `write`. For simplicity, we shall ignore most of this procedure's idiosyncrasies, and concentrate on procedure calls of the form '`write (E)`'. The effect of such a procedure call depends on the type of *E*. There are several possibilities. For example, if *E* is of type Character, a single character will be written out. Or if *E* is of type String, a sequence of characters will be written out. Or if *E* is of type Integer, an integer value will be converted to a sequence of characters (a decimal literal padded with spaces), and that sequence of characters written out. In reality, the identifier `write` simultaneously denotes several distinct procedures, each having its own type. This is an example of *overloading*.

Now consider the Pascal built-in function `eof`. This takes an argument variable of *any* file type, and tests for end-of-file on that file variable. The function's type is File(τ) $\rightarrow$ Truth-Value, where τ stands for *any* type. This function is said to be *polymorphic*. (This word literally means 'many-shaped'.) It accepts arguments of different types, e.g., File(Character) and File(Integer), but operates uniformly on all of them.

We must be careful not to confuse the distinct concepts of overloading and polymorphism. Overloading means that a (small) number of distinct abstractions just happen to have the same identifier; these abstractions do not necessarily have related types, nor do they necessarily perform similar operations on their arguments. Polymorphism is a property of a single abstraction that has a (large) family of related types; the abstraction operates uniformly on its arguments, whatever their type.

It may be seen that overloading does not increase the language's expressive power, as it could easily be eliminated by renaming the overloaded abstractions. Thus the Pascal `write` procedures could be renamed `writechar`, `writestring`, etc., with nothing worse than a small loss of notational convenience. Polymorphism does provide a genuine gain in expressive power, however, since a polymorphic abstraction may take arguments of an unlimited variety of types.

Pascal is inconsistent: all abstractions explicitly defined by the programmer are monomorphic, but many of the built-in abstractions are overloaded or polymorphic. More modern languages (such as Ada and ML) have largely avoided such inconsistency by making overloading or polymorphism uniformly available for both built-in and defined abstractions. This results in greater convenience and power for the programmer to exploit, and fewer special cases to memorize.

Another concept found only in embryo form in Pascal is that of *inheritance*. Consider the subrange type defined by '**type** Size = 28..31'. The set of values of this type is:

$$\text{Size} = \{28, 29, 30, 31\} \subset \text{Integer}$$

Therefore any operation that expects an Integer value will happily accept a value of type Size. For example, a function of type Integer $\rightarrow$ Truth-Value can be applied to an argument of type Size, and thus the function will behave as if it also had type Size $\rightarrow$ Truth-Value. The type Size is said to *inherit* all the operations of type Integer.

A Pascal subrange type inherits all the operations of its parent type. Otherwise, no Pascal type inherits any operations from another distinct type. At the opposite extreme, the object-oriented languages provide comprehensive support for inheritance.

In the remainder of this chapter we shall examine overloading, polymorphism, and inheritance in more detail.

7.2   Overloading

In discussing issues of scope and visibility, in Section 4.3, we assumed that within a particular block each identifier denotes at most one entity. Here we relax this assumption.

We first consider the possibility that an identifier or operator can simultaneously denote more than one function. (Recall, from Section 2.6.3, that we may view an expression like 'n+1' as a function call, where the operator '+' denotes a function. From this point of view, an operator is a kind of identifier.)

An identifier or operator is said to be **overloaded** if it simultaneously denotes two or more distinct functions. In general, overloading is acceptable only where each function call is unambiguous, i.e., where the function to be called can be identified uniquely using available type information.

In Pascal and ML, only identifiers and operators denoting built-in abstractions may be overloaded.

Example 7.2
In Pascal, the operator '–' simultaneously denotes five distinct functions:

- integer negation   (a function in Integer → Integer)
- real negation   (a function in Real → Real)
- integer subtraction   (a function in Integer × Integer → Integer)
- real subtraction   (a function in Real × Real → Real)
- set difference   (a function in Set × Set → Set)

No ambiguity can arise. In function calls such as '–y' and 'x–y', the number of actual parameters and their types uniquely determine which function is being called.   □

In Ada, both identifiers and operators may be overloaded by the programmer.

Example 7.3
The operator '/' in the Ada standard environment simultaneously denotes two distinct functions:

- integer division   (a function in Integer × Integer → Integer)
- real division   (a function in Real × Real → Real)

For example, the function call '7/2' yields 3, and '7.0/2.0' yields 3.5.
   The following Ada function definition further overloads the operator '/':

```
function "/" (m, n : Integer) return Float is
begin
    return Float (m) / Float (n);
end;
```

(The function body calls the real-division function.) This overloading makes '/' also denote:

- real division of integers   (a function in Integer × Integer → Real)

Using this function, the function call '7/2' yields 3.5.
   Because the functions for integer division and real division of integers differ only in their result types, in general the identification of '/' in a function call will depend on the context as well as the number and types of actual parameters. (In the right-hand column below we will use different symbols to distinguish among the three functions: ÷ for integer division, / for real division, and ∻ for real division of integers.)

```
n : Integer;  x : Float;
...
x := 7.0/2.0;        – computes 7.0/2.0 = 3.5
x := 7/2;            – computes 7∻2 = 3.5
n := 7/2;            – computes 7÷2 = 3
n := (7/2)/(5/2);    – computes (7÷2)÷(5÷2) = 3÷2 = 1
```

Some function calls will be ambiguous, even taking context into account:

$$x \; := \; (7/2)\,/\,(5/2)\,; \qquad - \text{computes} \; (7 \div 2) \div (5 \div 2) \; = \; 3 \div 2 \; = \; 1.5$$
$$\textit{or} \; (7 \div 2)/(5 \div 2) \; = \; 3.5/2.5 \; = \; 1.4$$

$\square$

We can characterize overloading in terms of the types of the overloaded functions. In Pascal and ML, the parameter types of the overloaded functions are always distinct. In Ada, it is sufficient for the parameter *or* result types of the overloaded functions to be distinct.

More generally, consider an identifier or operator I that denotes both a function f_1 of type $S_1 \rightarrow T_1$ and a function f_2 of type $S_2 \rightarrow T_2$. (Recall that this covers functions of several arguments: S_1 or S_2 could be a Cartesian product.) There are two kinds of overloading:

- *Context-independent overloading* (as in Pascal and ML) requires that S_1 and S_2 be distinct. Consider the function call '$I\ (E)$'. If the actual parameter E is of type S_1, then I here denotes f_1 and the result is of type T_1; if E is of type S_2, then I here denotes f_2 and the result is of type T_2. With context-independent overloading, the function to be called is always uniquely identified by the type of the actual parameter.
- *Context-dependent overloading* (as in Ada) requires that S_1 and S_2 be distinct *or* that T_1 and T_2 be distinct. If S_1 and S_2 are distinct, the function to be called can be identified as above. If S_1 and S_2 are not distinct, but T_1 and T_2 are distinct, context must be taken into account to identify the function to be called. Consider the function call '$I\ (E)$', where E is of type S_1 ($\equiv S_2$). If the function call occurs in a context where an expression of type T_1 is expected, then I must denote f_1; if the function call occurs in a context where an expression of type T_2 is expected, then I must denote f_2. With context-dependent overloading, it is possible to formulate expressions in which the function to be called cannot be identified uniquely, as we saw in Example 7.3; but the language must prohibit such ambiguous expressions.

As well as functions, some languages allow overloading of procedures, and even overloading of literals. It is a simple matter to extend the above characterization to these cases. (See Exercises 7.2 and 7.3.)

7.3 Polymorphism

In a **polymorphic** type system, we can write abstractions that operate uniformly on arguments of a whole family of related types. We saw in Section 7.1 that polymorphism crops up among the built-in abstractions of a basically monomorphic language like Pascal. However, ML was the first major programming language with a truly polymorphic type system, and we shall use ML to illustrate this important concept.

(To be exact, ML features a particular kind of polymorphism sometimes called *parametric polymorphism*. The topic of the previous section, *overloading*, is sometimes called *ad-hoc polymorphism*. The topic of Section 7.6, *inheritance*, is sometimes called *inclusion polymorphism*.)

7.3.1 Polymorphic abstractions

In ML it is a simple matter to define a polymorphic function. The key is to define such a function's type using *type variables*, rather than specific types. We shall introduce this idea by a series of examples.

Example 7.4
The following ML function accepts a pair of integers and returns their sum:

```
fun sum (x: int, y: int) = x + y
```

This function is of type Integer × Integer → Integer. The function call 'sum (13, 21)' will yield 34.

Now consider the following function, which accepts a pair of integers and simply returns the second of them:

```
fun second (x: int, y: int) = y
```

This function is also of type Integer × Integer → Integer. The function call 'second (13, 21)' will yield 21. The function call 'second (13, true)' would be illegal, because the argument pair does not consist of two integers. The function call 'second (13)' or 'second (1983, 2, 23)' would also be illegal, because the argument is not a pair at all.

But why should second be restricted to accepting a pair of *integers*? There is nothing in the function body that is specifically an operation on integers, so the function's argument could in principle be any pair of values whatsoever. It is in fact possible to define second in this way:

```
fun second (x: σ, y: τ) = y
```

This function is said to be of type $\sigma \times \tau \to \tau$. Here σ and τ each stands for *any* type whatsoever.

Now the function call 'second (13, true)' is legal. Its type is determined as follows. We can match the argument type, Integer × Truth-Value, to the function type, $\sigma \times \tau \to \tau$, by systematically substituting Integer for σ and Truth-Value for τ. Therefore, the type of the result is Truth-Value (and its value will be *true*).

Consider the function call 'second (name)', where the value of name is the string pair ("Jeffrey", "Watt"). This function call is also legal. We can match the argument type, String × String, to the function type, $\sigma \times \tau \to \tau$, by uniformly substituting String for both σ and τ. In this case the type of the result is String (and its value will be "Watt").

The function second is polymorphic. That does not imply that it accepts just any argument. A function call like 'second (13)' or 'second (1983, 2, 23)' is still illegal, because the argument type cannot be matched to the type $\sigma \times \tau \to \tau$. The allowable arguments are just those values that have types of the form $\sigma \times \tau$, i.e., pairs.

□

A type like $\sigma \times \tau \rightarrow \tau$ is called a *polytype*, because it can be thought of as deriving a family of many types. Here σ and τ are *type variables*; each stands for an unknown type. (Type variables are conventionally written as Greek letters.)

The family of types derived by a polytype is obtained by taking all possible *systematic* substitutions of types for type variables. In the case of $\sigma \times \tau \rightarrow \tau$, the family includes Integer × Truth-Value → Truth-Value and String × String → String. It does not include Integer × Truth-Value → Integer, nor Integer → Integer, nor Integer × Integer × Integer → Integer. In other words, each type in the family is the type of a function that accepts a pair of values and returns a result of the same type as the second component of the pair.

Example 7.5

The function of Example 7.1 could be written as follows if Pascal allowed us to define polymorphic functions:

```
function disjoint (s1, s2 : set of τ) : Boolean;
  begin
  disjoint := (s1 * s2 = [])
  end
```

The type of disjoint would be $\wp\tau \times \wp\tau \rightarrow$ Truth-Value. As such it could be applied to any pair of arguments of the same set type:

```
var   chars : set of Char;
      ints1, ints2 : set of 0..99;
...
if disjoint (chars, ['a','e','i','o','u']) then ...
if disjoint (ints1, ints2) then ...
```

The polytype $\wp\tau \times \wp\tau \rightarrow$ Truth-Value derives a family of types that includes $\wp$ Character × $\wp$ Character → Truth-Value, $\wp$ Integer × $\wp$ Integer → Truth-Value, and many others.

□

Example 7.6

The following defines the integer identity function in ML:

```
fun id (x: int) = x
```

This function is of type Integer → Integer, and maps any integer to itself.

The following defines the polymorphic identity function:

```
fun id (x: τ) = x
```

This function is of type $\tau \rightarrow \tau$. It represents the following mapping:

$$id = \{ \ \textit{false} \mapsto \textit{false}, \textit{true} \mapsto \textit{true},$$
$$..., -2 \mapsto -2, -1 \mapsto -1, 0 \mapsto 0, 1 \mapsto 1, 2 \mapsto 2, ...,$$

$$\text{“”} \mapsto \text{“”}, \text{“a”} \mapsto \text{“a”}, \text{“ab”} \mapsto \text{“ab”}, ...,$$
$$...\}$$

i.e., it maps *any* value to itself.   □

We conclude this subsection with a couple of examples that more convincingly demonstrate the expressive power of polymorphic functions.

Example 7.7
The following defines twice to be a function that takes an argument function *f*, and returns a new function *g* such that $g(x) = f(f(x))$, i.e., it applies *f* twice to *x*.

```
fun twice (f: τ -> τ) =
        fn (x: τ) => f (f (x))
```

Both the argument and result of twice are functions of type $\tau \to \tau$. Therefore twice itself is of type $(\tau \to \tau) \to (\tau \to \tau)$.

The following defines fourth to be the function that maps each integer to its fourth power:

```
val fourth = twice (sqr)
```

The standard function sqr has type Integer $\to$ Integer. This matches the argument type of twice, and therefore the function call 'twice (sqr)' has type Integer $\to$ Integer.   □

Example 7.8
The following defines o to be an operator that takes two functions *f* and *g* and returns their composition – i.e., a function *h* such that $h(x) = f(g(x))$.

```
fun op o (f: β -> γ, g: α -> β) =
        fn (x: α) => f (g (x))
```

The function o has parameters of types $\beta \to \gamma$ and $\alpha \to \beta$, respectively, and its result is of type $\alpha \to \gamma$.

The following illustrate some possible uses of this operator:

```
val even = not o odd
fun twice (f: τ -> τ) = f o f
```

                                      □

7.3.2   Parameterized types

Consider 'file of τ' in Pascal. We can think of **file** as a parameterized type, which can be specialized to ordinary types by substituting actual types for τ, as in 'file of Char' and 'file of Real'. Other parameterized types in Pascal are **set** and **array**.

A *parameterized type* is a type that has other type(s) as parameters. Parameterized types are essential in any language with a system of composite types. We can specify the properties of Pascal files, arrays, and sets, without concern for the actual types of their components.

In a monomorphic language, only built-in parameterized types are provided; the programmer cannot define new parameterized types. In Pascal, for example, we can define particular types of homogeneous pair:

```
type IntPair  = record fst, snd : Integer end;
     RealPair = record fst, snd : Real end
```

but we *cannot* define homogeneous pairs in general:

```
type Pair (τ) = record fst, snd : τ end;
     IntPair  = Pair (Integer);
     RealPair = Pair (Real)
```

Likewise, we can define particular types of homogeneous list:

```
type CharList = ...;
     IntList  = ...;
var  line : CharList
```

but we cannot define homogeneous lists in general:

```
type List (τ) = ...;
var  line : List (Char)
```

In ML it is easy to define such parameterized types, as illustrated by the following examples.

Example 7.9
Consider the following ML parameterized type definition:

```
type τ pair = τ * τ
```

In this definition τ acts as a type parameter, denoting an unknown type. The definition makes the identifier pair denote a parameterized type. (Note that a parameterized type identifier (e.g., pair) *follows* its type parameter (e.g., τ) in the ML syntax.)

An example of using pair would be 'int pair'. By substitution of int for τ, we see that this is equivalent to 'int * int'; thus it denotes a type in which each value is a pair of integers. Another example would be 'real pair', denoting a type in which each value is a pair of real numbers. □

Example 7.10
The following ML type definition defines homogeneous lists in general:

```
datatype τ list = nil | cons of (τ * τ list)
```

Now 'int list' denotes a type in which each value is a list of integers.

Now we can define some polymorphic functions on lists:

```
fun hd (l: τ list) =    (* first element of a list *)
       case l of
```

```
                    nil          => ...    (* error *)
                    cons(h,t)    => h
      and tl (l: τ list) =    (* remaining elements of a list *)
              case l of
                    nil          => ...    (* error *)
                    cons(h,t)    => t
      and length (l: τ list) =    (* length of a list *)
              case l of
                    nil          => 0
              |  cons(h,t) => 1 + length (t)
```

(In fact, list, hd, tl, and length are all predefined in ML.)   □

In order to avoid being restricted to the notation of any particular programming language, we shall use notation such as Pair(τ) and List(τ) for parameterized types. Thus we can rewrite the type definitions of Examples 7.9 and 7.10 as equations:

$$\text{Pair}(\tau) = \tau \times \tau \tag{7.1}$$
$$\text{List}(\tau) = \text{Unit} + (\tau \times \text{List}(\tau)) \tag{7.2}$$

Comparing (7.2) with equation (2.20) in Section 2.4.1, we see that List(τ) = τ^*.

Using this notation, we can define the parameterized types of Pascal as follows:

$$\text{Array}(\sigma, \tau) = \sigma \rightarrow \tau \tag{7.3}$$
$$\text{Set}(\sigma) = \wp\sigma \tag{7.4}$$

where, in (7.3) and (7.4), σ is restricted to a primitive discrete type.

The types of the functions defined in Example 7.10 are as follows: hd is of type List(τ) $\rightarrow$ τ; tl is of type List(τ) $\rightarrow$ List(τ); and length is of type List(τ) $\rightarrow$ Integer.

7.3.3   Polytypes

A *polytype* is a type that contains one or more type variables. The following are examples of polytypes:

$$\text{List}(\tau) \quad \text{List}(\tau) \rightarrow \tau \quad \text{List}(\tau) \rightarrow \text{Integer}$$
$$\tau \rightarrow \tau \quad \sigma \times \tau \rightarrow \tau \quad (\beta \rightarrow \gamma) \times (\alpha \rightarrow \beta) \rightarrow (\alpha \rightarrow \gamma)$$

A *type variable* generally stands for any type. A polytype derives a whole family of types, obtained by systematic substitution of an actual type for each type variable. For example, the polytype $\tau \rightarrow \tau$ derives a family of types that includes Integer $\rightarrow$ Integer, String $\rightarrow$ String, List(Real) $\rightarrow$ List(Real), etc., but *not* String $\rightarrow$ Integer.

A type that contains no type variables is called a *monotype*. In a monomorphic language (such as Pascal), all types are monotypes.

If we are to talk about *the* type of a polymorphic abstraction such as hd, tl, or length (Example 7.10), we must view a polytype as being itself a type. We must therefore be able to define the set of values of a polytype.

In general, the set of values of any polytype is the *intersection* of all types that can be derived from it. This statement seems paradoxical at first sight, but a couple of examples will justify it.

Example 7.11
What is the set of values of the polytype List(τ)? Consider first the set of values of each type derived from List(τ). The type List(Integer) includes all (finite) lists of integers, including the empty list. The type List(Truth-Value) includes all (finite) lists of truth values, including the empty list. The type List(String) includes all (finite) lists of strings, including the empty list. These types, and all others derived from List(τ), have (only) the empty list in common. See Figure 7.1.

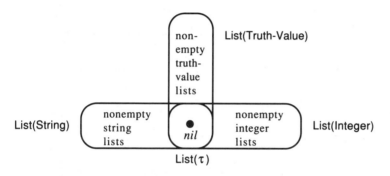

Figure 7.1 The polytype List(τ) as an intersection of monotypes.

Every nonempty list has a monotype, determined by the type of its components. Only the empty list has type List(τ). Therefore the type List(τ) is the intersection of the types List(Integer), List(Truth-Value), List(String), and so on.   □

Example 7.12
What is the set of values of the polytype $\tau \rightarrow \tau$? Consider first the set of values of each type derived from $\tau \rightarrow \tau$. The type Integer $\rightarrow$ Integer includes the integer identity function, the successor function, the absolute value function, the squaring function, and many others. The type String $\rightarrow$ String includes the string identity function, the string replication function, the space trimming function, and many others. The type Truth-Value $\rightarrow$ Truth-Value includes the truth value identity function, the logical negation function, and a couple of others. If we similarly consider the sets of values of other types derived from $\tau \rightarrow \tau$, we find that an identity function is common to all of them.

The polymorphic identity function *id* of Example 7.6, when applied to an integer argument, will always map that integer to itself. In fact, we might as well regard the integer identity function as being the same function as *id*. (The integer identity function will never be applied to a noninteger, because of type checking, so we do not care what it would do with a noninteger argument.) Similarly, we might as well regard the string identity function, the truth value identity function, and all the others as being the same function as *id*. Thus *id* is common to Integer $\rightarrow$ Integer, String $\rightarrow$ String,

Truth-Value → Truth-Value, and so on. The same cannot be said of any of the other functions mentioned in the previous paragraph.

In fact, the type $\tau \to \tau$ is the *intersection* of the types Integer → Integer, String → String, Truth-Value → Truth-Value, and so on. See Figure 7.2.   □

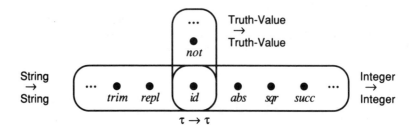

Figure 7.2 The polytype $\tau \to \tau$ as an intersection of monotypes.

7.4 Type inference

Up to now we have been assuming that, in a statically typed language, the type of every variable, parameter, etc., must be explicitly stated. This is clearly the case in a Pascal variable declaration, '**var** $I : T$ ', and in a Pascal function declaration, such as '**function** I (I': T') : T; B'. But consider the Pascal constant definition, '**const** $I = E$'; here the type of the declared constant is given implicitly by the type of E.

The latter is a very simple example of what we call *type inference*. The type of a declared entity is inferred, rather than explicitly stated. Type inference can be carried much further. In ML, types only occasionally have to be stated explicitly by the programmer.

7.4.1 Monomorphic type inference

So far we have been writing ML function definitions in the form '**fun** I (I': T') = E', relying on the result type's being inferred from the function body E, but explicitly stating the type of the formal parameter I'. In fact, even the latter is unnecessary, and we can write simply '**fun** I (I') = E'. The type of I' is then inferred from its applied occurrences in E. (And similarly for functions with several parameters.)

Example 7.13
Consider the following ML function definition:

```
fun even (n) =
```

```
(n mod 2 = 0)
```

Assume that the operator 'mod' has type Integer × Integer → Integer. From the subexpression 'n mod 2' we can infer that n must be of type Integer (otherwise the subexpression would be ill-typed). Then we can infer that the function body is of type Truth-Value. Therefore even is of type Integer → Truth-Value.   □

ML adopts a *laissez-faire* attitude to typing. The programmer can voluntarily state the type of a declared entity, or leave the compiler to infer the type.

In longer pieces of program than Example 7.13, however, it is unwise to rely too much on type inference. Consider a very large function definition, written without any types being stated explicitly. A (human) reader might have to scan several pages simply to discover the type of the function. Even the author of the function definition can get into difficulties: a slight programming error in the function body might confuse the compiler, causing it to produce obscure error messages, or even to infer a different type from the one intended by the programmer. So explicitly stating types, even if redundant, is good programming practice.

7.4.2   Polymorphic type inference

Type inference sometimes yields a monotype, as in the previous subsection, but only when the available clues are strong enough. In Example 7.13, the function body contained a monomorphic operator, mod, and two integer literals. These clues were enough to allow us to infer a monotype for the function.

In general, the available clues are not so indicative: the function body might be written entirely in terms of polymorphic functions. Indeed, it is conceivable that the function body might provide no clues at all. In these circumstances, type inference will yield a polytype.

Example 7.14
Consider the following ML function definition:

```
fun id (x) = x
```

Let τ be the type of x. There is no clue as to what τ is, but we can infer that the function result will also be of type τ. Therefore the type of id is $\tau \rightarrow \tau$. This function is, in fact, the polymorphic identity function of Example 7.6.   □

Example 7.15
Consider the following definition of an operator o:

```
fun op o (f, g) =
        fn (x) => f (g (x))
```

We can see, from the way they are used, that both f and g are functions; moreover, we can see that the result type of g must be the same as the argument type of f. Let the types of f and g be $\beta \rightarrow \gamma$ and $\alpha \rightarrow \beta$, respectively. The type of x must be α, since it is used as an argument of g. Therefore, the subexpression 'f (g (x))' is of type γ, and the expression '**fn** (x) => f (g (x))' is of type $\alpha \to \gamma$. Therefore, o is of type $(\beta \to \gamma) \times (\alpha \to \beta) \to (\alpha \to \gamma)$.

In fact, o is the operator that takes two functions and returns their composition, as in Example 7.8.   □

Example 7.16
Recall the following ML type definition from Example 7.10:

> **datatype** τ list = nil | cons **of** (τ * τ list)

Recall also the polymorphic functions on lists defined in Example 7.10. We can abbreviate each function definition by relying on type inference, e.g.:

```
fun length (l) =                    (* length of l *)
        case l of
            nil        => 0
          | cons(h,t) => 1 + length (t)
```

The result type of length is clearly Integer, since one limb of the *case* expression is an integer literal (and the other is an application of the operator '+'). The *case* expression also tells us that the value of l is either nil or of the form 'cons (..., ...)'. This allows us to infer that l is of type List(τ). We cannot be more specific, since there is no clue as to what τ is. Thus length is of type List(τ) $\to$ Integer.   □

7.5   Coercions

A *coercion* is an implicit mapping from values of one type to values of a different type. Typical examples of coercions are mapping integers to real numbers, and mapping characters to one-character strings. A coercion is performed automatically whenever the context demands it.

Consider a context in which an operand of type T is expected but an operand of type T' (not equivalent to T) is supplied. The programming language may allow a coercion in this context, provided that the language also defines a unique mapping from type T' to type T.

This is illustrated by the Pascal expression 'sqrt (n)', where the function sqrt expects an argument of type Real, but n is of type Integer. Now there is an obvious mapping from Integer to Real, namely:

$$\{..., -2 \mapsto -2.0, -1 \mapsto -1.0, 0 \mapsto 0.0, 1 \mapsto 1.0, 2 \mapsto 2.0, ...\}$$

Accordingly, Pascal does provide a coercion from Integer to Real, and the expression 'sqrt (n)' is legal.

On the other hand, there is no obvious unique mapping from Real to Integer: would we map 3.5 to 3 or to 4? So Pascal provides no coercion from Real to Integer, and instead requires the programmer to use an explicit transfer function (trunc or round) that makes clear which mapping is desired. If Pascal did provide a coercion from Real to Integer, the choice of mapping would be arbitrary, and would be a burden on the programmer's memory.

Some languages, notably PL/I and Algol-68, are very permissive in respect of coercions. For example, Algol-68 allows the following coercions, among others: from an integer to a real number, and from a real number to a complex number (*widening*); from a reference to a variable to the current value of that variable (*dereferencing* – see Section 3.5.2); from any value to an array with that value as a single component (*rowing*); from any value to the corresponding tagged value in a disjoint union (*uniting*); from any value to () (*voiding*).

More modern languages tend to minimize or even eliminate coercions altogether. At first sight this might seem to be a retrograde step. However, coercions do not fit well with overloading (Section 7.2) and polymorphism (Section 7.3), concepts widely thought to be more useful than coercion. In place of coercions, Ada provides a rather systematic way of mapping from one type to another type, using the name of the latter type as a transfer function. The Pascal expression 'sqrt (n)' would be written in Ada as 'sqrt (Float (n))', assuming that sqrt expects an argument of type Float.

7.6 Subtypes and inheritance

If we consider a type *T* to be a set of values, it seems natural to consider what significance can be attached to its subsets. We call each subset a *subtype* of *T*.

The concept of subtype is a fruitful and surprisingly pervasive notion in programming. We often declare a variable (or parameter) to be of type *T*, knowing that it will range over only a subset of the values of type *T*. If we can declare the variable's *subtype*, and thus specify more exactly what values it might take, this tends to make the program easier to understand, and sometimes more efficient. However, not all languages recognize the concept of subtype.

Pascal recognizes only one restricted kind of subtype. We can define *subranges* of any discrete primitive type *T*. As the terminology suggests, each subrange type is a contiguous range of values from *T*, and is thus a subtype of *T*.

Example 7.17
Consider the following Pascal declarations:

```
type  Natural = 0..maxint;
      Small   = -3..+3;
var   i : Integer;
      n : Natural;
      s : Small
```

The subtypes defined here are illustrated in Figure 7.3.

Following these declarations, the assignments 'i := n' and 'i := s' are always safe to perform since the assigned values, although unknown, are certainly in the type of i. Likewise, it is always safe to assign to n any value of type '28..31'.

On the other hand, assignments like 'n := i', 's := i', 'n := s', and 's := n' are unsafe. Each of them requires a run-time range check, to ensure that the assigned value is actually in the type of the variable being assigned to.

Similarly, if we define a function that expects an argument of type Integer or Natural or Small, some function calls will be safe, but others will require run-time range checks.   □

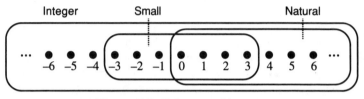

Figure 7.3 Subtypes of Integer.

Ada recognizes a much wider variety of subtypes than Pascal. We can define subranges of all primitive types, including real types. We can define a subtype of an array type by freezing its index bounds. We can define a subtype of a record type by freezing specially designated components called *discriminants*.

Example 7.18
The following Ada declarations define some subtypes of primitive types (compare Example 7.17):

```
subtype Natural is Integer range 0..Integer'last;
subtype Small   is Integer range -3..+3;
subtype Probability is Float range 0.0..1.0;
```

The following Ada declarations define an array type and some of its subtypes:

```
type    String  is array (Integer range <>)
                            of Character;
subtype String5 is String (1..5);
subtype String7 is String (1..7);
```

The values of type String are character arrays of all lengths. The values of subtype String5 are arrays of exactly five characters. The values of subtype String7 are arrays of exactly seven characters. See Figure 7.4.

The following Ada declarations define a record type and some subtypes:

```
type    Sex is (f, m);
type    Person (gender : Sex) is
                    record
                        name : String (1..8);
                        age  : Integer range 0..120;
                    end record;
```

```
subtype Female is Person (gender => f);
subtype Male   is Person (gender => m);
```

The values of type Person are triples, each consisting of a component gender of type {*f, m*}, a component name that is an array of exactly eight characters, and a component age of subtype {0, ..., 120}. The gender component is designated as a discriminant, and thus may be frozen if desired. The values of subtype Female are those triples in which the gender component is *f*, and the values of subtype Male are those triples in which the gender component is *m*. See Figure 7.5.   □

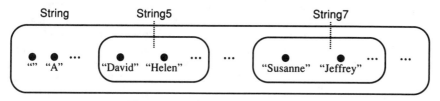

Figure 7.4 Array subtypes in Ada.

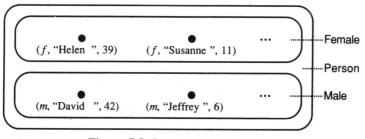

Figure 7.5 Record subtypes in Ada.

Thus each language recognizes certain subsets of types as subtypes – but not *arbitrary* subsets. For example, in no programming language can we declare an integer variable that ranges over the prime numbers only. We can declare a record variable that ranges over the set {*jan, ..., dec*} × {1, ..., 31}, but we cannot declare a record variable that ranges over the proper calendar dates only (i.e., excluding pairs such as (*feb*, 30) and (*apr*, 31)).

Let us now examine the general properties of subtypes. A necessary condition for *S* to be a subtype of *T* is that $S \subseteq T$. A value known to be in *S* can then safely be used wherever a value of type *T* is expected.

Suppose that *U* is not a subtype of *T*, but *U* and *T* do overlap. Then a value known to be in *U* may be used where a value of type *T* is expected only if a run-time check establishes that the value is actually in *T*. This is a kind of run-time type check, but much simpler and more efficient than the full run-time type checks implied by a dynamically typed language.

Wherever overlapping types exist, we cannot uniquely state the (sub)type of every value. For example, Figure 7.3 shows that the value 2 is not only in the type Integer but also in the subtypes Natural and Small, and indeed in numerous other subtypes of Integer. But we can uniquely state the (sub)type of every *variable*, provided that the programming language requires the (sub)type of each variable to be explicitly declared.

Associated with each type T are a number of operations applicable to values of type T. Each of these operations will also be applicable to values of any subtype S of T. We can think of S as **inheriting** all the operations associated with T. For example, a function of type Integer $\rightarrow$ Truth-Value will be inherited by all the subtypes of Integer, such as Natural and Small.

The term *inheritance* comes from object-oriented programming. An object a has one or more (hidden) components, which may be accessed by operations associated with a. A second object b might be declared to have all the components of a (and maybe additional components). Then it is sensible for b to inherit all the operations associated with a (and maybe additional operations, accessing the components unique to b). We can think of each object as a record. The following example illustrates this kind of inheritance.

Example 7.19

Consider the following ML type definitions:

```
type point  = {x: real, y: real}
type circle = {x: real, y: real, r: real}
type box    = {x: real, y: real, w: real, d: real}
```

These record types model points, circles, and boxes (rectangles) on the xy plane. For a circle or box, the components x and y are the coordinates of its center.

Given a value of type point, the most basic operations that can be applied to it are to access its components x and y. But these same operations can also be applied to a circle value (and additionally its component r can be accessed), or to a box value (and additionally its components w and d can be accessed).

These observations suggest that we could consider circle and box to be subtypes of point. ML itself does not allow that, but we could imagine an extension to ML that does. To be consistent, other operations associated with the type point should be inherited by its subtypes.

First consider the following function:

```
fun remoteness (p: point) =
        sqrt (sqr (p.x) + sqr (p.y))
```

This function can be called with any point argument, and will return the distance of that point from the origin. If circle and box were subtypes of point, remoteness could also be called with any circle or box argument, and would return the distance from the origin of that circle or box's center. So far so good.

But now consider the following function abstraction:

```
fun moved (p: point, xshift: real, yshift: real) =
        {x = p.x + xshift, y = p.y + yshift}
```

This function can be called with any `point` argument, and will return a `point` result: the original point displaced horizontally and vertically by a given amount. If `moved` were called with a `circle` argument, it would still return a `point` result: the circle's *center* displaced by a given amount. In effect, the information contained in the `circle` argument's `r` component would be discarded. A similar effect would be observed if `moved` were called with a `box` argument.

The type of `moved` is Point × Real × Real → Point. We would, however, prefer this function applied to a `point`, `circle`, or `box` argument to return a `point`, `circle`, or `box` result (respectively). In other words, we want the type of `moved` to be τ × Real × Real → τ, where τ is constrained to be a subtype of `point`. The following hypothetical notation would achieve this effect:

```
fun moved (p: τ ⊆ point,
           xshift: real, yshift: real) =
     p \ x => (p.x + xshift)
       \ y => (p.y + yshift)
```

(The hypothetical notation '*R* \ *I* => *E*' is supposed to take a record *R*, and yield a new record of the same type, in which component *I* has the value of *E* but all other components have the same value as in *R*.)

Finally, consider the following function:

```
fun area (p: point) = 0.0
```

which is of type Point → Real. We would *not* want this version of `area` to be inherited by all the subtypes of `point`. To prevent such inheritance, we might provide alternative versions of `area` for the subtypes `circle` and `box`:

```
fun area (c: circle) = pi * sqr (c.r)
fun area (b: box)    = b.w * b.d
```

However, other subtypes of `point` might sensibly inherit the original version of the `area` operation. An example might be a subtype `coloredpoint`, with a component of type `color` added to the `x` and `y` components. This illustrates that fine control of inheritance is sometimes needed.   □

The hypothetical extension to ML illustrated in Example 7.19 would force us to modify our view of records. If we view each record as an ordered tuple, then clearly Circle = Real × Real × Real and Box = Real × Real × Real × Real are not subtypes of Point = Real × Real; indeed, these types are not comparable at all. Instead, we must view each record as an *unordered* tuple of *labeled* values. Then we can define our types as follows:

Point = {*p* | *p* is a record that contains
             a Real value labeled x and a Real value labeled y}

Circle = {*c* | *c* is a record that contains
             a Real value labeled x and a Real value labeled y and
             a Real value labeled r}

Box   = {*b* | *b* is a record that contains
             a Real value labeled x and a Real value labeled y and
             a Real value labeled w and a Real value labeled d}

Now clearly Circle ⊂ Point and Box ⊂ Point. This view of records is illustrated in Figure 7.6.

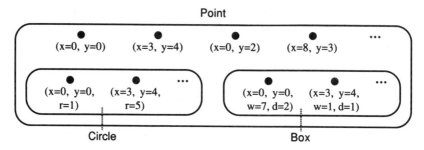

Figure 7.6 Record subtypes in an object-oriented language.

7.7   Further reading

Much of the material in this chapter is based on an illuminating survey paper by Cardelli and Wegner (1985). The authors propose a uniform framework for understanding (parametric) polymorphism, abstract types, subtypes, and inheritance. Then they use this framework to explore the consequences of combining some or all of these concepts in a single language. (No major language has yet attempted to combine them all.)

For another survey of type systems see Reynolds (1985). Unlike Cardelli and Wegner, Reynolds adopts the point of view that the concepts of coercion and subtype are essentially the same. For example, if a language is to provide a coercion from Integer to Real, then Integer should be defined as a subtype of Real. From this point of view, subtypes are not necessarily subsets.

The system of polymorphic type inference used in languages like ML and Miranda is based on a type inference algorithm independently discovered by Hindley (1969) and Milner (1978). ML's polymorphism and type inference are described in Wikström (1987), and Miranda's in Bird and Wadler (1988).

For a detailed discussion of overloading in Ada, see Ichbiah (1979).

Exercises 7

7.1   Suppose that the operator '&' (denoting concatenation) is overloaded, with types Character × Character → String, Character × String → String, String × Character → String, and String × String → String. Is this overloading context-dependent or context-independent? Identify each occurrence of '&' in the following expressions:

```
c & s
(s & c) & c
s & (c & c)
```

where c is a Character variable and s is a String variable.

7.2   Adapt the characterization of overloading at the end of Section 7.2 to cover procedures. Is the overloading of procedures context-dependent or context-independent?

Consider a language in which the operator '/' is overloaded, with types that include Integer × Integer → Integer and Integer × Integer → Real. The language also has an overloaded procedure write whose argument may be of several types, including Integer and Real. Find examples of procedure calls in which the procedure to be called cannot be identified uniquely.

7.3   Adapt the characterization of overloading at the end of Section 7.2 to cover literals. Is the overloading of literals context-dependent or context-independent?

Consider a language in which the operator '/' is overloaded, with types Integer × Integer → Integer and Real × Real → Real (and the other arithmetic operators similarly). The language has no integer-to-real coercion. It is now proposed to treat the literals 1, 2, 3, etc., as overloaded, with types Integer *and* Real, in order to allow expressions like '1/x', where x is of type Real. Examine the implications of this proposal.

7.4   Add to the group of ML list functions defined in Example 7.10: (a) a function to reverse a given list; (b) a function to concatenate two given lists; (c) a function to return the *i*th component of a given list. State the type of each function, using the notation defined at the end of Section 7.3.2.

7.5   Define the following polymorphic list-transforming functions in ML: (a) 'map (f, l)' returns a list in which each component is obtained by applying the function f to the corresponding component of list l; (b) 'filter (f, l)' returns a list consisting of every component x of list l such that f(x) yields *true*. State the types of map and filter.

7.6*   Define a parameterized type Set(τ) in ML (or any suitable language). Equip it with operations similar to those in Exercise 6.11, and state the type of each operation.

7.7   Infer the types of the following ML functions, given that the type of not is Truth-Value → Truth-Value, and that the type of o is ($\beta \rightarrow \gamma$) × ($\alpha \rightarrow \beta$) → ($\alpha \rightarrow \gamma$).

```
fun negation (p) = not o p;
fun cond (b, f, g) =
        fn x =>
            if b (x) then f (x) else g (x)
```

7.8   Infer the types of the following ML list functions, given that the type of '+' is Integer × Integer → Integer:

```
fun sum1 (l) =
        case l of
            nil => 0
          | cons(h,t) => h + sum1 (t);
fun insert (z, f, l) =
        case l of
            nil => z
          | cons(h,t) =>
                f (h, insert (z, f, t))
fun sum2 (l) = insert (0, (op +), l)
```

Compare the functions sum1 and sum2.

7.9   Show that, in Ada, two subtypes of a primitive type may overlap, but two subtypes of an array or record type are always disjoint.

7.10*   Make a list of the coercions allowed in your favorite language. Specify the mapping performed by each coercion.

CHAPTER EIGHT

Sequencers

Sequential, conditional, and iterative compositions of commands, discussed in Section 3.5, allow us to program a variety of control flows. Each of these control flows has a single entry and a single exit. Such control flows are adequate for most, but not all, purposes.

A *sequencer* is a construct that varies the normal flow of control, and thus allows more general control flows to be programmed. In this chapter we study several kinds of sequencer:

- *jumps*
- *escapes*
- *exceptions*

In so doing, we follow the trend in language design away from jumps and towards higher-level sequencers such as escapes and exceptions.

8.1 Jumps

A sequential, conditional, or iterative command has a flowchart with a single entry and a single exit. A simple command, such as an assignment, obviously has a single-entry single-exit flowchart. (See Figure 8.1.) By induction, therefore, any command formed by composition of simple, sequential, conditional, and iterative commands also has a single-entry single-exit flowchart.

A *jump* is an explicit transfer of control from one program point to another program point, its destination. Jumps appear in many languages, typically in the form 'goto *L*'. Here *L* is a *label* (usually an identifier) that denotes some program point. Attaching a label to a command, as in '*L* : *C* ', binds the label *L* to a particular program point. (Later in this section we shall see that a label actually denotes more than just a program point.)

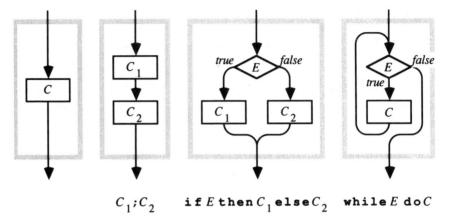

$$C_1;C_2 \qquad \text{if } E \text{ then } C_1 \text{ else } C_2 \qquad \text{while } E \text{ do } C$$

Figure 8.1 Flowcharts of simple, sequential, conditional, and iterative commands.

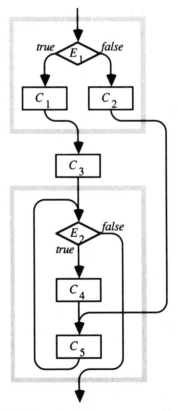

Figure 8.2 Flowchart of a program with a jump.

Example 8.1

Consider the following program fragment:

```
begin
if E₁ then C₁ else begin C₂; goto L end;
C₃;
while E₂ do
    begin
    C₄;
L: C₅
    end
end
```

The corresponding flowchart is shown in Figure 8.2. It has identifiable subcharts for the various commands. The subcharts of the *if* and *while* commands are outlined for emphasis.

The flowchart as a whole has a single entry and a single exit. But the subchart of the *if* command has two exits, and the subchart of the *while* command has two entries.   ☐

Unrestricted jumps allow any command to have many entries and many exits. They tend to give rise to 'spaghetti' programs, so called because their flowcharts are thoroughly tangled.

'Spaghetti' programs tend to be hard to understand. It is worth reflecting on why this is so. Simple commands like assignments are largely self-explanatory. Even composite single-entry single-exit commands can be understood more-or-less in isolation. But jumps are not self-explanatory at all. For example, what effect does the jump 'goto L' have on the flow of control? It might be a forward jump that causes commands to be skipped, or a backward jump that causes commands to be repeated. We cannot tell until we locate the label L, which might be pages away.

Still worse effects result from treating program points as values, allowing them to be passed as arguments or even stored – see Exercise 8.2.

Every major language places some restriction on jumps. Typically, the scope of a label is the block immediately containing its binding occurrence. In Fortran, with its flat block structure, jumps are therefore restricted to within a block (subprogram). In Algol, with its nested block structure, it is possible to jump within a block, or from one block out to an enclosing block, but never into a block from outside. The jump in Example 8.1 would be legal in both of these languages.

In Pascal, labels are subject to the scope rules, as in Algol, but there is a further restriction. In 'L: C' a jump to L is legal from anywhere in C; and in 'begin ...; L: C; ... end' a jump to L is legal from anywhere in the bracketed command. A jump may not transfer control from outside a composite (conditional or iterative) command to any of its subcommands, nor from one subcommand to another. In Example 8.1, the jump 'goto L' would be legal in Pascal if L's binding occurrence were in front of the *while* command, or in front of the command C_3, or in front of the *if* command. But in fact L's binding occurrence is inside the *while* command, so the jump would be illegal in Pascal. That does not imply that the flowchart of Figure

8.2 cannot be programmed in Pascal: we simply rewrite the *while* command in terms of the equivalent conditional and unconditional jumps. Since the resulting program fragment would hardly be more readable, Pascal's restriction on jumps is still not strong enough to prevent 'spaghetti' programming.

The mere existence of sequencers in a programming language radically modifies its semantics. For example, so far we have assumed that the sequential command 'C_1; C_2' is executed by first executing C_1 and then executing C_2. But this is correct only if C_1 terminates normally. If a sequencer causes exit from C_1, then C_2 might be skipped (or C_1 might be repeated). Likewise, the obvious way to define the effect of executing a loop – that the loop is repeated after the loop body has been executed – is correct only if the loop body terminates normally.

Now let us consider the semantics of jumps. If we consider only flowchart programs such as Figure 8.2, the effect of a jump is fairly obvious. But a jump out of a block is more complicated, in that any variables local to the block must be deleted. A jump out of a procedure body is also more complicated, in that the current procedure activation must be abandoned.

Example 8.2
Consider the following Pascal block:

```
type  Natural = 0..maxint;
var   n, w : Natural;

procedure print (num, width : Natural);
   var digit : 0..9;
   begin
   if width = 0 then goto 9;
   if num >= 10 then print (num div 10, width - 1);
   digit := num mod 10;
   write (output, chr (ord ('0') + digit))
   end;

begin
...
print (n, w)
...;
9:
...
end
```

If w is zero, the procedure will promptly perform the jump '**goto** 9'. The jump will cause the procedure activation to be abandoned, and all local variables to be deleted.

Now suppose that w is 3, and that n is 1983. Then four recursive activations of the procedure will be in existence when the jump is performed. (These are activations with the argument pairs (1983, 3), (198, 2), (19, 1), and (1, 0), respectively.) Each activation will have its own complement of local variables. The jump will abandon all these activations and delete all these variables.   □

Further complications arise when a jump's destination label is inside the body of a recursive procedure: which recursive activations are abandoned when the jump is performed? To deal with this possibility, we have to make a label denote not simply a program point, but a program point *within a particular activation of the enclosing procedure*. Thus jumps, superficially so simple, in fact introduce unwanted complexity into the semantics of a high-level language. Moreover, this complexity is *unwarranted*, since wise programmers in practice avoid using jumps in complicated ways. In the rest of this chapter, we study sequencers that are both higher-level than jumps and more useful in practice.

8.2 Escapes

An *escape* is a sequencer that terminates execution of a textually enclosing command. In flowchart terms, an escape is a direct transfer of control to the exit of an enclosing subchart. With escapes we can program single-entry *multiexit* control flows.

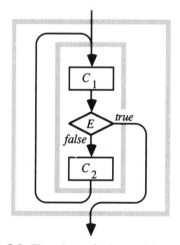

Figure 8.3 Flowchart of a loop with an escape.

In Ada, the *exit* sequencer terminates an enclosing loop. The simplest loop is '**loop** C **end loop;**', which causes the loop body C to be executed indefinitely. Termination can be achieved by including one or more *exit* sequencers within the loop body. In the following loop, there is a single (conditional) *exit* sequencer:

loop
    C_1

```
    exit when E;
    C₂
end loop;
```

The corresponding flowchart is shown in Figure 8.3. Note that the loop body (inner outline) has one entry and two exits. One of the exits follows execution of C_2 (after which the loop body is repeated); the other is a consequence of the escape (which terminates the loop). But note that the loop as a whole (outer outline) has a single exit.

The following example illustrates a more complicated use of the *exit* sequencer.

Example 8.3

The following Ada loop searches a diary, month by month and day by day, for the first entry that matches a given keyword:

```
diary    : array (Month, Day) of DiaryEntry;
keyword : String (1..10);
keydate : Date := default date;
...
search:
for amonth in Month loop
    for aday in Day loop
        if matches (diary(amonth,aday), keyword) then
            keydate := (m => amonth, d => aday);
            exit search;
        end if;
    end loop;
end loop;
```

By default, 'exit' terminates the smallest enclosing loop. Here we wish to terminate the outer loop, so we name the outer loop `search`, and write the escape as 'exit search'. (See also Exercise 8.4.)   □

Ada's *exit* sequencer can be used to terminate loops only. It would be more consistent to have an escape that terminates *any* command. Such an all-purpose escape might be similar in form to the *exit* sequencer of Example 8.3; the only difference would be to allow *any* command to be named like the loop in the example. (See Exercises 8.5 and 8.6.)

Another important kind of escape is the *return* sequencer. This is used in Ada to terminate execution of a procedure or function body. A procedure body is (in effect) a command, so in this case the *return* sequencer is just an ordinary escape. But a function body, although in the form of a command, has to determine the function's result; in this case the *return* sequencer includes an expression that is evaluated to yield the result.

Example 8.4

The following Ada function returns the greatest common divisor of two positive integers:

```
function gcd (i, j : Positive) return Positive is
    m : Positive := i;  n : Positive := j;
    r : Natural;
begin
   loop
      r := m mod n;
      if r = 0 then  return n;  end if;
      m := n;  n := r;
   end loop;
end;
```

The sequencer 'return n;' escapes from the function body, setting the function result to be the value of n.   □

Escapes are usually restricted so that they cannot transfer control out of procedures. For example, an Ada *return* sequencer must terminate the immediately enclosing procedure (or function) body. And although an Ada loop can contain a block that in turn contains a procedure definition, no *exit* sequencer inside the procedure body may terminate that loop. Without such restrictions, escapes would be capable of terminating procedure activations, causing complications similar to those of nonlocal jumps, discussed in Section 8.1.

The most drastic escape of all is *halt*, which terminates the whole program. Sometimes this escape is provided as an explicit sequencer (as in Fortran). Sometimes it is loosely disguised as a standard procedure (as in some dialects of Pascal and C). In either case, it usually has an argument (typically an integer or a string) that will be returned to the user of the program, and can be used to represent the reason for the halt.

8.3 Exceptions

What should happen when an arithmetic operation overflows, or an input–output operation cannot be completed? When such an *exceptional condition* arises, the program cannot continue normally. In many languages, the program simply halts with some sort of diagnostic message. Such a reaction is much too inflexible, however, making it difficult or impossible to make a program both modular and robust.

A program (or individual module) is said to be *robust* if it recovers from exceptional conditions, rather than just halting. When an exceptional condition arises, control is transferred to a *handler*, a part of the program that specifies recovery from the exceptional condition.

Typically, an exceptional condition is detected at some low level of the program or support software, but a handler is more naturally located at some higher level. For example, suppose that an application program attempts to read a nonexistent record from a file. This exceptional condition would be detected in the filestore software, but a handler should be located in the application program itself. Furthermore, the program might contain several calls to the filestore software, reading records for different purposes. Probably the most approriate recovery action will depend on the purpose for which the record was read. Thus we might need several handlers specifying different recoveries from the same kind of exceptional condition. For all these reasons, escapes and even jumps are unsuitable for transferring control to a handler from the point where the exceptional condition is detected.

A common technique for handling exceptional conditions is to equip each abstraction *P* with a *result code*. (This could be a global variable, a result parameter, or a function result.) When called, *P* sets its result code to indicate whether it was successful or, if not, which exceptional condition it detected. Afterwards *P*'s result code can be tested. One disadvantage of this technique is that the program tends to get cluttered by tests on result codes. An even more serious disadvantage is that the programmer might forgetfully or lazily omit to test a result code. In fact, the default handler is to ignore an exceptional condition!

Here we describe a better solution. An **exception** is an indication or signal that an exceptional condition has arisen. The operation that issues the signal is said to **raise** the exception. Exceptions cannot be ignored: if an exception is raised, the program will halt unless a corresponding handler has been provided. However, every exception *can* be handled, and the programmer has complete control over what the handler does. Each handler is associated with a particular exception, such as overflow or an input–output error.

PL/I was the first major language with a general form of exception handling. An *on* command associates a handler command with a given exception *e*. Thereafter, if any operation raises exception *e*, the associated handler command is executed and then the offending operation is resumed. The handler associated with a given exception may be updated at any time. Both properties – the highly dynamic nature of the exception-handler association, and the fact that the offending operation is resumed – make PL/I exceptions hard to understand, and we shall not consider them further here.

Exceptions have been incorporated more successfully in Ada. A handler for any exception *e* may be attached to any command *C*. If *C* (directly or indirectly) raises *e*, execution of *C* is abandoned and control is transferred to the handler.

Example 8.5
Given the following Ada declarations:

```
type Month is (jan, feb, mar, ..., nov, dec);
rainfall : array (Month) of Float;
```

we are required to read and process weather data for each month of the year.
    The following procedure reads the data:

```
procedure get_weather_data is
begin
    for amonth in Month loop
        begin
            get (rainfall(amonth));
        exception
```

```
        when data_error =>
            put ("Invalid data for "); put (amonth);
            skip_data_item; rainfall(amonth) := 0.0;
      end;
    end loop;
end;
```

This illustrates how we can recover from reading ill-formed data. The standard procedure get will raise the exception data_error if the input data item is not a well-formed real literal. We have attached a handler for data_error to the command 'get (...);'. (This handler writes a warning message, skips the offending data item, and substitutes zero for the missing number.) Thus if get raises data_error, the procedure call is abandoned, and the handler is executed instead. This completes execution of the '**begin** ... **end**' command inside the loop, and execution of the loop itself can then continue. Thus the remaining weather data will be read normally.

The following main program calls get_weather_data. It illustrates another exception handler, this time responding to incomplete input data:

```
procedure main is
begin
    get_weather_data;
    process_weather_data;
exception
    when end_error =>
        put ("Incomplete data");
end;
```

The standard procedure get will raise the exception end_error if all the input data have already been read. The body of get_weather_data does not handle this exception. Therefore, if end_error is raised, this exception will be propagated by the command that calls get, and by the command that calls get_weather_data, to the handler in the above block. As a consequence, process_weather_data will not be called. □

Although not illustrated by Example 8.5, we can attach different handlers for the same exception to different commands in the program. We can also attach handlers for several different exceptions to the same command.

Ada exceptions have the following important properties:

- If a command raises an exception but has no handler for that exception, the command *propagates* the exception. If a procedure or function body propagates an exception, the corresponding procedure or function call also propagates the exception.
- Any command that propagates an exception is *not* resumed.
- Certain exceptions are built-in, and are raised by built-in operations that cannot be performed. Examples are arithmetic overflow and out-of-range array indexing.
- Further exceptions can be declared by the programmer, and can be raised explicitly when the program itself detects an exceptional condition.

It is relatively easy to define the semantics of exceptions. In general, a command

C may either terminate normally or propagate an exception (or not terminate at all). In the sequential command '$C_1; C_2$', C_1 is executed first; if it terminates normally, then C_2 is executed next; but if C_1 propagates an exception e, then the sequential command itself propagates e and C_2 is not executed. In any other composite command, similarly, if a subcommand propagates an exception e, the composite command itself propagates e.

Only a command with a handler for e can stop propagation of e:

```
begin
   C
exception
   when e => C'
end;
```

Here, if *C* propagates the exception e, *C* is abandoned and *C'* is executed instead. Thereafter, execution of the program continues normally (unless *C'* itself raises an exception).

Although ML is a functional language, its exception mechanism is quite similar to Ada's. The main difference is that exceptions work at the expression level:

```
E
handle
   e => E'
```

If exception e is raised during the evaluation of expression *E*, that evaluation is abandoned and *E'* is evaluated instead.

8.4   Further reading

Böhm and Jacopini (1966) proved that every flowchart can be programmed entirely in terms of sequential, *if*, and *while* commands. Their theorem is only of theoretical interest, however, since the elimination of multientry and multiexit control flows requires us to introduce auxiliary truth-valued variables and/or to duplicate commands. This awkwardness justifies the existence of sequencers in programming languages.

The dangers of jumps were exposed in a famous letter by Dijkstra (1968b). An extended discussion of the use and abuse of jumps, in a language like Pascal, may be found in Knuth (1974).

A variety of loops with multiple exits have been proposed by Zahn (1974).

A discussion of exceptions may be found in Chapter 12 of Ichbiah (1979). This includes a demonstration that exception handling can be implemented efficiently – with negligible overheads on any program unless it actually raises an exception.

A careful description of the semantics of jumps in Pascal may be found in BSI (1982) or ANSI/IEEE (1983). Read this description, and note how difficult jumps are to describe precisely.

The term *sequencer* has been used by Tennent (1981). Tennent discusses the semantics of sequencers in terms of *continuations*, a very powerful semantic concept beyond the scope of this textbook. Tennent also proposes a sequencer abstraction – an application of the abstraction principle – but this proposal has not been taken up in any major language.

Exercises 8

8.1   (a) Rewrite the following program fragment entirely in terms of conditional and unconditional jumps. Explain why this makes the fragment harder to read.

```
p := 1;   m := n;   a := b;
while m > 0 do
    begin
    if odd (m) then
        p := p * a;
    m := m div 2;
    a := sqr (a)
    end
```

(b) Draw the flowchart corresponding to this program fragment. Outline the subcharts corresponding to the *while* command, the *if* command, and the bracketed sequential command. Note that these subcharts are properly nested.

8.2*   (a) Consider a language (such as Algol-60) in which program points may be passed as arguments to a procedure. Explain why use of this feature can make a program hard to understand. (b) Consider a language (such as PL/I) in which program points are first-class values, and thus can be assigned, etc. Explain why use of this feature can make a program even harder to understand. (c) Show that the effect of passing a program point as an argument can be achieved, indirectly, in Pascal.

8.3   A hypothetical form of loop, '**repeat** C_1 **while** E **do** C_2', was discussed in Section 3.5.7. Draw its flowchart. Compare it with the Ada loop whose flowchart is given as Figure 8.3.

We classify this hypothetical loop as a single-entry single-exit control flow, but the Ada loop as a single-entry multiexit control flow. What is the distinction? (*Hint:* the Ada loop can have any number of *exit* sequencers in its body.)

8.4   Rewrite the Ada code of Example 8.3 to avoid using any sequencer. You will need to replace the *for* loops by *while* loops, and to introduce auxiliary variables. Is your code more or less readable than the original code?

8.5   Suppose that Example 8.3 is to be modified to assign the default date to keydate *only* if the search fails. Where should the assignment be placed? Would your job be easier if Ada had an all-purpose escape allowing exit from *any* command?

8.6   The language C has a *continue* sequencer that terminates the current iteration of the enclosing loop, thus causing the next iteration (if any) to be started immediately. Show that this can be understood in terms of an all-purpose escape.

8.7   Rewrite the Ada program of Example 8.5 using result codes rather than exceptions. Each result code is to be an *out* parameter of type {*ok, end-error, data-error*, ... }. Compare and contrast the result-code and exception handling versions.

8.8   Provide the package of Example 6.10 and Exercise 6.10 with exceptions, which are to be raised on attempting to append an item to a full queue and on attempting to remove an item from an empty queue.

8.9   Provide your text-buffer package of Exercise 6.8 with an exception, which is to be raised on attempting to exceed the capacity of the buffer.

8.10   Provide your input–output package of Exercise 6.3 with exceptions, which are to be raised on attempting to read past end-of-file, on attempting to read ill-formed input data, etc.

CHAPTER NINE

Concurrency

9.1 Perspectives on concurrency

Historically, *concurrency* was introduced into computing systems with a view to improved performance. The earliest computers were serial machines that processed data one bit at a time. An order-of-magnitude increase in speed was achieved by hardware that processed data in words of several (typically, 32) bits at once.

Further improvements in performance were achieved by arranging for input–output and CPU operations to proceed in parallel. This immediately introduced concurrent programming. To exploit this new opportunity, elaborate buffering schemes were devised, with the aim of decoupling the progress of a computation as much as possible from the timing constraints imposed by the need to synchronize with input–output devices.

The resulting increase in complexity was too much to expect the application programmer to cope with, and it was precisely at this stage that operating systems were introduced, to assume much of that burden. Operating systems are thus the archetypal concurrent programs.

Multiprogramming systems attempt to utilize resources that would otherwise be wasted, by running two or more jobs concurrently. When a job is held up, waiting for the end of an input–output operation that cannot be fully overlapped by buffering, the system passes control of the CPU to a lower-priority job that is able to run. At the end of the awaited input–output operation, the low-priority job is preempted and the high-priority job is resumed. If the high-priority job is input–output limited and the low-priority job is CPU limited, they coexist symbiotically, allowing full use to be made both of the input–output device and of the CPU. Similarly, multiprogramming two jobs that use different sets of input–output devices can let otherwise idle equipment be more fully utilized.

Multiaccess systems extend this principle, allowing many jobs to be run, each on behalf of a user at an interactive terminal. Multiprogramming shares the CPU and input–output devices, but multiaccess systems must also provide main storage for a large number of jobs whose combined demand may exceed the physical capacity of the computer. Various techniques of swapping and paging meet this need, by allowing large-capacity backing store devices to be used as repositories for jobs that have been preempted. The sharing of main storage and input–output resources can be so effective, and the consequent expectations of users so buoyant, that the bottleneck becomes a shortage of CPU time. *Multiprocessor* systems deal with this by providing computers in which several CPUs operate simultaneously on separate jobs in a shared main store.

The recent development of fast local area networks has boosted interest in *distributed* computer systems, consisting of several complete computers that can operate independently but also intercommunicate efficiently. These have the potential for both higher (aggregate) performance and greater reliability than centralized systems based on the same hardware technology.

Contemporary with this, more sophisticated users are making demands that take concurrency out of the limited domain of operating system design and make it an issue for application programmers once again.

An application area in which concurrency has a long history is that of simulation. If we regard a well-written program as one with a structure that reflects the properties of a real-world system, it follows that a good simulation program should have internal concurrency that models the concurrency of the real-world system being simulated.

Another example of this is provided by iconic user interfaces, which represent components of a computer system graphically. Operations on these components are invoked by manipulating their graphical images with the help of a pointing device such as a mouse. The user may be simultaneously holding down modifier keys on a keyboard, moving the mouse and clicking its buttons, or dragging a cursor through different areas of the screen and so activating the objects portrayed there.

In a conventional sequential programming language it is both tedious and difficult to write applications driven by such an interface. The essentials of the application tend to be swamped by code that exists only to coordinate the various interdependent operations being invoked by the user. Languages such as the object-oriented Smalltalk, which deal more naturally with concurrency, are well suited to such applications.

Interest in concurrency is also being stimulated by new computer architectures, which aim to exploit concurrency in the quest for previously unattainable performance.

Array processors provide a large number of computational elements (typically 100 or more) that operate simultaneously on different parts of the same data structure. By this means extremely high performance is achieved on suitable tasks – essentially, those for which the data are naturally structured as rectangular, or other regular, arrays. Problems in linear algebra, which arise in science, engineering, and economics, are a rich source of applications for such systems.

Dataflow computers are a new, unconventional, approach aimed at extracting the maximum concurrency from a computation. They may be especially suitable for functional programming languages.

Connectionism, or *parallel distributed processing*, is another, radically different, approach based on the modeling of neural networks in living brains. Some think that this is the way to realize the dream of artificial intelligence.

The study of concurrent programming aims to provide a unified conceptual framework in which all of these developments may be set. Structured programming has shown how to write sequential programs whose complexity grows in proportion to their length. But sequential programs have important properties that make them (relatively) intellectually manageable: determinism, speed independence, freedom from deadlock, and freedom from starvation. These properties are not shared by concurrent programs, in general, so it is important to find ways to organize such programs so that they remain comprehensible. It must immediately be admitted that computer science is still far from achieving this goal.

9.2 Programs and processes

A *sequential process* is a totally ordered set of events, each event being a change of state in (some component of) a computing system. A *sequential program* is a text that specifies the possible state changes of a sequential process, whereas a *concurrent program* specifies the possible state changes of two or more sequential processes. No ordering need be defined between the state changes of any pair of processes. Thus they are said to execute *concurrently*, and they may even execute *simultaneously*.

The most obvious example of a sequential process is the execution of a program in a language like Pascal or Fortran. The events constituting such a process are the updating of variables of the program. These events are totally ordered by the sequencing rules of the language, which define how control is transferred from command to command.

Note that, because of the total ordering, we can associate the state changes of a sequential process with the passage of real (physical) time.

If we consider the execution of a machine code program on a simple computer, the same holds good, except that the sequencing rules are given by the definition of the computer architecture, and that not only storage but also registers (including the program counter) are components of the state.

At the most primitive level, state changes might not be totally ordered in time. For example, during an assignment, the bits of the source operand may be copied concurrently into the destination operand. However, it is not possible to examine the bits of the destination operand independently, to monitor the order in which they change. As far as the programmer is concerned, they all change at once. This departure from strict sequentiality is therefore irrelevant, because it is not observable.

For the sake of speed, some implementations of a computer architecture may allow even greater departures from strictly sequential execution of a program.

Pipelining allows several instructions to be executing at once, each at a different phase in its progress. For example, a processor may be capable of pipelining three instructions, one in the instruction-fetch phase, one in the instruction-decode phase, and one in the instruction-execute phase. If each phase takes one clock cycle, such a processor can complete one instruction in every clock cycle. This is three times faster than a simpler implementation that does no pipelining and would therefore take three clock cycles for each instruction. Provided that the pipelining has no observable side effects, the departure from sequentiality again is irrelevant to the programmer. Computer architects achieve this by designing interlocks into the hardware to ensure that pipelined execution has no effect on the outcome. For example, if two instructions are in the pipeline at the same time, and the second depends on a result computed by the first, the computer will hold up the pipeline to ensure that the result becomes available before any attempt is made to use it.

Similarly, a high-level language might allow some latitude as to the ordering of operations within a program. In a language where expressions have no side effects, for example, subexpressions may be evaluated in any order or even concurrently. We can preserve the notion of a sequential process by looking at a large enough unit of action, such as the evaluation of a complete expression, or the execution of a complete command.

9.3   Problems with concurrency

We now turn to a consideration of the ways in which concurrent programs differ from sequential programs.

9.3.1   Nondeterminism

Sequential programs are nearly always deterministic. A deterministic program (see Section 3.5.5) follows a sequence of steps that can be predicted in advance, if we know its inputs. Thus its behavior is reproducible, which is very important because it makes testing feasible.

There are some constructs that do introduce a degree of nondeterminism into sequential programs. Consider the collateral command 'C_1, C_2' (Section 3.5.5): one subcommand might update variables that are inspected by the other, so the collateral command's behavior depends on the order in which the subcommands are executed. Other examples are the nondeterministic conditional command (Section 3.5.6), and the collateral evaluation of subexpressions where one subexpression may have side effects on another (Section 3.6.1). In each of these cases, the language processor is free to decide the order of execution, and a given program might behave differently under different language processors. But, in practice, a particular language processor will fix the order of execution. Thus the program's behavior is still reproducible.

A concurrent program, on the other hand, is likely to be highly nondeterministic. The order of execution of processes is unpredictable, even under a particular language processor, since it may be influenced by run-time conditions. Usually we attempt to write programs that are effectively deterministic (Section 3.5.5), an effectively deterministic program being one whose net effect is predictable. However, an (incorrect) concurrent program might behave as predicted most of the time, but deviate from its predicted behavior intermittently and irreproducibly. Such problems are among the most difficult to diagnose in programming.

9.3.2   Speed dependence

A sequential program is ***speed-independent*** because its correctness does not depend on the rate at which it is executed. This is a property so basic that we tend to take it for granted. Among other benefits, it allows computer manufacturers to produce a range of architecturally compatible machines that differ in speed and cost. The same software runs correctly on all models in the range, thanks to speed independence.

A concurrent program may be ***speed-dependent***, in general, as its outcome may depend on the *relative* speeds of execution of its component sequential processes. Consequently, small random fluctuations in the speed of processors and input–output devices, and variations in scheduling priority, may lead to nondeterminism.

Where *absolute* speeds must be taken into account, for example in an embedded computer system that synchronizes with external equipment, we have a ***real-time*** program.

9.3.3   Deadlock

Deadlock is a situation in which a set of processes are prevented from making any further progress by their mutually incompatible demands for additional resources. Deadlock can occur in a system of processes and resources if, and only if, the following conditions all hold together:

- *Mutual exclusion:* processes are given exclusive access to the resources they require.
- *Wait and hold:* processes continue to hold previously allocated resources while waiting for a new resource demand to be satisfied.
- *No preemption:* resources cannot be removed from a process until it voluntarily relinquishes them.
- *Circular wait:* there may be a cycle of resources and processes in which each process is awaiting resources that are held by the next process in the cycle.

We can depict the progress of a pair of processes using a simple graph with two time axes, as in Figure 9.1. A step in the direction of the vertical axis indicates process 1 running for that interval, and the horizontal axis similarly corresponds to process 2. The locus thus traced is the *joint progress path* for the two processes.

In the case of processes sharing a single processor, a step in the execution of process 1 (2) is indicated by a line segment parallel to the vertical (horizontal) axis. In a multiprocessor both processes may be running simultaneously, resulting in a line whose slope is determined by the relative speeds of their two processors. (The joint progress path cannot move down, or to the left, as that would imply a reversal of execution, with state changes being undone!)

In Figure 9.1 we indicate resource requirements by labeling segments of each axis. Projecting these segments defines a number of regions of the progress space that are of particular interest. A deadlock becomes inevitable if the joint progress path enters the *unsafe* region, and deadlock actually takes hold when it reaches both boundaries of the *infeasible* region.

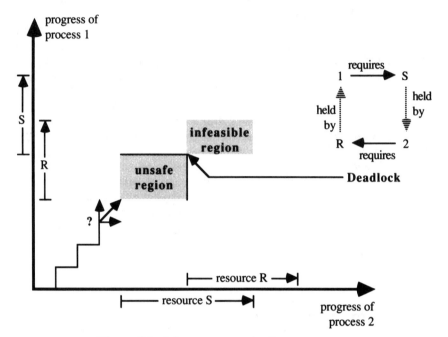

Figure 9.1 Joint progress path of two processes.

There are several approaches to the problem of deadlock.

Perhaps the most common approach, even now, is to *ignore* deadlock and hope that it will not happen often enough to have a serious effect on reliability. When deadlock does strike, the system's operators must deal with it as best they can (probably by restarting the whole system). This attitude is less and less defensible in an era of highly concurrent systems with strong reliability requirements.

A more principled approach is to allow deadlocks to take place, but to undertake to *detect* them and to *recover* from them automatically, so that the system as a whole keeps running. This involves aborting some of the processes involved, and should be done in such a way as to minimize the cost of the work lost. In real-time systems, especially, this might not be an acceptable (nor even possible) strategy, for the processes to be aborted might be critical. An alternative is to *roll back* the execution of some processes to a point before they entered the unsafe region. This is done by restoring the state of the processes as they were when recorded at an earlier *checkpoint*. Execution can then be resumed, but this time suspending the rolled-back process until the danger has passed. Again, this strategy may not be workable in a real-time system.

An alternative is to *prevent* deadlocks by removing one or more of the preconditions. Since some resources must be granted for exclusive use, and since forcible preemption of resources may be tantamount to aborting the process involved, just two possibilities remain:

(a) Eliminate the wait-and-hold condition by requiring that a process requests, at once, all the resources it will need.
(b) Eliminate the circular-wait condition by imposing a total ordering on resources and insisting that they be requested in that order.

Method (a) can lead to poor utilization of resources if processes are forced to acquire them prematurely. Method (b) may be better in this regard if the total ordering is well chosen, but it requires considerable programming discipline, and cannot be appropriate for good utilization in all cases.

Finally, the schedulers of the system can actively *avoid* deadlock by steering the joint progress path so that it never enters an unsafe region. The maximum resource requirement must be declared to the schedulers in advance (but need not be reserved at once). The *banker's algorithm* (to be discussed in Section 11.3) can determine whether a resource request can be safely granted, using CPU time proportional to p^2r for p processes and r resources.

9.3.4 Starvation

A concurrent system has the property of *finite progress* if it is guaranteed that every process will make nonzero progress over a sufficiently long (but finite) span of time. To meet this condition the system must be (a) free of deadlock, and (b) scheduled fairly. *Scheduling* is the allocation of resources to processes so as to further some objective, such as good response time or high CPU utilization. *Fair scheduling* ensures that no process needing a resource is indefinitely prevented from obtaining it by the demand from other processes.

An example of a fair scheduling rule is to make the processes that need a resource queue for it in first-come first-served order. This guarantees that, if the resource becomes available often enough, a process needing it will eventually make its way to the head of the queue and so gain access to the resource. An example of an unfair rule is one that gives preferential access to high-priority processes, for it might indefinitely delay a low-priority process should there always be a high-priority demand waiting to be serviced. The term **starvation** is used when a process is prevented indefinitely from running by unfair scheduling.

9.4 Process interactions

Section 3.5.4 introduced the notation '$C; K$' for the sequential composition of commands C and K, and Section 3.5.5 the notation 'C, K' for their collateral composition. The difference is that in sequential composition all of the actions of C must be completed before any of the actions of K are begun; whereas, in collateral composition, the actions of C and K may be interleaved arbitrarily.

However, neither notation admits the possibility that the commands C and K

may be executed *simultaneously*. In order to express this we use the **parallel command**, '*C* | | *K*', which is the concurrent composition of *C* and *K*. (The symbol ' | | ' is used to suggest parallelism.) Note carefully that '*C* | | *K*' does not *require* simultaneous execution of the steps of *C* and *K* , but does permit it; the notation also permits collateral execution and sequential execution, each a special case of concurrency.

Concurrent programs are distinguished from sequential programs by the presence of operations that cause interactions between processes. We now go on to consider the kinds of interaction that may take place between commands that are composed concurrently.

9.4.1   Independent processes

We say that commands *C* and *K* are **independent** if any component action C_i of *C* may be executed in any time relationship to any component action K_j of *K* , without effect on the meaning of the program. If *C* and *K* are independent, it follows that the sequential composition '*C* ; *K*', in which *all* of the C_i precede *all* of the K_j, is equivalent to the sequential composition '*K* ; *C*'. Equivalent, too, are '*C* , *K*' and '*C* | | *K*'. It follows that the concurrent composition of independent processes is deterministic.

This is an important result, because it provides the basis for multiprogramming systems, which may run independent jobs collaterally, and multiprocessing systems, which may run them simultaneously. Provided that the jobs *are* independent, the users and operators of such a system need take no special precautions arising from the concurrency.

Unfortunately it is undecidable, in general, whether commands *C* and *K* are independent. However, a sufficient condition is that neither command updates a variable that the other inspects or updates. This criterion has the advantage that it can be checked at compile-time (provided that there is no aliasing). However, we have to define *variable* in its widest sense: essentially, any component of the system whose state can be both inspected and changed. (See the discussion in Section 3.4.)

9.4.2   Competing processes

We say that commands *C* and *K* **compete** if each must gain exclusive access to the same resource *r* for some of their actions. Let *C* be the sequence 'C_1; C_2; C_3', and let *K* be the sequence 'K_1; K_2; K_3'. None of C_1, C_3, K_1, or K_3 uses *r*, and any of them may be a skip. We assume that C_1 and K_1 are independent, and that C_3 and K_3 are independent. However, C_2 and K_2 must not take place simultaneously nor overlap in time, for both require exclusive access to *r*. They are called **critical sections** with respect to the resource *r*. So '*C* | | *K*' may be executed in either of the following ways:

$$...; \ C_2; \ ...; \ K_2; \ ...$$

...; K_2; ...; C_2; ...

but *not* as:

...; C_2 || K_2; ...

Thus 'C || K' has two possible outcomes, which are exactly the outcomes of the sequences 'C; K' and 'K; C' respectively. Which of these outcomes actually happens will depend on the relative speeds at which C and K are executed, and so is not in general predictable.

If the effect of a critical section depends on the state of the resource when it is acquired, and if it changes the state of the resource, then the system 'C || K' is nondeterministic in general. To ensure determinism the processes must agree the order in which they will acquire r, and to achieve this they must communicate with each other.

9.4.3   Communicating processes

Let C and K be commands structured as before. We say there is *communication* from C to K if the action C_2 must entirely precede the action K_2. Then 'C || K' has the same outcome as 'C; K'.

C_2 must precede K_2 because it produces some information that K_2 consumes. It is useful to extend this to a chain of processes, each consuming the output of the preceding process and producing input for the next. In software, as well as in hardware, such a chain is commonly known as a *pipeline*.

Example 9.1
The Unix operating system's command language provides the notation 'C_1 | C_2'. This means that the commands C_1 and C_2 are executed concurrently, with the output from command C_1 becoming the input to C_2. The notation can easily be extended to a longer pipeline, 'C_1 | ... | C_n'. In this way commands that were written independently may be composed, contributing much to the power of the user interface.

The MS-DOS operating system's command language also provides this notation, but does not support concurrent execution. It therefore implements the command 'C_1 | C_2' as if the user had issued the sequence of two commands 'C_1>f; C_2<f', where C_1 writes its output (in its entirety) to a temporary file f, then C_2 runs and reads its input from that temporary file.   □

Processes C and K *intercommunicate* if there is communication in both directions. This makes the possible outcomes of 'C || K' very much more numerous. We are therefore forced to impose a severe discipline on the forms of intercommunication permitted, if we want to preserve the intellectual manageability of our programs.

This is very reminiscent of the restrictions that structured programming imposes on sequential control flow. There is an analogous proliferation of notations for concurrent structures that are thought to be beneficial by the designers of concurrent programming languages. Unfortunately, there is nothing in concurrent programming that corresponds to the theorem of Böhm and Jacopini (1966), which assures us that a small, fixed set of control structures is capable of expressing all possible sequential algorithms. The choice of concurrent control structures is therefore more controversial, and different choices are suitable for different applications.

9.5   Low-level concurrency primitives

In this section we consider operations at a low level of abstraction that affect concurrency, either by creating it, by destroying it, or by controlling it. These are important both to provide a basis for understanding higher-level constructs and because they show how the higher-level constructs may be implemented.

9.5.1   Process creation and control

The most primitive operations relevant to process creation are the following:

* *create* a new, dormant process
* *load* a program into it
* *start* its execution
* *suspend* its execution
* let a process *stop* itself at the end of its execution
* let its creator *wait* for it to stop, and
* *destroy* it

It is often convenient to combine *create*, *load*, and *start* into one operation, usually called *fork*. When this is done, *wait* and *destroy* may also be combined into a single operation, *join*.

Fork is often defined so that the new process gets as its program an exact copy of its parent's. There must be a means by which the parent process and its offspring can subsequently be made to follow different paths through this program. One method is to give an address as a parameter to *fork*, so that the parent continues at the instruction following the *fork*, whereas the offspring continues at the given address. An alternative method that is more convenient for use in a high-level language is employed in the Unix operating system. The Unix *fork* operation is a parameterless function that returns an integer. In the parent process this integer is the process identification of the newly created offspring, but in the offspring process it is zero.

Example 9.2
A common fragment of a Unix concurrent program (such as the *shell*, the command language interpreter) is the following:

```
child_id := fork;
if child_id = 0 then
```

child's program
else
continue parent's program

Unix has no *join* operation. A process is automatically destroyed at termination. A *wait* operation is provided that suspends a parent until any one of its offspring stops. It is a function that returns the offspring's process identification, also passing back the offspring's final status (e.g., 'terminated normally', 'failed due to time limit expiry', etc.) through an argument variable. The *join* operation can be programmed thus:

```
repeat
    id := wait (status)
until id = child_id
```

□

The low-level primitives are quite general, letting us create any desired system of concurrently active processes. In this they resemble *goto* sequencers, which allow us to set up any sequential control flow. They also have an analogous disadvantage, namely that a simple scan of the program text does not suffice to reveal that control flow, which develops dynamically.

Constructs that express process creation, but have the desirable single-entry single-exit property, have been proposed, notably by Edsger Dijkstra and Tony Hoare. Dijkstra's construct is of the form:

parbegin C_1; ...; C_n **parend**

which causes commands $C_1, ..., C_n$ to be executed concurrently, and waits for them all to terminate before proceeding. Hoare's notation is the construct '$B | | C$' that we have been using.

So much for process creation and termination. We also need operations to enable orderly competition and communication. First we will present these in rather an abstract manner; later we will describe various alternative realizations.

To make the critical sections of competing processes disjoint in time, primitive operations *acquire(r)* and *relinquish(r)* are used to gain and give up, respectively, exclusive access to a resource *r*. If *r* is already allocated, *acquire(r)* blocks the process that executes it, i.e., holds it up. When *relinquish(r)* is executed by the process to which *r* is allocated, *r* is made free to be reallocated, and processes waiting to gain control of *r* are rescheduled. One of them will be able to complete its *acquire(r)* operation and in turn get exclusive access to *r*.

A similar pair of operations provides for interprocess communication. The most basic communication possible transmits a single bit of information – the fact that some condition *c* (i.e., some circumstance of interest to the receiving process) now obtains. This is effected by a *transmit(c)* operation in the sender and a *receive(c)* operation in the receiver. The receiver is blocked until a corresponding transmission is made.

An important choice is how selective the transmission is. Some versions communicate with a specific receiving process. Others are 'broadcast' operations that make the transmission available to any interested receiver.

Another choice is what happens when no process is waiting to receive at the time of transmission. In some versions the transmission is lost. In others the transmission is stored until a receive operation is performed.

In practice we usually need to communicate more than one bit, but appropriate operations are definable on the basis of such primitives.

9.5.2   Interrupts

Exceptional conditions (such as overflow or division by zero) occur comparatively infrequently. But when one does occur, it is important to become aware of it and to act accordingly. By testing after every arithmetic operation, a program can guarantee that timely action will be taken. However this is at the expense of larger, slower programs and great inconvenience for the programmer.

A better mechanism is the *trap*. The hardware checks each operation and, if an exceptional condition arises, forces a jump to a routine that will deal with it. To let the program be resumed after making any necessary adjustments, a return address is noted. At the end of the trap routine it is possible to go back to the point where the problem was detected. The trap is thus, in effect, an unforeseen procedure call.

The end of a concurrent input–output operation is another condition to which the CPU should respond quickly. Again, it would not normally be efficient to test repeatedly for this, so, when autonomous input–output transfers were introduced, the end of each input–output operation was made to cause a trap. Such traps, because they originate from causes independent of the process running at the time, are called *interrupts*. If we view the activity of the input–output device as an external process, we can treat the interrupt as a mechanism for interprocess communication.

This is extended, in many operating systems, to a facility whereby one (internal) process can interrupt another, a well-known example being the Unix `signal` system call.

In most computer systems there is only one CPU, and multiple processes are supported by multiprogramming, in which control of the CPU is switched rapidly from one process to another. This happens whenever a blocked process, of higher priority than the process currently running, becomes unblocked and ready to run (in response to an end-of-transfer interrupt). A process can therefore give itself exclusive use of the CPU by ensuring that no interrupt will occur. This can be achieved in various ways, depending on the computer architecture, but it is usually possible either to ignore interrupt requests completely, or to defer acting upon them.

A process that has exclusive use of the CPU has, in effect, exclusive use of the whole system, including any shared variables. So switching off interrupts provides an implementation of *acquire*, and restoring them implements *relinquish*. Of course, this is a rather heavy-handed way of gaining exclusivity, and it has its disadvantages. If interrupts are inhibited too often or for too long, it may become impossible for a system to meet its real-time constraints. Many computer architectures classify interrupts into several priority levels, depending on the urgency of communication with the external device. This makes it possible to inhibit only those classes of interrupt that may lead to competition over a shared variable. Designing a system's data and control structures to use such an interrupt system effectively requires considerable experience and finesse.

9.5.3 Spin locks

On a multiprocessor, several processes may be executing simultaneously. Manipulating the interrupt system of such a machine does not readily provide a means of mutual exclusion, for preventing one CPU from responding to interrupts does nothing to exclude access to a shared variable by processes running on the other CPUs.

In these, and other, circumstances a different mechanism must be used – the **spin lock**. A spin lock is a 'busy-waiting loop', in which a process waits for access to a shared resource by repeatedly testing a flag that indicates whether the resource is free.

Spin lock algorithms depend upon the fair serialization of concurrent main storage fetch and store operations by the CPU–store interface. That is, they assume that accesses to the same storage location initiated concurrently are performed sequentially, and that no process is starved of storage cycles. Given these properties it is possible to program fair spin locks – algorithms that implement the *acquire(r)* and *relinquish(r)* operations without starving any competing process of access to *r*.

This is no small feat, as the history of the subject shows. It was first achieved by the mathematician Dekker, and presented by Dijkstra (1968a) with an illuminating preamble, in the form of a series of incorrect attempts that illustrate the subtleties faced by the programmer who deals in access to shared variables. Here we shall follow that development.

We assume that there are two processes, numbered 1 and 2, and that each is executing a program of the following form (*self* being either 1 or 2), with a cyclic pattern of accesses to *r* :

```
repeat
      noncritical code for process self;
      acquire(r);
      critical section for process self;
      relinquish(r)
until  process self is finished
```

The first idea is to use a variable `turn`, initialized to either 1 or 2, that indicates which of the two processes has permission to enter its critical section. Each process *self* implements the exclusion primitives as follows, where {*self, other*} = {1, 2}:

```
acquire:
      while turn = other do  (* skip *)

relinquish:
      turn := other
```

This certainly guarantees that only one of the processes can enter its critical section. However, it is too rigid, because they are forced to enter their critical sections alternately. Should either be held up in its noncritical code, the other will be locked out of its critical section after at most one more cycle.

A second attempt uses an array `claimed`, with one truth-valued component for each process, indicating whether that process has claimed the right to enter its critical section. Both components of `claimed` are initialized to `false`. Each process *self* implements the exclusion primitives as follows:

acquire:
```
while claimed[other] do (* skip *);
claimed[self] := true
```

relinquish:
```
claimed[self] := false
```

This fails if process 1 (say) is held up between finding `claimed[2]` to be `false` and setting `claimed[1]` to `true`. A 'window of opportunity' then opens for process 2 to enter its loop and discover `claimed[1]` to be still `false`. Both processes will now set their elements of `claimed` to `true` and may go on to enter their critical sections concurrently. Thus mutual exclusion is not guaranteed.

We might attempt to rectify this fault as follows:

acquire:
```
claimed[self] := true;
while claimed[other] do (* skip *)
```

But now a problem arises if process 1 (say) is held up after setting `claimed[1]` to `true`, but before entering the loop. This allows process 2 to do the same. Now both processes will discover that the other is claiming the shared resource. Consequently both must loop indefinitely and neither will enter its critical section.

To correct this fault we allow each process, while looping, to withdraw its claim temporarily. This gives the other process an opportunity to go ahead:

acquire:
```
claimed[self] := true;
while claimed[other] do
   begin
   claimed[self] := false;
   while claimed[other] do (* skip *);
   claimed[self] := true
   end
```

This idea works (albeit rather inefficiently) in most circumstances, but it has one fatal flaw. If both processes run at exactly the same speed, and perfectly in phase, both may step through the code abreast, in which case neither will ever discover that the other process has offered it a chance to proceed. Thus this attempt is speed-dependent.

Dekker's algorithm combines the best features of these four failed attempts. It uses both `turn` and `claimed`, initialized as before:

acquire:
```
    claimed[self] := true;
    while claimed[other] do
        if turn = other then
            begin
            claimed[self] := false;
            while turn = other do (* skip *);
            claimed[self] := true
            end
```

relinquish:
```
    turn := other;
    claimed[self] := false
```

Dekker's algorithm is rather complex, and is hard to generalize to more than two processes while preserving fairness. *Peterson's algorithm*, discovered as recently as 1981, is free of these defects:

acquire:
```
    claimed[self] := true;
    turn := other;
    while claimed[other] and (turn = other) do
        (* skip *)
```

relinquish:
```
    claimed[self] := false
```

It is both simple and fair, with a maximum delay proportional to n^2 entries to the critical section, in the generalization to n processes. That it took almost 20 years to discover so simple an algorithm is eloquent of the difficulty humans find in thinking about concurrent systems.

Spin locks are clearly very wasteful of CPU time and store cycles. Unless the waiting time is expected to be very short, it would be advantageous to block the waiting process each time around the loop, until there is a better chance of its being able to continue. However, this is not always possible. Consider, for example, access to the CPU scheduler's data structures, which also must be modified under mutual exclusion. The spin locks used to achieve this cannot themselves contain calls on scheduler operations (such as *block*). These spin locks may be bottlenecks significantly limiting the performance of highly concurrent systems.

9.5.4   Events

An *event* represents a class of state changes, the occurrence of which must be communicated among a set of processes. This is effected by the operations *event-wait(e)* and *event-signal(e)*. When a process executes *event-wait(e)*, it is blocked, awaiting the next occurrence of an event in the class identified by *e*. The operation *event-signal(e)* makes all processes that are waiting for *e* ready to run again.

Example 9.3
Events can be used to program a blocking version of the spin lock *acquire(r)*
operation. With each resource *r* we associate an event *r-freed* that is signaled period-
ically. Then (using Peterson's algorithm) we have:

    acquire:

```
claimed[self] := true;
turn := other;
while claimed[other] and (turn = other) do
      event-wait (r-freed)
```

                                              □

Considered as communication primitives, events have the following important
drawbacks:

- The wait and signal operations are not commutative, for the time sequence *event-
signal(e)* in process 1, followed by *event-wait(e)* in process 2, leaves process 2
waiting for a signal that has come and gone.
- The *event-signal(e)* operation awakens *all* processes blocked on event *e*, so that
transmit is interpreted as 'broadcast'. One-to-one transmission requires the use of
auxiliary data to identify the intended recipient. All other awakened processes must
test this data, note that the signal is not for them, and repeat the wait operation.
Selective waiting is therefore subject to considerable overhead.
- Events are not useful for mutual exclusion, so separate provision must be made for
that (e.g., spin locks or interrupt management).

Despite their several disadvantages, it is noteworthy that the combination of
interrupt management and events is the basis for synchronization in the very successful
Unix family of operating systems.

9.5.5   Semaphores

Formally, a ***semaphore*** is a variable of an abstract type that may be accessed only by
three primitive operations: *sema-initialize(s, n)*, *sema-wait(s)*, and *sema-
signal(s)*.

    These operations are defined in terms of their effects on three integer values
associated with *s*: *waits(s)* is the number of completed *sema-wait(s)* operations;
signals(s) is the number of completed *sema-signal(s)* operations; and *initial(s)* is
the value given by *n* in the single allowed *sema-initialize(s, n)* operation. Any
sequence of wait and signal operations on *s* must leave invariant the relation:

$$0 \leq waits(s) \leq signals(s) + initial(s) \qquad (9.1)$$

To achieve this, a process will be blocked within an incomplete wait operation until it
can complete without violating (9.1). That is to say, if a process executes *sema-
wait(s)* when *waits(s)* = *signals(s)* + *initial(s)*, then it will be blocked. It will
not resume until some other process completes an invocation of *sema-signal(s)*, thus

increasing the value of *signals(s)*.

If several processes are waiting on the same semaphore, it is not defined which of them will be resumed by a given signal. This provides a degree of freedom that the designer can exploit to include the appropriate scheduling criteria for the application. We only require that these criteria be fair. (This is the *strong semaphore*. Some researchers use a *weak semaphore* that does not stipulate fairness.)

By contrast with events, semaphore operations are commutative because unawaited signals are remembered (by virtue of the invariant). Consequently semaphore-based program are less susceptible to speed dependence induced by programming errors.

Again unlike events, the semaphore signal operation awakens only one process – *transmit* here is more like 'send a telegram' than 'broadcast'. This allows highly selective and efficient communication. (Admittedly, it is less easy to broadcast, if that is what is required.)

A further advantage over events is that semaphores can be used both for mutual exclusion and for communication.

To program mutual exclusion we associate with each shared resource *r* a semaphore *r-mutex*. Each process using *r* brackets its critical sections with *sema-wait(r-mutex)* and *sema-signal(r-mutex)* operations, doing duty for *acquire(r)* and *relinquish(r)* respectively.

Simple communication is effected in the same manner. For each condition *c* to be transmitted, allocate a semaphore *c-sem*. The *transmit* and *receive* operations become *sema-signal(c-sem)* and *sema-wait(c-sem)*, respectively. This reveals a deep connection between mutual exclusion and communication that was not apparent with events because their primitives do not commute.

Example 9.4
Large quantities of data can readily be communicated using an auxiliary buffer variable. Declare the semaphores *nonempty* and *nonfull*.

> *parent process:*
>> *sema-initialize(nonempty, 0);*
>> *sema-initialize(nonfull, 1)*
>
> *sender:*
>> *sema-wait(nonfull);*
>> *place data in buffer;*
>> *sema-signal(nonempty)*
>
> *receiver:*
>> *sema-wait(nonempty);*
>> *take data from buffer;*
>> *sema-signal(nonfull)*

□

Semaphores have a serious disadvantage, which is shared equally by events, and indeed by all of the low-level primitives. This disadvantage is that the connection between any given resource or condition and the associated semaphore operations is entirely a matter of convention. The convention is respected when the programmer remembers to invoke these operations at appropriate points in the program, but this cannot be enforced by compile-time checks. It is easy to forget a wait or signal operation, with disastrous results.

The problem is that these primitives are at too low a level of abstraction, and so allow a badly structured program to be written as readily as a well structured one. (Semaphores were introduced by Dijkstra (1968c) with the aim of improving on interrupt management as a means of synchronization in an operating system. Their invention predated the attack on *goto* sequencers in Dijkstra (1968b), which was the genesis of structured programming.)

Semaphores are perhaps most appropriately treated as machine-level operations, and some computer architectures include semaphore instructions. They show that semaphore signaling is competitive with interrupts even for communication with input–output devices. Semaphores implemented in software (e.g., using spin locks) incur a greater cost, perhaps one or two orders of magnitude more.

9.5.6   Messages

When processes run on a network of computers (not sharing main storage), spin locks, events, and semaphores cease to be appropriate. Instead, the network provides a data communication service that supports process interaction by the exchange of *messages*. It is possible to use message passing as the basis for shared-store systems as well, because of the ease of reimplementation as a distributed system. Indeed the first known message-based operating system was for a single-CPU shared-store environment, described in Brinch Hansen (1973). However, message passing does attract greater overheads than (say) the use of semaphores, and this can be crucial in real-time systems.

A message passing operation implies a link between processes that can carry the message. Such a link may either be explicitly identified, or implied by the identities of the sender and receiver processes. An explicitly identified link may be known as a *message queue*, a *mailbox*, or the like; such a link may allow communication between an arbitrary number of senders and receivers. An implicitly identified link can support only one-to-one communication and the sender must know the process identification of the receiver, although the process identification of the sender need not be passed to the receiver. There is also a question of whether the link supports communication in one direction only (*simplex*), in both directions alternately (*half duplex*), or in both directions concurrently (*full duplex*).

Like any variable, the lifetime of a link may be bounded by the activation of the communication procedure (local), by the lifetime of the communicating processes (global), or by operations outside these processes (persistent), the latter being most common with the mailbox variety.

The most characteristic primitive operations on a link include:

- *connect* a process to a link
- *disconnect* a process from a link

- *send* a message on a link
- *receive* a message from a link, or wait for its arrival
- *test* for a message from a link

A message may consist of (a copy of) data belonging to the sender, or of a reference to shared data, the former being more common in distributed systems and the latter in shared-storage systems. Messages may be fixed or variable in length, and links may have a fixed capacity or be able to expand and contract to meet demand. When a sender has dispatched a message, it may be blocked pending a reply, so that communication proceeds synchronously. Alternatively, a sender may be free to continue after a send operation, so that communication is asynchronous.

The designer of a message-based system thus has a great number of alternatives to explore, and such systems have indeed been very diverse.

9.5.7   Remote procedure calls

A disadvantage of basing a design on message passing is that the division of the system into processes is strongly reflected in the program text. Operations within the same process are invoked by procedure calls and those in other processes by message passing. This poses a maintenance problem when the distribution of functions among processes is changed.

It is possible to avoid this, and retain the advantages of procedural notation, by exploiting the **remote procedure call**. The run-time environment determines where a procedure is provided, and communicates synchronously with that site to call it.

The site that provides the procedure may, on receiving a remote call, create a process to implement the operation. Alternatively, a *server* process at the remote site may receive all calls for a procedure and provide that service in turn. The choice is determined by the relative cost of process creation as against communication, and by the degree of concurrency desired. Both of these are pragmatic issues rather than questions of principle.

9.6   Structured concurrent programming

Although often defined in terms of single-entry single-exit control flows, structured programming is more usefully viewed as the effort to make each program express clearly what it means. That is, the concern is to make obvious in its text the essential structures that underlie a program. These include data flow relationships and algebraic relationships among types, as well as control flow relationships. We go on from there to observe a heuristic principle (not an invariable law) that *simple* relationships are both technically sufficient and psychologically preferable.

Language designers have largely succeeded in creating sound and workable structures for sequential imperative programming, and many have now turned their attention to the problems raised by concurrency and distribution. There is a proliferation of ideas in this domain that is reminiscent of the ferment of activity in the early 1970s, before the present consensus on sequential imperative programming emerged. This section presents only a few of the highlights from the work done in structured concurrent programming.

9.6.1 Conditional critical regions

Independently, both Tony Hoare and Per Brinch Hansen suggested the *conditional critical region* as a well-structured notation encompassing both mutual exclusion and communication.

The crux of the proposal is that every variable shared between processes must be declared as such. Any variable not so declared is local to one particular process, and the compiler can easily check that no such variable is accessed by another process.

The *region command* is a special composite command that delimits a critical section (region) with respect to a shared variable. Typically it is of the form '**region** *V* **do** *C* ', where *V* identifies the shared variable. A shared variable may be accessed only within a *region* command. Again, this can easily be checked by the compiler. At most one process is allowed to be executing within a particular *region* command, so that mutual exclusion is automatic. This is easily implemented using a semaphore.

The *await command*, allowed only within a *region* command, blocks a process until a given truth-valued expression involving the shared variable takes the value *true*. While waiting, a process relinquishes its possession of the shared variable. When it resumes, its possession of the shared variable is reacquired.

Example 9.5
The following pseudo-Pascal code implements a bounded queue of messages:

```
type MessageBuffer =
        shared record
            size, front, rear : 0..capacity;
            items : array [1..capacity] of Message
        end;

procedure sendmessage
              (newitem : Message;
               var buffer : MessageBuffer);
    begin
    region buffer do
      begin
      await buffer.size < capacity;
      buffer.size := buffer.size + 1;
      buffer.rear := buffer.rear mod capacity + 1;
      buffer.items[buffer.rear] := newitem
      end
    end;
```

```
procedure receivemessage
              (var olditem : Message;
               var buffer : MessageBuffer);
    begin
    region buffer do
      begin
      await buffer.size > 0;
      buffer.size := buffer.size - 1;
      olditem := buffer.items[buffer.front];
      buffer.front := buffer.front mod capacity + 1
      end
    end
```

□

As Example 9.5 shows, the conditional critical region highlights the points of interaction between processes, with minimal conceptual clutter:

- Both mutual exclusion and communication are provided in full generality, with no need for auxiliary flags or variables.
- Mutual exclusion is guaranteed at compile-time.
- Transmission of conditions is automatic and implicit. A process that establishes a condition need not even be aware that the condition is of interest to any other process.
- Reception is simple, explicit, and commutes with transmission.

These properties greatly improve the modularity of programs written in terms of conditional critical regions. However, they are achieved at the cost of busy-waiting: the command 'await *E* ' must be implemented in terms of a loop that repeatedly evaluates *E*.

9.6.2 Monitors

Given the attractions of conditional critical regions, it is perhaps surprising that they have not figured in a major programming language. The main reason was that Hoare and Brinch Hansen (again!), inspired by a suggestion of Dijkstra, soon proposed yet another notation that has become a standard feature in concurrent programming languages.

The argument is simple: for greatest modularity, processes should be coupled as loosely as possible to any variables they share. This implies that all operations on such variables should be segregated into suitable procedures. Why not take the further step of encapsulating each shared variable in a module, treating it as an object? (See Section 6.3.) And, having done that, why not arrange for automatic mutual exclusion on calling an operation exported by the module? The *monitor* is such a module, combining encapsulation with mutual exclusion and synchronization. Concurrent Pascal, described in Brinch Hansen (1977), and Modula, described in Wirth (1977), are two influential Pascal-like languages that adopt monitors as their way of structuring concurrency.

Example 9.6

The following monitor, written in Modula, implements a bounded queue of messages:

```
INTERFACE MODULE queue_monitor;
DEFINE   sendmessage,
         receivemessage;    (* exported operations *)
...

TYPE MessageBuffer =
         RECORD
             size, front, rear : 0..capacity;
             items : ARRAY 1..capacity OF Message
         END;
VAR  buffer : MessageBuffer;
     nonfull, nonempty : signal;

PROCEDURE sendmessage (newitem : Message);
   BEGIN
   IF buffer.size = capacity THEN wait (nonfull);
   buffer.size := buffer.size + 1;
   buffer.rear := buffer.rear MOD capacity + 1;
   buffer.items[buffer.rear] := newitem;
   send (nonempty)
   END;

PROCEDURE receivemessage (VAR olditem : Message);
   BEGIN
   IF buffer.size = 0 THEN wait (nonempty);
   buffer.size := buffer.size - 1;
   olditem := buffer.items[buffer.front];
   buffer.front := buffer.front MOD capacity + 1;
   send (nonfull)
   END;

BEGIN  (* initialization of buffer *)
buffer.size := 0;
buffer.front := 1;
buffer.rear := 0
END queue_monitor
```

□

Each `signal` variable declared in Example 9.6 is in fact a queue of processes waiting for permission to proceed within the monitor. The `wait` operation blocks a process and places it at the end of the nominated queue. While waiting on a signal queue, a process gives up its exclusive use of the monitor. The `send` operation unblocks the process at the head of the nominated queue. When it resumes, it regains its exclusive use of the monitor.

Like semaphores or events, signals are associated with (truth-valued) conditions only by convention, enforced by conditional commands of the monitor. This allows a more efficient implementation of interprocess communication than is possible with the *await* command, but at the cost of more work for the programmer (and more opportunity for error). Compare the clarity of the logic in Examples 9.5 and 9.6.

9.6.3 Rendezvous

The difficulties associated with shared variables in distributed systems (and, in some sense, *all* systems are distributed) led many researchers to concentrate on well-structured communication. Hoare (1978) proposed the notation that has come to be called *communicating sequential processes (CSP)*.

The essential feature of CSP is that processes interact only by means of unbuffered (synchronous) communication, or **rendezvous**. In order to rendezvous, each of the two processes involved executes a command that indicates its willingness to communicate with the other. This is a kind of input command in the receiver, and a kind of output command in the sender. Either process blocks if the other process has not yet reached its rendezvous point. When both processes have reached their rendezvous points, data are copied from the sender to the receiver; thereafter both are set free to continue independently. As Hoare himself stressed, CSP was more of a thought experiment than a practical tool, but it has inspired many subsequent developments, including the programming languages occam and Ada.

The occam language has been used as a design tool in the development of the Transputer parallel processing element, and also as the Transputer's system programming language.

Ada was the first major programming language to incorporate structured concurrent programming. A *task* module is in some ways similar to a package. The body of a task module may be executed as a concurrent process. Global variables are accessible by a task body, as a normal consequence of Ada's scope rules, so tasks may interact by their effect on shared variables. However, Ada provides no support for such interactions: it lacks a built-in mutual exclusion construct, and the programmer is responsible for ensuring that sharing of variables has no harmful effects.

Instead, the preferred mode of communication between tasks is the rendezvous, which is encouraged by a rich set of language features. A task may export some *entries*, which resemble remote procedures. (In fact, entries are the *only* operations that may be exported by a task.) The sender task communicates by means of an *entry call*, which is syntactically similar to a procedure call, and which passes arguments to the nominated entry. The receiver task communicates by means of an *accept* command, a composite command that has access to the arguments from the entry call. The sender is blocked until the entry call is served, and waits in a first-come first-served queue. The receiver is blocked at an *accept* command for an entry with no outstanding calls. Additional language features allow for bounded nondeterminism in accepting calls, and offer the option not to wait if no rendezvous can be achieved.

Since reception takes place at the behest of the receiver, it is possible to ensure that communication always follows a strict protocol: an entry call has no effect on the receiver until the latter chooses to respond to it. This is an advantage of rendezvous over message passing and remote procedure calls, where callers must arrange to communicate in the correct sequence.

Example 9.7
The following Ada task module implements a buffer abstract type, with a buffer having capacity for a single message:

```
task type MessageBuffer is
   entry store (newitem : in Message);
   entry fetch (olditem : out Message);
end MessageBuffer;
...
task body MessageBuffer is
   storeditem : Message;
begin
   loop
      accept store (newitem : in Message) do
         storeditem := newitem;
      end;
      accept fetch (olditem : out Message) do
         olditem := storeditem;
      end;
   end loop;
end MessageBuffer;
```

Note how the control structure of the task ensures that messages are alternately stored and fetched, and that no attempt can be made to fetch from an empty buffer.

The following variable declaration:

```
urgent, pending : MessageBuffer;
```

creates two tasks of type `MessageBuffer`. Each of these tasks runs concurrently with the process that elaborated the declaration. They can now be called independently to store and fetch messages:

```
msg : Message;
...
pending.store (msg);
...;
pending.fetch (msg);   urgent.store (msg);
```

where, for example, 'pending.store (msg);' is a call to the entry store in the task pending, passing the value of msg as an argument.

Tasks can also be created dynamically. Every evaluation of the allocator '**new** MessageBuffer' would create a new task of type MessageBuffer. Thus the number of concurrently active processes in an Ada program need not be determined in advance.

□

Nondeterministic choice is provided by the *selective wait* command, which allows a task to respond to the first of a selection of entry calls (or to any one of them if several are outstanding). Acceptance can be made conditional in each case. This makes it easy to write monitor-like tasks, with no need for a mutual exclusion mechanism.

Example 9.8

The following Ada task module implements a semaphore abstract type:

```
task type Semaphore is
    entry initialize (n : in Integer);
    entry wait;
    entry signal;
end Semaphore;
...
task body Semaphore is
    count : Integer;
begin
    accept initialize (n : in Integer) do
        count := n;
    end;
    loop
        select
            when count > 0 =>
                accept wait do
                    count := count - 1;
                end;
        or
                accept signal;
                count := count + 1;
        end select;
    end loop;
end Semaphore;
```

This algorithm will accept calls to both `wait` and `signal`, provided that as the semaphore invariant (9.1) would not be violated. When (9.1) would otherwise be violated, calls to `wait` are ignored for the time being. This task could be used as follows:

```
nrfull, nrfree : Semaphore;
...
nrfull.initialize (0);
nrfree.initialize (nrslots);
...
nrfree.wait;
nrfull.signal;
```

□

9.7 Further reading

There is a wide-ranging anthology of original papers on concurrent programming in Gehani and McGettrick (1988). Distributed systems are treated in depth by Coulouris and Dollimore (1988). The theory of communicating processes is advanced in Hoare (1985).

Exercises 9

9.1   List some components of a computer system, and give examples of the different states that each component may adopt.

9.2   List some important examples of concurrency: (a) in computer systems; and (b) in the 'real world'.

9.3   The PDP-11 architecture has a `wait` instruction that halts the CPU until the next interrupt is requested. How could such an instruction be used in conjunction with spin locks? What effect would it have on performance? What changes in the *relinquish* operation would be necessary to use `wait` in this way on a multiprocessor?

9.4   Suggest two alternative implementations of the event abstract type.

9.5   Use semaphores to implement a buffer with capacity for *n* data items.

9.6*   The hypothetical primitive '**start** *C*' (not part of Ada) causes the command *C* to be executed in a new process, concurrent with the one that executes the *start* primitive. The new process shares all presently existing variables with its parent, but subsequently created variables are not shared.

Using the *start* primitive, modify the following sequential procedure so that as many components as possible of sum are computed concurrently.

```
type Matrix is array (1..n, 1..n) of Float;

procedure add (a, b : in Matrix;
                    sum : out Matrix) is
begin
  for i in 1 .. n loop
    for j in 1 .. n loop
        sum(i,j) := a(i,j) + b(i,j);
    end loop;
  end loop;
end;
```

How many processes can be active concurrently in your version?

Assume that starting a process takes time T, and that executing the assignment command takes time t. In what circumstances would the concurrent version be faster than the sequential version?

9.7*   Using the *start* primitive of Exercise 9.6, modify the following procedure so that as many as possible of the nodes of the tree `atree` are visited concurrently.

```
type TreeNode;
type Tree    is access TreeNode;
type TreeNode is record
                     datum : ...;
                     left, right : Tree;
                 end record;

procedure traverse (atree : Tree; ...)' is
begin
   if atree.left /= null then
      traverse (atree.left, ... );
   end if;
   if atree.right /= null then
      traverse (atree.right, ... );
   end if;
   ...;   -- process atree.datum here
end;
```

If the tree has n nodes, how many processes can be active concurrently in your version? What kinds of processing operations could be performed in the sequential version that could not be performed in the concurrent version?

9.8   (a) Why must processes that share variables (normally) arrange for time-wise disjoint access to them?

(b) Give a simple example of what can go wrong without mutual exclusion.

(c) Give an example of concurrent operation on a shared variable that does **not** require the software to arrange mutual exclusion.

(d) Define the semaphore operations *wait* and *signal*, and state the semaphore invariant.

(e) A *binary* semaphore is limited so that *wait* and *signal* operations must be applied to it strictly in alternation. This allows it to be implemented as a single bit. Show how a general semaphore G can be implemented using binary semaphores.

9.9   Hoare has proposed a simpler form of the *region* command than Hansen, in which the *await* clause is restricted to the start of the region, with no preceding commands. Give a simple example to show that this is not equivalent to the more general form due to Hansen. Is the difference of any importance?

CHAPTER TEN

The Imperative Programming Paradigm

In the rest of the book we shall view programming languages from a different perspective. So far we have studied individual concepts. Now we examine how these concepts are selected and put together to design complete programming languages.

It is as important for the language designer to decide which concepts to omit as to decide which ones to include. Often the language designer is forced to compromise, because a particular combination of concepts would make the language hard to use, to understand, or to implement.

The language designer has in mind a particular style of programming for which the language is intended to be suitable. A seemingly minor design decision like including or omitting a particular data type can have a significant influence on the way the language is used. A major design decision such as omitting the concept of storage altogether, or basing the whole language on the concept of encapsulation, must imply a really distinctive style – or *paradigm* – of programming.

In the 1980s a variety of programming paradigms became very popular, including object-oriented programming, functional programming, and logic programming. Each of the remaining chapters of this book explains one of the major paradigms, examining it through the medium of one or two representative languages.

In this chapter we look at *imperative programming*, which is the oldest but still the dominant paradigm. First we identify the key characteristics of imperative programming. Then we discuss the design of two important imperative languages, Pascal and Ada.

10.1 Imperative programming

Imperative programming is so called because it is based on commands that update variables held in storage. (The Latin word *imperare* means 'to command'.) This paradigm has a relatively long history, because language designers as early as the 1950s recognized that variables and assignment commands constitute a simple but useful abstraction from the memory fetch and update of machine instruction sets. Because of their close relationship with machine architectures, imperative programming languages can be implemented very efficiently, at least in principle.

The imperative paradigm is still dominant today. The overwhelming majority of commercial software currently in use or under development is written in imperative languages. The great majority of professional programmers are skilled mainly or exclusively in imperative programming. (Furthermore, the concurrent and object-oriented programming paradigms discussed in Chapters 11 and 12 are really subparadigms of imperative programming, so their practitioners are also imperative programmers.)

It might be argued that the continuing dominance of the imperative paradigm is due entirely to inertia. After all, the dominant individual languages are Basic, Cobol, and Fortran, not the later and much better-designed Pascal and Ada, so inertia is certainly a factor!

However, there is a more fundamental reason for the importance of the imperative paradigm, and that is related to the very nature and purpose of programming. Programs are written to model real-world processes affecting real-world objects, and such objects often possess a state that varies with time. Variables naturally model such objects, and imperative programs naturally model such processes.

Example 10.1
Consider an automatic pilot program. The aircraft has a state, consisting of its position, speed, attitude, payload, fuel load, etc. In order to perform its function, the automatic pilot program must model the aircraft's state. Since the state changes with time, it is most naturally modeled by a group of updatable variables. □

Variables are also used in imperative programming to hold intermediate results of computations. However, such use of variables is not a *key* characteristic of imperative programming.

Example 10.2
Compare the following alternative versions of the power function in Pascal:

```
(a) function power (b : Real; n : Integer) : Real;
       var p : Real; i : Integer;
       begin
       p := 1.0;
       for i := 1 to abs (n) do
          p := p * b;
       if n >= 0 then
          power := p
       else
          power := 1.0 / p
       end

(b) function power (b : Real; n : Integer) : Real;
       begin
       if n = 0 then
          power := 1.0
```

```
else if n > 0 then
   power := b * power (b, n-1)
else
   power := 1.0 / power (b, -n)
end
```

Version (a) works by iteration; it uses local variables to accumulate the product and to control the iteration. Version (b) works by recursion, and needs no local variables at all.   □

   This example illustrates the fact that powerful concepts, in this case recursion, can often be exploited to reduce the need for variables to hold intermediate results. But variables remain the most natural way to model real-world objects that possess state.

   Neither Pascal nor Ada is sufficiently rich to eliminate all use of variables to hold intermediate results. However, an imperative language with a sufficiently rich variety of expressions could, in principle, be designed. Then commands could be used more sparingly, to model changes of state only.

10.2   Case study: Pascal

Pascal was designed around 1970 by Niklaus Wirth, who intended it to be a language suitable for teaching the fundamentals of programming. As an educational language Pascal has proved marvelously successful. Moreover, as legions of students trained in it have become professional programmers, Pascal has been widely adapted for systems and applications programming too.

   The reasons for Pascal's success are clear, at least in retrospect. Its simplicity and compactness allow it to be learned by novices in a few months, and by experienced programmers in a week. Its judicious selection of program and control structures provides effective support for structured programming. Its rich variety of data types allows data to be described accurately. Finally, Pascal was carefully designed to be simple and efficient to implement, and free availability of a model implementation (the Zürich portable compiler) allowed use of the language to spread rapidly.

   It is also clear, in retrospect, that Pascal could have been designed better. Nevertheless, its failings are just as instructive as its successes!

10.2.1   Values and types

Pascal's type system was discussed in Chapter 2. The combination of record, variant record, array, and pointer types allows a variety of data structures to be defined, created, and manipulated.

   Pascal is statically typed, and compile-time type checks eliminate a large class of programming errors. A further class of errors, such as attempting to index an array with an out-of-range value, or attempting to follow the *nil* pointer, can be trapped by run-time checks.

Example 10.3
Consider the following declarations:

```
type Letter  = 'A'..'Z';
var   profile : array [Letter] of
                        record
                              frequency : 0..maxint;
                              followers : set of Letter
                        end
```

This array variable might be processed as follows:

```
var letter1, letter2 : LETTER;
...
for letter1 := 'A' to 'Z' do
   begin
   write (profile[letter1].frequency);
   for letter2 := 'A' to 'Z' do
      if letter2 in profile[letter1].followers then
         write (letter2)
   end
```

Notice that a compiler can deduce that the value of letter1 will always be in the range 'A' through 'Z', so the array access profile[letter1] needs no run-time range check.   □

Example 10.3 illustrates some characteristic features of Pascal's type system: (a) we can define a subrange of an existing discrete primitive type; (b) we can choose any discrete primitive type for the index of an array; (c) we can freely choose the type of the components of an array; (d) we can use sets (provided that the elements are of a discrete primitive type).

It also illustrates that a *for* command may be used to iterate over the indices of any array, or over the range of potential elements of any set, since like them the control variable may be of any discrete primitive type.

Example 10.4
It is desired to declare a telephone directory that can be searched efficiently either by name or by number. Here the directory is represented by a pair of binary trees, one ordered by name, and the other ordered by number:

```
type Customer    = record
                        customername    : Name;
                        customeraddress : Address;
                        customernumber  : Number
                   end;
```

```
            NameTree    = ^ NameNode;
            NameNode    = record
                              keyname      : Name;
                              details      : ^ Customer;
                              left, right  : NameTree
                          end;
            NumberTree  = ^ NumberNode;
            NumberNode  = ...;   (* analogous to NameNode *)
    var     directory   : record
                              byname    : NameTree;
                              bynumber  : NumberTree;
                          end
```

This is a fairly complicated data structure, but the above type definitions make the structure reasonably clear. Several distinct pointer types are used here, and it would be easy to confuse them in pointer operations. Suppose that n is of type `NameTree`. Any attempt to assign to n a pointer of type `NumberTree`, or to access n^.`customernumber`, would be prevented by a compile-time type check. Any attempt to access n^.`keyname` when n's value is *nil* would be prevented by a run-time check.   □

Thus programming with pointers in Pascal is as safe as it can ever be, and certainly safer than in a language with untyped pointers (such as PL/I). Nevertheless, pointer manipulation is fundamentally error-prone, as discussed in Section 3.4.2. Pointers are best used to implement objects and abstract types, where the explicit pointer manipulation is localized and (notionally) hidden. (See Example 10.5 below.)

Pointers in practice have two distinct roles. The first role is to implement recursive types. In Example 10.4, the binary trees were implemented using pointers. The second role is sharing. In Example 10.4, two binary trees both contained pointers to shared records of type `Customer`; each customer's details were recorded in a single place. The alternative to sharing is to duplicate the shared data. Thus sharing saves storage, but more importantly it reduces the risk of data inconsistency as new operations are written to access the data.

The first role would be redundant if the language supported recursive types directly. The implications of such a design were discussed in Section 3.4.2. It should be remembered that recursive types were not well understood when Pascal was designed. Furthermore, one of Wirth's design criteria was a simple computational model to allow programmers to visualize clearly how efficiently their programs would run. Seen in this light, his decision not to provide recursive types directly was reasonable.

10.2.2   Expressions

Pascal's repertoire of expressions is very limited. It has no conditional expressions of any kind, and no block expressions. It has no nontrivial expressions of composite type, due to the lack of aggregates and the fact that functions cannot have composite results.

These omissions force the programmer to use commands in situations where expressions would otherwise be sufficient. For example, the only way to construct a record (or array) value is by assigning one at a time to the components of a record (or array) variable. Moreover, a function body is in effect a command. Pascal is consequently very much an imperative language.

10.2.3 Commands and sequencers

Pascal has a fairly rich repertoire of commands. The *if* and *case* commands provide for conditional execution. The *while* and *repeat* commands provide for indefinite iteration, and the *for* command for definite iteration. These commands can be composed freely, allowing a variety of single-entry single-exit control flows to be programmed naturally.

The only way to program more general control flows in Pascal is by using the *goto* sequencer. Pascal restricts its use in order to avoid the worst abuses, such as jumping into a loop or into a block. Programmers can use *goto* sequencers in a disciplined fashion, e.g., to escape from loops and blocks; but it is still possible to abuse them to write 'spaghetti' programs. Pascal requires that each label intended as the destination of a *goto* sequencer must be declared at the top of the enclosing block; such a label declaration serves as a useful danger signal to readers of the program!

10.2.4 Declarations

In Pascal we can declare constants, types, variables, and procedure and function abstractions. See Section 4.4 for a full discussion of declarations in Pascal.

Declarations can be placed only at the head of a block. Since a block can occur only as a program body, procedure body, or function body, programmers are forced to group all their declarations in a comparatively small number of places. There are no block commands (as such) and no block expressions, so a declaration needed only for a small part of the program has to be given a wider scope than we would wish.

More seriously, Pascal declarations must be grouped by kind, in the order given in the first paragraph of this subsection. This makes it difficult to keep related declarations together. Suppose that a program is to be (logically) composed of modules A and B, where each module has its own constants, types, variables, and abstractions. Pascal does not support modules as such, but at least it would be desirable to group together all the declarations of module A, and similarly to group together all the declarations of module B. Instead the modules have to be intertwined, making it awkward to manage them separately:

const
>   *definitions of constants for module A;*
>   *definitions of constants for module B;*

type
>   *definitions of types for module A;*
>   *definitions of types for module B;*

```
var
        declarations of variables for module A ;
        declarations of variables for module B ;

    definitions of abstractions for module A ;
    definitions of abstractions for module B
```

10.2.5 Abstractions

Pascal is typical among imperative languages in supporting only procedure and function abstractions. Abstractions in Pascal are not first-class values. They can be passed as arguments to other abstractions, but they cannot be assigned, nor used as components of composite values.

There are four parameter mechanisms: value, variable, procedural, and functional parameters. These allow (first-class) values, references to variables, procedure abstractions, and function abstractions (respectively) to be passed as arguments.

Pascal originally had constant parameters, which complied well with the correspondence principle, as discussed in Section 5.2.3. However, they were later replaced by value parameters: a design change of unclear motivation.

Procedures and functions are the only kinds of module supported by Pascal. The concept of encapsulation is not directly supported, but can be used to inform the design of particular Pascal programs. However, the programmer must exercise care and self-discipline – not a very firm basis for programming in the large!

Example 10.5
A 'module' for handling stacks of characters could be implemented by the following group of declarations:

```
type Stack    = ^ StackNode;
     StackNode = record
                    top  : Char;
                    rest : Stack
                 end;

procedure clear (var thestack : Stack);
   begin
   thestack := nil
   end;

procedure push  (var thestack : Stack;
                     newitem : Char);
   var newstack : Stack;
   begin
   new (newstack);
   newstack^.top  := newitem;
   newstack^.rest := thestack;
```

```
      thestack := newstack
   end;

procedure pop     (var thestack : Stack;
                    var olditem  : Char);
   begin
   olditem  := thestack^.top;
   thestack := thestack^.rest
   end;

function empty (thestack : Stack) : Boolean;
   begin
   empty := (thestack = nil)
   end
```

The programmer can then use these abstractions as if `Stack` were an abstract type, by abstaining from writing any code that depends on the particular representation chosen for `Stack`:

```
var symbol : Char;  symbolstack : Stack;
...
clear (symbolstack);  push (symbolstack, '*');  ...;
while not empty (symbolstack) do
   begin  pop (symbolstack, symbol);  ... end
```

Provided that the programmer faithfully adheres to this discipline, the `Stack` representation could be changed without affecting the rest of the program. However, the Pascal compiler cannot enforce such a discipline. The `Stack` representation is visible throughout the scope of the above declarations. Therefore any change in the `Stack` representation *potentially has effects throughout that scope*. (See also Exercise 10.1.)

□

It is impossible in Pascal to parameterize abstractions with respect to the types of values on which they operate. Declarations for stacks of strings, stacks of integers, etc., would be similar to the declarations of Example 10.5, but would have to be reproduced manually (or by a preprocessor). A single program using several types of stack would have to include a complete group of declarations for each distinct type of stack. (See also Exercise 10.3.)

10.3 Case study: Ada

If Fortran and Cobol are elderly programming languages, Pascal is middle-aged. It does not, of course, support concepts developed in the 1970s and later (e.g., recursive types, encapsulation, polymorphism, concurrency, exceptions). Nevertheless, it was so successful in satisfying its limited design aims that it begat a whole family of *Pascal-like* languages, in much the same way as its own ancestor Algol-60.

The most important of Pascal's descendants is Ada. This was designed in the late 1970s to be a general-purpose language, suitable in particular for implementation of large-scale and embedded systems. The Ada design team was large, and received inputs from a still larger number of interested persons, but the design effort was dominated by Jean Ichbiah. As a consequence, Ada is a large but reasonably coherent language.

To classify Ada as a Pascal-like language might be misleading. Only about half of Ada is directly comparable to Pascal (although that half corrects most of Pascal's design flaws and is notationally richer). The other half supports important concepts such as encapsulation, generics, exceptions, and concurrency, and in these respects Ada extends far beyond Pascal.

This section is a (necessarily brief) overview of Ada. Only the sequential part of the language is covered. Ada as a concurrent programming language will be discussed in Chapter 11.

10.3.1 Values, types, and subtypes

Ada's selection of primitive and composite types is similar to Pascal's. Ada like Pascal does not support recursive types directly; they must be programmed using pointers.

Ada complies well with the type completeness principle. Unlike Pascal, constants of any type can be defined, and functions can have results of any type.

Ada supports the concept of *subtype* more systematically than Pascal. Every kind of type can have subtypes, as discussed in Section 7.6. However, Ada makes an important distinction between types and subtypes: a subtype is not itself a type. Each type declaration creates a new and distinct type. (The language uses name equivalence of types.) Each subtype declaration merely binds an identifier to a subtype of an existing type.

Each value belongs to one and only one type. The set of all possible Ada values is partitioned into disjoint types. However, a given type may contain many, possibly overlapping, subtypes, all of which share the same operations.

Example 10.6
Consider the following subtype declarations from Example 7.18:

```
subtype Natural is Integer range 0..Integer'last;
subtype Small   is Integer range -3..+3;
```

The value 2 belongs to many subtypes, including `Natural` and `Small`, but it belongs to only one *type*, `Integer`.

Now consider the function declared here:

```
function "**" (i : Integer; n : Natural)
                return Integer;
```

In a function call, e.g., 'j**k', the compiler simply checks that both j and k are of type `Integer` (or any subtype thereof). However, a run-time check may be needed to ensure that the value of k is actually is of subtype `Natural`.

Finally, consider the procedure declared here:

procedure increment (i : **in out** Integer);

In a call of this procedure, the argument may be a variable of type Integer *or any subtype thereof.* (The corresponding procedure in Pascal would accept only an Integer variable as argument. A subtype like Natural would be considered to be a distinct type in Pascal.)   □

10.3.2 Expressions

In Ada we can write nontrivial expressions of every type. In particular, aggregates allow records and arrays to be constructed from their components. However, Ada has no conditional expressions or block expressions, and a function body is a command (in effect). Thus Ada, like Pascal, forces the programmer to resort to commands for any computation that is too complicated for its limited repertoire of expressions.

10.3.3 Commands and sequencers

Ada's repertoire of commands is much the same as Pascal's. However, Ada's *exit* and *return* sequencers, discussed in Section 8.2, allow single-entry multi-exit control structures to be programmed as easily as single-entry single-exit control structures. Ada also has a *goto* sequencer, but this is an obsolete feature that seems to have no useful application!

Ada was the first major language to include a secure form of exception handling. See Section 8.3 for a full discussion.

10.3.4 Declarations

Ada allows the programmer to declare types and subtypes, constants and variables, procedure and function abstractions, packages, tasks, and exceptions. Declarations may be located in block commands, which allow the scope of a declaration to be restricted as much as desired by the programmer. Procedure and function bodies are, in effect, block commands. Declarations may also be grouped in packages (discussed in Section 10.3.6 below).

10.3.5 Abstractions

Ada supports procedure and function abstractions. Abstractions are not first-class values; indeed they cannot even be passed as arguments to other procedure and function abstractions. (In this respect, Ada is weaker even than Fortran!)

Ada's parameter mechanisms were designed on the principle that the direction of data flow (into and/or out of the abstraction) should be evident. The kinds of parameter are:

- *In parameter:* the formal parameter is a constant, and is bound to the argument (a first-class value).
- *In out parameter:* the formal parameter is a variable, and permits both inspection and updating of the argument (a variable).
- *Out parameter:* the formal parameter is a variable, and permits only updating of the argument (a variable).

For primitive types, the above effects must be achieved by copy. This makes *in* parameters behave (roughly) like value parameters, and the others like value-result and result parameters, respectively. (See Section 5.2.1.)

For composite types, there is an implementation choice: the above effects may be achieved either by copy or by reference. The latter choice would make *in* parameters behave like constant parameters, and the others (roughly) like variable parameters – complete with the possibility of aliasing. (See Section 5.2.2.)

Example 10.7

Compare the following Ada procedures with those of Examples 5.8 and 5.9:

```
type Vector is array (1..n) of Float;

procedure add (v, w : in Vector;
                sum : out Vector) is
begin
   for i in 1 .. n loop
      sum(i) := v(i) + w(i);
   end loop;
end;

procedure normalize (u : in out Vector) is
   s : Float := 0.0;
begin
   for i in 1 .. n loop
      s := s + u(i)**2;
   end loop;
   s := sqrt (s);
   for i in 1 .. n loop
      u(i) := u(i) / s;
   end loop;
end;
```

Since the type Vector is composite, these parameters could be implemented either by copy or by reference. Either way, the procedure call 'add (a, b, c)' will have the expected effect. (See also Exercise 10.4.)   □

An Ada function may not have *out* or *in out* parameters. This prevents a function from updating variables supplied as arguments, but is only a half-hearted attempt to discourage side effects. The function body (which is, in effect, a block command) can update global variables, a concealed and therefore more dangerous kind of side effect.

10.3.6   Encapsulation

As discussed in Chapter 6, *packages* are used in Ada to declare abstract types, to declare objects, and to achieve encapsulation in general. The key concept is the division of a package into a package declaration and a package body. The essential purpose of the *package declaration* is to declare only those components that are to be exported, and thus specify the interface between the package and other modules. The purpose of the *package body* is to contain implementation details. These details include bodies of any exported abstractions, and declarations of any hidden components.

Example 10.8
The following package declaration declares an abstract (*private*) type Stack, together with appropriate operations. Compare with Example 10.5.

```
package char_stack_type is
   type Stack is limited private;
   procedure clear  (thestack : out Stack);
   procedure push   (thestack : in out Stack;
                     newitem  : in Character);
   procedure pop    (thestack : in out Stack;
                     olditem  : out Character);
   function   empty (thestack : Stack)
                     return Boolean;
private
   type StackNode;
   type Stack     is access StackNode;
   type StackNode is record
                        top  : Character;
                        rest : Stack;
                     end record;
end char_stack_type;
```

And here is the corresponding package body:

```
package body char_stack_type is

   procedure clear (thestack : out Stack) is
   begin
      thestack := null;
   end;

   procedure push  (thestack : in out Stack;
                    newitem  : in Character) is
   begin
      thestack :=
              new StackNode' (newitem, thestack);
   end;
```

```
procedure pop    (thestack : in out Stack;
                  olditem  : out Character) is
begin
   olditem  := thestack.top;
   thestack := thestack.rest;
end;

function empty (thestack : Stack)
                 return Boolean is
begin
   return (thestack = null);
end;

end char_stack_type;
```

This package could be used as follows:

```
use char_stack_type;   -- allows us to abbreviate the dot notation
symbol : Character;  symbolstack : Stack;
...
clear (symbolstack);  push (symbolstack, '*');  ...;
while not empty (symbolstack) loop
   pop (symbolstack, symbol);  ...;
end loop;
```

Unlike Example 10.5, there is no reliance here on the programmer's self-discipline. The Ada compiler will prevent any attempt to access the Stack representation. Values of type Stack can be manipulated only by calling the operations exported by the char_stack_type package. □

Assignment and equality tests are operations applicable to all Ada types, including abstract types – but not abstract types declared as *limited private*. When defining a recursive type, the programmer will normally declare it as limited, in order to avoid inconsistency in the results of assignment and equality tests. For example, assignment of a record or array value causes the whole value to be copied; but assignment of a value of recursive type would simply cause sharing, if the value is represented using pointers. (See also the discussion in Section 3.4.2, and Exercise 10.2.)

Where a package defines an abstract type, as in Example 10.8, the part of the package declaration between **private** and **end** defines the representation of the abstract type. Logically, this information should be located in the package body, along with the other implementation details. The reason for this inconsistency is that the Ada compiler must deduce how much space to reserve for values of the abstract type, and it must extract this information from the package declaration. (Declarations of constants and variables of the abstract type might have to be compiled before the package body. This possibility is especially relevant if the package is compiled separately; see Section 10.3.7.) This is a typical example of a design compromise motivated by implementation considerations.

10.3.7   Separate compilation

We have seen that a package is split into a package declaration and a package body. Similarly, a procedure can be split into a procedure declaration (its heading) and a procedure body, and a function can be split into a function declaration (its heading) and a function body. In each case, the module has a *declaration* that specifies its interface, and a *body* that contains its implementation details. This division supports *separate compilation* of modules.

Example 10.9
Consider a program that uses the `char_stack_type` package of Example 10.8. We could compile the `char_stack_type` declaration first, followed (in either order) by the `char_stack_type` body and the main program.

Subsequently, if the `char_stack_type` declaration is modified (an interface change), everything must be recompiled. But if only the `char_stack_type` body is modified (an implementation change), only the package body must be recompiled.

Notice that this is so only because the package is split into declaration and body. If the whole package had to be compiled as a single unit, then the smallest implementation change would force everything to be recompiled.   □

The Ada compiler ensures that modules are compiled (and recompiled) in a correct order. It also performs full type checks across module boundaries.

Contrast Ada's secure *separate compilation* with Fortran's and C's *independent compilation*. In these languages procedure and function calls are not type-checked at all. If an abstraction is called with the wrong number or type of arguments, the program will probably run wild. Nor is there any constraint at all on (re)compilation order.

10.3.8   Generics

As discussed in Section 6.4, Ada allows any package to be made *generic*, and then it can be parameterized with respect to values, variables, types, procedures, and functions on which it depends. Here we give one further example.

Example 10.10
The package of Example 10.8 can be made generic, with respect to the type of the items stored in the stack. Here is the generic package declaration:

```
generic
   type Item is private;
package stack_type is
   type Stack is limited private;
   procedure clear (thestack : out Stack);
   procedure push (thestack : in out Stack;
                   newitem  : in Item);
```

```
        procedure pop    (thestack : in out Stack;
                          olditem  : out Item);
        function  empty (thestack : Stack)
                          return Boolean;
  private
     type StackNode;
     type Stack     is access StackNode;
     type StackNode is record
                          top  : Item;
                          rest : Stack;
                      end record;
  end stack_type;
```

The corresponding package body is similar to that of Example 10.8, with systematic substitution of Item for Character.

This generic package could be instantiated and used as follows:

```
  package char_stack_type is
          new stack_type (Character);
```

and the resulting package char_stack_type could then be used exactly as at the end of Example 10.8.   □

Not only packages but also procedures and functions can be made generic. A generic procedure or function gives us an extra level of abstraction.

Example 10.11
The following declares a swapping procedure that is generic with respect to the type of the items being swapped:

```
  generic
     type Item is private;
  procedure swap (x, y : in out Item);
```

And here is the corresponding procedure body:

```
  procedure swap (x, y : in out Item) is
     xcopy : constant Item := x;
  begin
     x := y;  y := xcopy;
  end;
```

We instantiate this generic procedure by supplying an argument type to be bound to the type parameter Item:

```
  procedure swap_integers is new swap (Integer);
```

Now swap_integers denotes an ordinary (nongeneric) procedure with two *in out* parameters of type Integer. This procedure can be called in the usual manner:

```
a : array (1..n) of Integer;
...
swap_integers (a(i), a(i+1));
```

                                                             □

Note that an Ada generic procedure or function must first be instantiated in a declaration, which binds an identifier to the resulting ordinary procedure or function, before the latter can be called. Instantiation and call cannot be combined – see Exercise 10.5.

The importance of the concept of genericity should not be underestimated. Nearly all potentially reusable software is generic. For example, sorting and searching algorithms are generic with respect to the type of the values being sorted and searched. Even numerical algorithms are generic with respect to the real-number precision. (The traditional Fortran numerical library has one instance of every routine for each real-number precision.) Ada was the first major language to allow such generic software to be written. Nevertheless, the feature has not been entirely successful, due to implementation problems.

10.4   Further reading

Pascal was first described by Wirth (1971). Subsequently a large subset of Pascal was formally specified by Hoare and Wirth (1973). This effort exposed certain irregularities in the original design, prompting a language revision, which was described in Jensen and Wirth (1974). The international standard version of Pascal, see BSI (1982) or ANSI/IEEE (1983), clarified a number of obscurities in Wirth's descriptions, and also eliminated a couple of perceived deficiencies.

The design of Pascal generated plenty of debate. Two of the more constructive and influential criticisms were by Habermann (1973) and Welsh *et al.* (1977).

The standard description of Ada is Ichbiah (1983). Unusually and commendably, the Ada design team produced not only a language description but also a design rationale, see Ichbiah (1979). The rationale explores many important areas of programming language design and discusses the design decisions underlying (an earlier version of) Ada.

Ada was designed to meet requirements set out by the US Department of Defense (1978). Their intention was (and still is) to make Ada mandatory for all their new software contracts (except in data processing). Successive versions of the language design were published for public comment. Unsurprisingly in view of Ada's predestined importance, the debate that accompanied and followed the design process was vigorous, sometimes generating more heat than light. Some of the more notable contributions were by Hoare (1981), Ledgard and Singer (1982), and Wichmann (1984).

Exercises 10

10.1　Refer to Example 10.5. Change the `Stack` representation to an array.

　　　Which of the following Pascal commands (in which s and t are `Stack` variables) would have effects dependent on the `Stack` representation?

　　　　(a)　`s^.top := '*'`
　　　　(b)　`push (s, '*')`
　　　　(c)　`t := s^.rest`
　　　　(d)　`t := s`
　　　　(e)　`if s = t then ...`
　　　　(f)　`if s = nil then ...`

10.2　Repeat Exercise 10.1 for Ada, referring to Example 10.8 instead. Which of the corresponding Ada commands would be illegal, given that `Stack` is limited private? How would your answers be affected if `Stack` were declared to be private rather than limited private?

10.3**　Given the limitations of standard Pascal (no packages or generics), suggest how a project team could build and manage a library of 'modules', like that of Example 10.5, in order to encourage software reuse. It should be possible for programmers to construct, test, and modify such 'modules' individually, and to integrate them into application programs. What software tools would be needed, in addition to the standard Pascal compiler? How should 'modules' like that of Example 10.5 be written to be as reusable as possible?

10.4　Consider the procedure call 'add (a, b, c)' of Example 10.7. Show that the procedure call has the expected effect, whether the parameters are implemented by copy or by reference. Repeat for the procedure call 'add (a, b, b)'. Show that (harmless) aliasing can arise in this case.

10.5　It might be convenient for the instantiation and call of a generic procedure to be combined into a single command as follows (see Example 10.11):

　　　　`swap (Integer) (a(i), a(i+1));`

Ada does not permit this. Nevertheless, the same effect can be achieved (less concisely) by an Ada block command. Show how.

　　　The same effect *cannot* be achieved for a generic function. Why not?

10.6*　Investigate why Ada restricts generic instantiations to occur in declarations, and not in commands such as the one in Exercise 10.5.

10.7*　Consider each of the following controversial features of Ada: (a) exceptions; (b) generics; (c) overloading. Was each feature well designed, or could it have been better designed, or should it have been omitted altogether?

CHAPTER ELEVEN

The Concurrent Programming Paradigm

It would be a considerable exaggeration to claim that there is any such thing as *the* concurrent programming paradigm, for the discipline is still relatively immature, and many different approaches are being actively pursued. An unfortunate consequence of this is that concurrent programs must often be structured to conform with one particular concurrent hardware architecture, and do not adapt well to architectures that support dissimilar paradigms. Much research is being directed to a resolution of this problem, which is perhaps the main obstacle in the way of a much wider use of concurrency.

This chapter will focus on what may be termed the 'classical' approach to concurrent programming, based directly on the ideas of competition and communication introduced in Chapter 9. These ideas inform most of the concurrent programming that underlies systems presently available to end-users, including the major operating systems.

We will explore these important topics by means of a case study: an implementation of the banker's algorithm in Ada. The banker's algorithm is a scheduler that steers a set of competing processes away from deadlock. This will illustrate the concurrency features of Ada at their best and at their weakest, for scheduling is an application that does not sit well with the tasking mechanism, although it can be implemented (at some cost) by exploiting lower-level tasks that use Ada idiomatically. Our development of the banker's algorithm follows that given in Brinch Hansen (1973).

11.1 Ada tasking revisited

To set the scene, we need to become familiar with a little more of the Ada approach to concurrency. Recall that a process in Ada is called a *task* and that tasks interact by means of *entry calls* (see Section 9.6.3).

An *active task* is one that makes entry calls but does not itself export entries. (We may treat the main program as if it were an active task.) A *passive task* is one that exports entries but does not itself make entry calls. Passive tasks typically provide services, and active tasks typically make use of these services. For this reason passive tasks may also be termed *servers* and active tasks may also be termed *clients*.

Tasks that both make and accept entry calls are also possible, and may be useful, for example to delegate work on a basis of 'divide and conquer'. Tasks that do neither are uncommon. They must achieve their effect by changing global variables, at the expense of greatly increased intermodule coupling. Such designs are deprecated, although considerations of efficiency may tempt programmers in that direction.

Example 11.1

Here we show an Ada package called `synchronization` that declares passive task types useful for mutual exclusion and for low-level communication. We will use these later in our implementation of the banker's algorithm. For low-level communication we employ the `Event` type, defined in Section 9.5.4, with its operations `await` and `signal`. For mutual exclusion we employ a simple locking mechanism, the `Gate` type, that implements strictly alternating *acquire* and *relinquish* operations, called `lock` and `unlock` respectively.

Here is the declaration of `synchronization`:

```
package synchronization is

   task type Gate is
      entry lock;
      entry unlock;
   end Gate;

   task type Event is
      entry await;
      entry signal;
   end Event;

end synchronization;
```

And here is the body:

```
package body synchronization is

   task body Gate is
   begin
      loop
         select
            accept lock;
         or
            terminate;
         end select;
         select
            accept unlock;
         or
            terminate;
         end select;
      end loop;
   end Gate;
```

```
task body Event is
begin
   loop
      select
         accept signal;
         for i in 1 .. await'count loop
            select
               accept await;
            else
               null;
            end select;
         end loop;
      or
         terminate;
      end select;
   end loop;
end Event;

end synchronization;
```

The *accept* commands within Gate are enclosed in selective waits that offer a *terminate alternative*. This allows the server task to terminate if there are no outstanding calls on its entries and there are no active processes that might make such calls.

The treatment of the await entry in Event merits a fuller explanation. The function of Event is to wait for the occurrence of a signal, and then to allow every process waiting on that signal to proceed. This is effected by holding processes in the entry queue for await. When signal is called, the await entry queue is cleared out. The value of await'count is the number of tasks queued for await, so the *for* loop accepts every outstanding call. The *accept* command for await is enclosed in a selective wait with an *else* part. The latter is executed if there is no outstanding call in the queue. In this case the action taken is **null** (skip). This is made necessary by the fact that a task might time out or be aborted, thus withdrawing its entry call, after await'count is evaluated but before the entry call is accepted. Such complications are typical of the difficulties introduced by concurrency. □

An operation is **reentrant** if it works correctly even when called concurrently. Concurrent calls to a nonreentrant operation must be excluded. Example 11.2 illustrates how the synchronization package can be exploited to provide such exclusion.

Example 11.2
The standard package text_IO provides text input–output facilities, but it is not guaranteed to be reentrant. For example, concurrent calls to the string output procedure text_IO.put_line might well cause the two strings to be interleaved, or worse.

When two or more tasks are to use text_IO, it is necessary to ensure that they do so under mutual exclusion. The following package exports a string output procedure that meets this requirement by calling the operations of the Gate type.

First the package declaration:

```
package serialized_output is

    procedure put_line (s : in String);

end serialized_output;
```

Now the package body:

```
package body serialized_output is

    IO_gate : synchronization.Gate;

    procedure put_line (s : in String) is
    begin
        IO_gate.lock;
        text_IO.put_line (s);
        IO_gate.unlock;
    end;

end serialized_output;
```

When this put_line procedure is called, it prevents any other task from calling it concurrently by 'locking the gate'. Once the output command has completed, it 'opens the gate' again, allowing any other task calling this put_line to continue into text_IO. To be convinced of this, trace through the action of two calls made concurrently to this put_line.   □

11.2   Deadlock again

In this section we develop a simple concurrent program that illustrates how easy it is to introduce a deadlock.

Example 11.3
The package resource_definitions uses the code developed in Example 11.1 to implement a simple resource management system. For purposes of explanation, it includes comments that we will use to trace its flow of control.

First the package declaration:

```
package resource_definitions is

    type Process_Id is (p1, p2);    -- e.g.
    -- every process has an identification

    type Resource_Id is (disk, tape, modem);   -- e.g.
    -- every resource has an identification

    procedure acquire
                  (resource : in Resource_Id;
                   process  : in Process_Id);
```

```ada
procedure relinquish
             (resource : in Resource_Id;
              process  : in Process_Id);

end resource_definitions;
```

Now the package body:

```ada
package body resource_definitions is

   mutex : array (Resource_Id) of Gate;

   procedure acquire
                (resource : in Resource_Id;
                 process  : in Process_Id) is
   begin
      -- process bids for the resource
      mutex(resource).lock;
      -- process has the resource
   end;

   procedure relinquish
                (resource : in Resource_Id;
                 process  : in Process_Id) is
   begin
      mutex(resource).unlock;
      -- process has given up the resource
   end;

end resource_definitions;
```

The procedure trouble, which is intended to be called concurrently, uses the package to provide mutual exclusion:

```ada
use resource_definitions;

procedure trouble (res1, res2 : in Resource_Id;
                   proc : in Process_Id) is
   interval : constant Duration := 1.0;   -- seconds
begin
   acquire (res1, proc);
   delay interval;
   acquire (res2, proc);
   delay interval;
   ...;   -- critical section
   relinquish (res2, proc);
   relinquish (res1, proc);
end;
```

The following concurrent program calls trouble to illustrate how easy it is to get caught in a deadlock:

```
use resource_definitions;

procedure main is
begin

    declare
        task worker1;
        task worker2;

        task body worker1 is
        begin
            -- worker 1 is getting into trouble ...
            trouble (disk, modem, p1);
            -- ... worker 1 is now out of trouble
        end worker1;

        task body worker2 is
        begin
            -- worker 2 is getting into trouble ...
            trouble (modem, disk, p2);
            -- ... worker 2 is now out of trouble
        end worker2;

    begin
        null;
    end;    -- at this point await termination of both workers

    -- end of run
end;
```

The following trace is typical, and shows the program running into difficulties:

worker 2 is getting into trouble ...
worker 1 is getting into trouble ...
worker 2 bids for the modem
worker 1 bids for the disk
worker 2 has the modem
worker 1 has the disk
worker 2 bids for the disk – but worker 1 has it
worker 1 bids for the modem – but worker 2 has it

Deadlock has struck!   □

Example 11.4
As described in Section 9.3.3, we can prevent deadlocks by imposing a total ordering
on resources and by insisting that they be acquired consistently with that ordering. Here
we adapt the trouble procedure using this idea:

```
use resource_definitions;

procedure trouble (res1, res2 : in Resource_Id;
                   proc : in Process_Id) is
   interval : constant Duration := 1.0;   -- seconds
   r1 : constant Resource_Id := min (res1, res2);
   r2 : constant Resource_Id := max (res1, res2);
   -- the canonical ordering of resources is r1 followed by r2
begin
   acquire (r1, proc);
   delay interval;
   acquire (r2, proc);
   delay interval;
   ...;   -- critical section
   relinquish (r2, proc);
   relinquish (r1, proc);
end;
```

Here is a typical trace of this version in action:

worker 2 is getting into trouble ...
worker 1 is getting into trouble ...
worker 2 bids for the disk
worker 2 has the disk
worker 1 bids for the disk – but worker 2 has it
worker 2 bids for the modem
worker 2 has the modem
worker 2 has given up the modem
worker 2 has given up the disk
worker 1 has the disk
... worker 2 is now out of trouble
worker 1 bids for the modem
worker 1 has the modem
worker 1 has given up the modem
worker 1 has given up the disk
... worker 1 is now out of trouble
end of run

Now the program is deadlock-free and runs to completion.   □

11.3   The banker's algorithm

The banker's algorithm provides a more practical resource management interface than
the package declared in Example 11.3, for it is capable of resolving incompatible
requests for resources and ensuring that no deadlock ensues. It does this by suspending,

temporarily, processes whose demands cannot presently be guaranteed capable of satisfaction. Thus the algorithm is a *scheduler*. As it turns out, schedulers are not at all easy to write using the intertask communication primitives of the Ada language.

To see why this is so, let us consider the obvious way to go about it. A scheduler has to maintain data structures that model the state of allocation of the system's resources. Since competing processes may make concurrent calls on the scheduling operations, it is natural to implement the scheduler as a task that encapsulates the resource management data. Scheduling operations are then represented as entries and the problem of ensuring exclusive access to the data disappears.

The `acquire` entry examines the effect of allocating the resource to the caller, and allows the caller to proceed only if the resulting state of the system is *safe*, that is only if it is guaranteed to be deadlock-free. An outline of the algorithm for this operation might be as follows:

```
accept acquire
                (resource : in Resource_Id;
                 process  : in Process_Id) do
    new_state : system state;
begin
    new_state := current state;
    decrement the availability of the resource;
    increment the amount of the resource allocated to the caller;
    decrement the amount of the resource that may be claimed
        by the caller;
    if deadlock is possible in new_state then
        suspend the calling process until new_state is safe;
    end if;
    current state := new_state;
end;
```

Using either a conditional critical region (Section 9.6.1) or a monitor (Section 9.6.2), the command '*suspend the calling process until* new_state *is safe*' would pose no problem. However, Ada does not have an operation by means of which a called task may suspend its caller. In fact, there is no way for a task even to determine the identity of its caller! (That is why we had to declare the Process_Id type.)

This turns out to be an insurmountable obstacle to the implementation of the scheduler as a task. Instead we have to structure the scheduler as a package, the operations being exported as procedures, and we have to solve the resulting synchronization and mutual exclusion problems ourselves.

Example 11.5
Here is the declaration of the package `banker`. Its interface differs from `resource_definitions`. There is an important element of flexibility, in that `banker` can deal with resources that exist, and may be claimed, in varying quantities. An additional procedure, `notify_claim`, is declared. This allows processes to register their maximum claim for resources, which is necessary so that the algorithm can anticipate the possible future demands of processes it is to schedule.

```
package banker is

    type Process_Id is (p1, p2);    -- e.g.
    -- every process has an identification

    type Resource_Id is (disk, tape, modem);    -- e.g.
    -- every resource has an identification

    type Budget is array (Resource_Id) of Natural;
    -- there is a certain (limited, nonnegative) amount of each resource

    procedure notify_claim
                (claim    : in Budget;
                 process  : in Process_Id);

    procedure acquire
                (resource : in Resource_Id;
                 process  : in Process_Id);

    procedure relinquish
                (resource : in Resource_Id;
                 process  : in Process_Id);

end banker;
```

Ada's tasking model forces us to adopt a traditional approach to implementing the *acquire* operation. In effect we have to simulate a conditional critical region, and so we program a busy-waiting loop. The *acquire* operation becomes a procedure that invokes mutual exclusion to protect the scheduler data structures. It then simulates the effect of allowing the demanded allocation of resource. If this leads to a safe state, that state is allowed and exclusion is released. Otherwise the caller is suspended until the state of the system does change and the caller's resource demand can be reconsidered. This is repeated as often as necessary.

```
use synchronization;
package body banker is

    type Process_Account is
            record
                claim, loan : Budget;
                achievable  : Boolean;
            end record;
    -- Process_Account models the resource status of a process
    -- claim sets an upper bound on its future demands
    -- loan gives the amounts tentatively allocated to it
    -- achievable is true if it can run thence to its end

    type Account_List is
            array (Process_Id) of Process_Account;

    type Exposure is
            record
```

```
            balance : Budget;
            account : Account_List;
        end record;
```
-- Exposure *describes an actual or projected state of the system*
-- balance *gives the amounts in hand (i.e., not on loan) in that state*
-- account *gives the particulars of each process in that state*

```
global_mutex : Gate;
state_change : Event;

capital : constant Budget := (1, 1, 1); -- e.g.
```
-- capital *gives the amount of each resource owned by the system*

```
actual  : Exposure :=
    (balance => capital,
     account => (Process_Id =>
                 ((0, 0, 0), (0, 0, 0), false)
                )
    );

procedure notify_claim
                (claim   : in Budget;
                 process : in Process_Id) is
begin
    -- process notifies its claim
    global_mutex.lock;
    actual.account(process).claim := claim;
    global_mutex.unlock;
    state_change.signal;
end;

procedure dec (i : in out Integer) is
begin i := i - 1; end;

procedure inc (i : in out Integer) is
begin i := i + 1; end;

function projection (from : Exposure)
                return Exposure is
    given : Exposure := from;
    stabilized : Boolean;

    function completion_is_possible
                    (claim, balance : Budget)
                    return Boolean is
    begin
        for res in Resource_Id loop
            if claim(res) > balance(res) then
```

```
                           return false;
                     end if;
                end loop;
                return true;
           end;

           procedure redeem_loan
                        (loan : in Budget;
                         balance : in out Budget) is
           begin
              for res in Resource_Id loop
                 balance(res) :=
                         balance(res) + loan(res);
              end loop;
           end;
     begin -- projection
        loop
           stabilized := true;
           for proc in Process_Id loop
              declare
                 acc : Process_Account renames
                         given.account(proc);
              begin
                 if not acc.achievable and then
                     completion_is_possible (
                            acc.claim, given.balance);
                 then
                     redeem_loan (
                         acc.loan, given.balance);
                     acc.achievable := true;
                     stabilized := false;
                 end if;
              end;
           end loop;
           exit when stabilized;
        end loop;
        return given;
     end projection;

     function is_safe (proposed : Exposure)
                   return Boolean is
        eventual : constant Exposure
               := projection (proposed);
     begin
        return (eventual.balance = capital);
     end;
```

```
procedure acquire
                (resource : in Resource_Id;
                 process  : in Process_Id) is
   trial : Exposure;
begin
   loop
      -- the process bids for the resource
      global_mutex.lock;
      trial := actual;
      dec (trial.balance(resource));
      inc (trial.account(process).
              loan(resource));
      dec (trial.account(process).
              claim(resource));
      exit when is_safe (trial);
      global_mutex.unlock;
      -- process waits for the resource
      state_change.await;
   end loop;
   actual := trial;
   global_mutex.unlock;
   -- process has the resource
end;

procedure relinquish
                (resource : in Resource_Id;
                 process  : in Process_Id) is
begin
   global_mutex.lock;
   inc (actual.balance(resource));
   dec (actual.account(process).loan(resource));
   inc (actual.account(process).claim(resource));
   global_mutex.unlock;
   state_change.signal;
   -- process has given up the resource
end;

end banker;
```

□

Example 11.6
Using `banker` we can program a version of `trouble` that is guaranteed to be deadlock-free:

```
use banker;

procedure trouble (res1, res2 : in Resource_Id;
                   proc : in Process_Id) is
```

```
    interval : constant Duration := 1.0;  -- seconds
begin
    notify_claim (
          (disk=>1, tape=>0, modem=>1), proc);
    acquire (res1, proc);
    delay interval;
    acquire (res2, proc);
    delay interval;
    ...;   -- critical section
    relinquish (res2, proc);
    relinquish (res1, proc);
end;
```

A typical trace from this version might go as follows:

worker 2 is getting into trouble ...
worker 1 is getting into trouble ...
worker 2 notifies its claim for disk and modem
worker 1 notifies its claim for disk and modem
worker 2 bids for the modem
worker 1 bids for the disk
worker 2 has the modem
worker 1 waits for the disk – because to grant it now would be unsafe
worker 2 bids for the disk
worker 2 has the disk
worker 2 has given up the disk
worker 1 bids for the disk
worker 2 has given up the modem
worker 1 has the disk – it is safe now
... worker 2 is now out of trouble
worker 1 bids for the modem
worker 1 has the modem
worker 1 has given up the modem
worker 1 has given up the disk
... worker 1 is now out of trouble
end of run

□

11.4 Further reading

The major concurrent programming paradigms are surveyed, with many examples, by
Perrott (1987). The book by Bustard *et al.* (1988) discusses applications, including
simulation, and is to be commended for addressing the question of testing concurrent
programs. Burns (1985) describes the Ada model of concurrency in detail, while Jones

and Goldsmith (1988) do the same for occam. An *architecture independent* paradigm called Linda is proposed by Carriero and Gelernter (1989). A theory of *paradigm independent* concurrent programming is put forward by Chandy and Misra (1988).

Exercises 11

11.1 This is the 'dining philosophers' problem. Five hungry (and obstinate) philosophers sit at table with a bowl of spaghetti in the middle. Each needs two forks to eat, but only five forks are available, placed between their plates. (a) Construct a sequence of events in which the philosophers deadlock and die of hunger. (b) Modify the banker's algorithm as necessary, and use it to program a solution in Ada.

11.2 (a) The version of `banker` given in Section 11.3 is not very practical. Modify it to allow resources to be acquired and relinquished in varying quantities (not just one unit at a time).

(b) Modify `banker` to ensure that `notify_claim` is called before `acquire`, and that no attempt is made to relinquish a resource that has not previously been acquired.

11.3 Program an implementation of the banker's algorithm using conditional critical regions (see Section 9.6.1). Compare it with the version in Section 11.3.

11.4* Learn a monitor-based programming language such as Concurrent Pascal (Brinch Hansen 1977), Modula (Wirth 1977) or Pascal Plus (Bustard *et al.* 1988). Program an implementation of the banker's algorithm using monitors. Compare it with the version in Section 11.3.

CHAPTER TWELVE

The Object-oriented Programming Paradigm

The object-oriented programming paradigm is based on the concepts of *object* and *object class*. An object is a variable equipped with operations that have the exclusive right to access it. Object-oriented programming originated simply as a discipline for imperative programming. However, it is possible to construct programs entirely from objects and classes, and this leads to a distinctive style of programming.

In this chapter we briefly examine the object-oriented programming paradigm in general, and illustrate this with an overview of the prototypical object-oriented language, Smalltalk.

12.1 Object-oriented programming

A fundamental flaw of imperative programming is that global variables can potentially be accessed (and updated) by every part of the program. Large programs that lack any discipline for accessing global variables tend to be unmanageable. The reason for this is that no module that accesses a global variable can be developed and understood independently of other modules that also access that global variable.

This problem was recognized around 1970 by David Parnas, who advocated the discipline of *information hiding* as a remedy. His idea was to encapsulate each global variable in a module with a group of operations (such as procedures and functions) that alone have direct access to the variable. Other modules can access the variable only indirectly, by calling these operations. We now use the term *object* for such a module (or for the encapsulated variable itself). *Object-oriented programming* is a discipline that relies on objects to impose a modular structure on programs.

Object-oriented programming (of a sort) can be practiced even in simple imperative languages such as Pascal. However, the scope rules do not actually prevent improper access to an object from another module. Programmers must exercise self-discipline to avoid such improper access.

Object-oriented programming is more securely founded in an imperative language (such as Ada) that supports the concept of encapsulation. An object can be implemented by a package that exports operations accessing the variable, with the variable itself being a hidden component. The language's scope rules will then prevent any other module from accessing the hidden variable other than by calling the exported operations. Thus there is no reliance on the self-discipline of programmers who implement individual modules. The discipline is imposed by the program designer who decides in the first place how to decompose the program into modules.

Even in imperative languages that support encapsulation, the object-oriented discipline remains only an option, to be adopted or rejected by the program designer. A pure object-oriented language, on the other hand, removes this option by requiring every program to be constructed from objects. Such a language is Smalltalk, which is the topic of the next section.

What exactly is an object-oriented language? Smalltalk certainly is object-oriented, and Pascal certainly is not, but what about Ada? (See Exercise 12.1.) The following concepts are generally accepted as characteristic of object-oriented languages:

- *Objects* and *classes* are obviously fundamental concepts. An object class is a set of objects that share the same operations. (See Section 6.3 for a fuller discussion of objects and classes.)
- Objects (or at least references to objects) should be first-class values. Thus any operation may take an object as an argument, and may return an object as a result. Thus the concept of an object class is related to the concept of a type.
- *Inheritance* is also generally seen as a key concept. In this context, inheritance is the ability to organize object classes into a hierarchy of subclasses and superclasses, and for operations of a given class to be applicable to objects of a subclass. (See Section 7.6 for a fuller discussion of inheritance.)

The following concepts have also been advocated as characteristic of object-oriented languages, but remain controversial:

- *Dynamic typing* (see Section 2.5.1) is often advocated as a way to encourage flexibility. Software can be written to process objects of classes yet to be defined.
- *Dynamic binding* (see Section 4.3.3) is also often advocated to allow operations associated with a particular object to be selected at run-time, again in the interests of flexibility.

Example 7.19 illustrated the relationship of inheritance to type systems. The following example is similar, but uses the notation and terminology of object-oriented programming.

Example 12.1
Consider an object class Point. Each object of this class has a position on the *xy* plane; it might be equipped with operations to position it, to compute its *x* and *y* coordinates, to compute its distance from another point, to move it, and so on. First we give some examples (in Ada-like notation) of calling such operations.

Suppose that p is an object of class Point. To position point p at coordinates (5, –5), we might write the command:

```
p.place (5, -5);
```

To compute the *x* coordinate of point p, we might write the expression:

```
p.xcoord
```

and similarly for the *y* coordinate. The operations `xcoord` and `ycoord` are parameterless functions, each returning a distance.

To compute the distance of point p from another point q, we might write the expression:

```
p.distance (q)
```

The operation `distance` is a single-parameter function, also returning a distance. The parameter is itself an object of class `Point`. (Note that this notation is somewhat artificial, disguising the fact that p and q are interchangeable. This is quite revealing of the nature of object-oriented programming, in which *every* operation is associated with a particular object.)

To move point p by a distance of 2 units in the *x* direction and 3 units in the *y* direction, we might write the command:

```
p.move (2, 3);
```

Now let us sketch an implementation of the object class `Point`. First we must define a representation for each object of the class. One possibility is the following pair of hidden variables:

```
x, y : Float;
```

(So far we have assumed that each object contains a single hidden variable. However, there is no harm in allowing several variables; they could be viewed as components of a tuple.)

We can now define the operations along the following lines (again in Ada-like notation):

```
procedure place (xnew, ynew : in Float) is
begin
   x := xnew;  y := ynew;
end;

function xcoord return Float is
begin
   return x;
end;

function ycoord return Float is
   ...   -- similar

function distance (other : Point)
               return Float is
begin
   return sqrt ( (x - other.xcoord)**2
                + (y - other.ycoord)**2 );
end;
```

```
procedure move (xshift, yshift : in Float) is
begin
    x := x + xshift;  y := y + yshift;
end;
```

Here occurrences of x and y denote the hidden variables of the current object. For example, 'p.move(..., ...)' updates p.x and p.y.

We could now introduce an object class Circle, declaring it to be a subclass of Point. All objects of class Circle would, by default, inherit the operations place, xcoord, ycoord, distance, and move. This makes sense if we choose a distinguished point in each circle (its center, say) for the purposes of the distance operations. If c is an object of class Circle, then we can write:

c.xcoord	*-- yields the x coordinate of the center of* c
c.distance (p)	*-- yields the distance of the center of* c *from* p
p.distance (c)	*-- yields the distance of* p *from the center of* c
c.move (5, 0);	*-- move* c *by 5 units horizontally*

We could provide Circle with additional operations peculiar to circles, e.g.:

c.radius	*-- yields the radius of* c

The object class Circle would inherit from Point not only the exported operations but also the hidden variables x and y. Thus, to implement Circle we simply add those operations and hidden variables that are peculiar to circles. In this case we need only one additional hidden variable, r, to represent the circle's radius; then the definition of the operation radius is trivial.

We sometimes need to override the default inheritance. Suppose that the object class Point includes a parameterless operation draw, such that 'p.draw;' plots point p on a graphical device. By default, 'c.draw;' would plot only the *center* of circle c on the screen. To avoid this, the object class Circle should be provided with its own definition of draw.   □

12.2   Case study: Smalltalk

Smalltalk was developed at Xerox Palo Alto Research Center during the 1970s. The language evolved through several versions: Smalltalk-72, Smalltalk-76, and Smalltalk-80. (The differences between these versions will not concern us here.) Smalltalk was designed to be the single language of a self-contained interactive programming system, in which programs would be characterized by a high degree of modularity and dynamic extensibility. A typical Smalltalk processor allows the programmer to browse through the extensive library of class definitions, to create, edit, compile, and test new class definitions, and to construct programs from these components. Smalltalk provides good support for work in graphics and human–computer interaction.

Smalltalk is a very pure object-oriented language. *All* values in Smalltalk are objects. Even object classes are themselves objects, and control structures are just operations of appropriate classes. With these characteristics Smalltalk is very economical of concepts, but its syntax is idiosyncratic.

12.2.1 Objects and classes

Smalltalk has a rich variety of predefined object classes, many of which are named in Figure 12.1 (page 227).

Primitive objects are grouped into classes such as Boolean, Character, Integer, and Float. Literals such as 1 and 2 simply denote Integer objects. Likewise, false and true denote Boolean objects. (No primitive object is equipped with an updating operation, so these particular objects are constants.)

Integer is a typical primitive object class. Each Integer object is equipped with operations such as '+', '-', '*', '//' (integer division), 'squared', 'even', 'gcd:', etc. Suppose that m and n are Integer objects. The expression 'm even' requests m to test its own evenness; the result of this operation is a Boolean object, either false or true. The expression 'm gcd: n' requests m to return the greatest common divisor of its own value and that of n; the result is another Integer object. The expression 'm + n' requests m to return the sum of its own value and that of the Integer object n; the result is another Integer object. (This interpretation of ordinary-looking expressions like 'm + n' is unusual, but their results are what we would expect.)

These examples illustrate Smalltalk's several notations for requesting an operation to be performed. In each case the subexpression E_0 is evaluated to determine the *receiver* object, i.e., the object requested to perform the named operation. Any other subexpressions are evaluated to determine the arguments.

- '$E_0\ I$' requests the receiver object to perform the operation named I, with no arguments. Further examples are 'n squared' and 'n asFloat'.
- '$E_0 \otimes E_1$', where $\otimes$ is an operator symbol, requests the receiver object to perform the operation named $\otimes$, with the object yielded by E_1 as argument. Further examples are 'n * 4' and 'm >= n'.
- '$E_0\ I_1:\ E_1\ ...\ I_n:\ E_n$' requests the receiver object to perform the operation named '$I_1:\ ...I_n:$', with the objects yielded by $E_1, ..., E_n$ as arguments. (Note that the operation name is distributed between the subexpressions, the colons marking the break points.) A further example is 'm between: 1 and: n-1', where the operation name is 'between: and:'.

Composite objects are grouped into classes such as Bag, Set, Dictionary, Interval, LinkedList, Array, and String. Each of these classes provides a variety of operations, including all the ones we would expect.

Array is a fairly typical composite object class. Each Array object is equipped with operations such as 'at:' and 'at: put:'. Suppose that a is an Array object. The expression 'a at: n' requests a to return the object that is its nth component, and 'a at: n put: x' requests a to update its nth component to be the object x. A form of aggregate is provided to compose an Array object from its components, e.g.:

```
monthsize <- #(31 28 31 30 31 30 31 31 30 31 30 31).
...
monthsize at: 2 put: 29
```

Smalltalk is dynamically typed. Every object has a tag that identifies its class. A primitive operation (such as '+') will check an argument object's tag to ensure that its class is acceptable. Such checks are effectively dynamic type checks. The programmer can also check the class of an object explicitly.

One consequence of dynamic typing is that composite objects can be heterogeneous. For example, in a graphics program, a picture might be represented by a Set object whose components are (say) points, circles, and lines. Furthermore, we can later enrich the picture with components of different classes, such as rectangles, character strings, etc., *that were not even envisaged when the picture object was created*. Such a high degree of flexibility is not possible in a statically typed language. Some advocates of object-oriented programming argue that this flexibility more than compensates for the insecurity of dynamic typing.

12.2.2   Variables

Variables in a Smalltalk program always contain references to objects. Since Smalltalk is dynamically typed, a given variable can refer to objects of any class.

Smalltalk is an expression-oriented language. Evaluating an expression not only yields a result but also may produce side effects. Sometimes an expression is evaluated for its side effects only, its result being discarded. Expressions may be sequenced by '$E_1 . E_2$'; here E_1 is evaluated for its side effects only, and then E_2 is evaluated.

The result of an expression is always a *reference* to an object. It follows that the arguments passed to an operation, and the result returned by the operation, are also references to objects. (Elsewhere in this section, for the sake of brevity, we talk of arguments and results being objects, but really they are references to objects.)

There is an assignment expression of the form '$V <- E$'. Its result is the reference yielded by E. Its side effect is that the variable V is made to refer to the same object as E. For example:

```
n <- n - m.
m <- n
```

The latter assignment makes m and n (temporarily) refer to the same object. This kind of sharing is harmless for primitive objects, but dangerous for composite objects equipped with selective updating operations. Suppose that a refers to an Array object. Then:

```
b <- a.
a at: i put: x
```

makes b refer to the same Array object, and then updates one component of the shared object.

12.2.3 Control

Smalltalk has no built-in control structures, but conditional and iterative control structures are embedded within the object framework.

The key concept is the so-called *block*. Smalltalk blocks are in fact function abstractions. Here is an example of a parameterless block:

```
counter <- [ n <- n + 1 ]
```

This assigns a block to `counter`; the block body is not (yet) evaluated. If we subsequently call this block by 'counter value', however, the block body 'n <- n + 1' is evaluated, incrementing the variable n and also yielding the incremented value. (This particular block will yield a different result every time it is called.)

Blocks are objects of the class `BlockContext`, which provides the operation `value` for calling a block. Blocks with parameters are included. The following block has formal parameter i and body 'i + 1', i.e., it is the familiar successor function:

```
[ :i | i + 1 ]
```

The class `Boolean` provides an operation named 'ifTrue: ifFalse:', with two arguments that are parameterless blocks. When received by the object `true`, this operation calls (only) the first block; when received by `false`, it calls (only) the second block. For example:

```
n > 0 ifTrue: [ m / n ] ifFalse: [ 0 ]
```

Here 'm / n' will be evaluated only if the block enclosing it is called by the 'ifTrue: ifFalse:' operation, i.e., only if the result of 'n > 0' is `true`.

The class `BlockContext` provides an operation named 'whileTrue:', with an argument that is a parameterless block. The receiver object itself must be a parameterless block, one that will yield a `Boolean` result when called. The receiver object first calls *itself*; if the result is `true`, it calls the other block and then repeats the whole process; if the result is `false`, it terminates. For example:

```
m <- 0.
[ n > 0 ] whileTrue: [ n <- n // 2. m <- m + 1 ]
```

Definite iteration is provided by the operation 'do:'. Its receiver must be a composite object, and its argument a one-parameter block. For each component of the composite object, the block is called with that component as argument. For example:

```
total <- 0.
monthsize do: [ :size | total <- total + size ]
```

sums the (integer) components of the array object `monthsize`. The 'do:' operation can be used to traverse bags, sets, dictionaries, intervals, lists, and strings, as well as arrays.

12.2.4   Class definitions

An object class is defined by the following:

- the name of the class
- the name of its superclass
- the names of any hidden variables – each object of the class will have its own group of hidden variables, which will contain that object's current value
- the names and definitions of all operations associated with the class.

The Smalltalk processor handles these portions of a class definition separately; they are not combined into a single text as in conventional programming languages.

Example 12.2
We give here a Smalltalk definition of the object class `Point` illustrated in Example 12.1.

We choose to represent each point by its *x* and *y* coordinates. Therefore we introduce two hidden variables, x and y. Although we cannot declare this explicitly, our intention is that x and y will each contain a distance.

We define the various operations as follows:

```
placeat: xnew and: ynew
    x <- xnew.  y <- ynew

xcoord
    ^ x

ycoord
    ^ y

moveby: xshift and: yshift
    x <- x + xshift.  y <- y + yshift

distance: other
    ^ ( (x - other xcoord) squared
       + (y - other ycoord) squared ) sqrt

draw
```
draw a point with coordinates x *and* y *on the screen*

In the definition of each operation, x and y denote the hidden variables of the receiver object.

The body of the xcoord operation is '^ x'. This indicates simply that the value contained in x is to be returned as the result of the operation. The body of the distance operation is more complicated, but again the expression after '^' determines the result of the operation. The body of the 'placeat: and:' operation does not explicitly determine its result; by default, the result is a reference to the receiver object.   □

12.2.5   Inheritance

In Smalltalk, all object classes are arranged in a hierarchy of subclasses and superclasses. Any object of class *c* is also an object of every superclass of *c*. The hierarchy of predefined classes is illustrated in Figure 12.1.

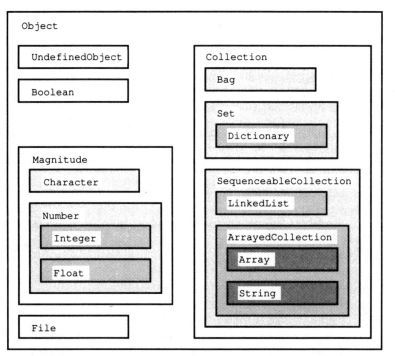

Figure 12.1 Hierarchy of classes in Smalltalk (simplified).

The operations associated with a class are automatically inherited by its subclasses. Note that *all* object classes are subclasses of Object, and therefore inherit the operations of that class.

In defining a new object class, the programmer specifies its (immediate) superclass, and thus places it in the hierarchy. By default, Object is taken as the superclass; thus the superclass of Point as defined in Example 12.2 is Object.

Example 12.3
We give here a Smalltalk definition of the object class Circle illustrated in Example 12.1. We define Circle to be a subclass of Point, which was defined in Example 12.2. Circle objects will therefore, by default, inherit the Point operations. If c is a Circle object and p is a Point object, then we can write:

```
c xcoord
c distance: p
p distance: c
c moveby: 5 and: 0
```

In addition, we want an operation to return the radius of `c`:

```
c radius
```

and one to initialize a circle:

```
c placeat: 3 and: 4 radius: 5
```

`Circle` will inherit the hidden variables `x` and `y` from `Point`. In addition we will need an hidden variable `r` to represent the circle's radius.

The `Circle` operations can now be defined like this:

```
placeat: xnew and: ynew radius: rnew
    x <- xnew.   y <- ynew.   r <- rnew

radius
    ^ r

draw
```
draw on the screen a circle with radius r and center at coordinates x, y

Note that '`c draw`' will perform the operation provided by `Circle`, *not* the one provided by `Point`.   □

Although each operation associated with a class is automatically inherited by all subclasses, any subclass may override this by defining an operation with the same name. If an object of class *c* is requested to perform an operation named *o*, then the class *c*, its superclass, its superclass's superclass, etc., are examined in turn until an operation named *o* is found. That operation is then performed. In Examples 12.2 and 12.3, if the operation named `draw` is requested, the effect will depend on whether the receiver is a `Point` object or a `Circle` object.

Because Smalltalk is dynamically typed, the class of the receiver object is not known until run-time, so the actual operation performed is not determined until run-time. Consequently, operation names are dynamically bound in Smalltalk. (On the other hand, variables and formal parameters of blocks are statically bound!)

12.3   Further reading

For criticisms of the undisciplined use of global variables in imperative programming, see Parnas (1972) and Wulf and Shaw (1973).

The prototypical object-oriented language was Simula-67, described in Dahl *et al.* (1970). Simula-67 introduced the concepts of objects, classes, and inheritance. However, Simula-67 lacked information hiding, so there was nothing to protect an object from unauthorized access other than programmers' self-discipline.

An overview of object-oriented programming, including its relationship to various programming languages, has been given by Cox (1986). For an account of object-oriented programming as a discipline for programming in Ada, see Booch (1987).

For a very full account of Smalltalk-80, including an overview, programming examples, descriptions of all predefined classes, and implementation details, see Goldberg and Robson (1983).

The new object-oriented language Eiffel suggests that the benefits of object-oriented programming can be achieved within a language that is statically typed and allows only a severely restricted form of dynamic binding. An overview of Eiffel may be found in Meyer (1989), and a detailed account in Meyer (1988).

Exercises 12

12.1* Ada is sometimes claimed to be an object-oriented language. Using the criteria listed in Section 12.1, formulate arguments both for and against this claim.

12.2 In Pascal, Ada, and some other languages, the types form a hierarchy not unlike the hierarchy of Smalltalk object classes. Choose one such language, and diagram its type hierarchy as in Figure 12.1. Apart from the specific choice of types in your language, in what respects is its type hierarchy similar to, and different from, Smalltalk's class hierarchy?

12.3 Refer to Examples 12.2 and 12.3. (a) Define object classes for other useful geometric objects, such as straight lines, rectangles, etc., placing them in an appropriate hierarchy. Each of these object classes must provide an operation draw. (b) Define an object class Picture, where each object is a set of geometric objects. Include an operation that draws the whole picture, by drawing all of its component objects.

12.4* Design, in Smalltalk or any suitable language, an object class Relation. Each object in this class should represent a binary relation. (See Section 14.1 for a discussion of relations.)

CHAPTER THIRTEEN

The Functional Programming Paradigm

We can often think of a program as implementing a mapping. The program takes some input values and maps them to output values. In imperative programming this mapping is achieved indirectly, by commands that read input values, manipulate them, and write output values. The commands of a program influence one another by means of variables held in storage. The relationship between two given commands can be completely understood only with reference to *all* the variables that they both access, and with reference to all the other commands that access these same variables. Unless the program is written with care and discipline, these relationships between commands can be very complicated and hard to understand.

In functional programming the mapping of input values to output values is achieved more directly. The program *is* a function (or a group of functions), typically composed from simpler functions. The relationships between functions are very simple: one function can call another, or the result of one function can be used as an argument to another function. Variables, commands, and side effects are excluded; instead programs are written entirely within the language of expressions, functions and declarations. This might sound like a virtuoso performance designed to show off the programmer's skill, on a par with riding a bicycle with no hands. But in functional programming the lack of storage is compensated by extensive exploitation of other powerful concepts, notably *higher-order functions* and *lazy evaluation*.

13.1 Functional programming

Functional programming is characterized by the use of expressions and functions; imperative programming by the use of variables, commands, and procedures. Of course, imperative languages also have expressions and functions, but often this part of the language is impoverished.

Example 13.1
Consider some Pascal code for manipulating complex numbers:

```
type Complex = record re, im : Real end;
var  i, w, y, z : Complex;

procedure add (c1, c2 : Complex;
                  var sum : Complex);
   begin
   sum.re := c1.re + c2.re;
   sum.im := c1.im + c2.im
   end;
...
i.re := 0.0;  i.im := 1.0;
add (w, y, z);
add (z, i, z)
```

Pascal lacks record constants, record aggregates, and functions with record results, so we have to make extensive use of assignment commands and procedures to compensate.

Contrast this with Ada code for the same purpose:

```
type Complex is
        record re, im : Float; end record;

i : constant Complex := (re => 0.0, im => 1.0);
w, y, z : Complex;

function "+" (c1, c2 : Complex) return Complex is
begin
   return (re => c1.re + c2.re,
           im => c1.im + c2.im);
end;
...
z := w + y + i;
```

With a richer sublanguage of expressions, Ada allows us to achieve the same effect much more conveniently. □

The richer the expression sublanguage, the less we need to resort to commands and variables. (See also Example 10.1.) However, a purely functional language excludes commands and variables altogether. But why be dogmatic about excluding them? Why not combine the expression part of the best functional language with the command part of a good imperative language, to design a language better than either? Unfortunately, some of the most powerful functional features – notably lazy evaluation – fit badly with side effects. Attempting to provide them both in the same language leads to unmanageable complexity and error-prone programming. We do not know how to achieve an elegant synthesis of the imperative and functional paradigms. In practice, languages either adopt limited functional features and retain variables (such as ML) or banish variables entirely (such as Miranda).

Example 13.2
As an illustration of the functional programming paradigm, let us translate an

imperative version of the factorial function, in Pascal, into a functional version, in ML. The Pascal version is:

```
function factorial (n : Integer) : Integer;
  var f : Integer;
  begin
  f := 1;
  while n > 0 do
    begin
    f := f * n;
    n := n - 1
    end;
  factorial := f
  end
```

The functional equivalent of iteration is recursion: we translate the loop above into a function that recurses once for each loop iteration. The local variables, which take different values on each iteration, correspond naturally to parameters that take different values on each call. Thus we translate the loop into the following ML function, which returns the computed factorial as its result:

```
fun factorialloop (n, f) =
        if n > 0
        then factorialloop (n - 1, f * n)
        else f
```

The factorial function itself simply calls loop with an 'initial' value of 1 for f:

```
fun factorial (n) = factorialloop (n, 1)
```

Translation between paradigms is not usually so straightforward. Global variables, for example, cannot simply be replaced by local parameters. Neither is there any implication that the translation is a 'good' functional program, or that it is 'better' than the original Pascal. In fact, the function could better be written directly in the functional style:

```
fun factorial (n) =
        if n > 0
        then n * factorial (n - 1)
        else 1
```

What the example does illustrate is that doing without local variables and loops poses no fundamental problems for the functional programmer.   □

We now examine some of the concepts that are especially useful in functional programming languages.

13.1.1 Pattern matching

Pattern matching is a common concept in modern functional languages. We have touched on it briefly, in the context of *case* expressions in ML (see Section 2.6.4). However, pattern matching is more pervasive than that. In particular, it can be exploited in function definitions.

Example 13.3
Consider the following:

```
datatype shape =
           point
         | circle of real           (* radius *)
         | box of (real * real)     (* width, height *)
fun area (point)     = 0.0
  | area (circle r) = pi * sqr (r)
  | area (box(w,h)) = w * h
```

Here the type Shape is the disjoint union Unit + Real + (Real × Real), with tags *point*, *circle*, and *box*. The function `area` is of type Shape → Real, and is defined by three equations. The first equation is applicable only if the argument is *point* () and thus matches the pattern 'point'; in that case the function immediately returns the result 0.0. The second equation is applicable only if the argument is a value such as *circle* 5.0 and thus matches the pattern 'circle r'; in that case the identifier r is bound to the value 5.0, for the purpose of evaluating the right-hand-side expression 'pi * sqr (r)'. The third equation is applicable only if the argument is a value such as *box* (2.0, 3.0) and thus matches the pattern 'box (w, h) '; in that case the identifiers w and h are bound to the values 2.0 and 3.0, respectively, for the purpose of evaluating the right-hand-side expression 'w * h'. □

In general, a function may be defined by several equations, each with a different left-hand side. Each equation's left-hand side contains a *pattern* in its formal parameter position. The pattern must match the function's argument for the equation to be applied. A pattern looks just like an expression, but each free identifier in the pattern is a *binding* occurrence. The pattern *matches* an argument if these identifiers can be given values making the pattern and the argument equal; whereupon these identifiers are bound to these values for the purpose of evaluating the right-hand side of the equation.

Defining functions by several equations in this way is a popular idiom, because it is concise, clear, and recalls familiar mathematical notation. Moreover, the equations can (with care) be understood independently as true statements about the function, and this facilitates reasoning about the function.

13.1.2 Values and types

By and large, functional languages provide similar types to other languages: truth-values, integers, strings, records, disjoint unions, and so on. But since selective updating is ruled out, composite values must be manipulated differently. Where an imperative programmer would update a single component of a composite variable, a functional programmer must make a copy of a composite value that differs from the original in a single component.

Example 13.4
Consider the type of integer binary trees, defined in ML as follows:

```
datatype tree =  null
              | node of (tree * int * tree)
```

An imperative programmer would define a procedure that inserts a new integer into a given tree by selective updating. A functional programmer must define an insertion function that returns a new tree containing the new integer, as well as all the integers in the original tree. The original tree itself remains unmodified. The following function does this, and has type Integer × Tree → Tree:

```
fun insert (newitem, null) =
        node (null, newitem, null)
  | insert (newitem, node(left,olditem,right)) =
        if newitem <= olditem
        then node (insert (newitem, left),
                     olditem,
                     right)
        else node (left,
                     olditem,
                     insert (newitem, right))
```

At first sight, this function copies an entire tree to make a small modification, which would be horrendously inefficient. But if we study insert closely, we see that only the nodes lying on a path from the root of the tree to the point of insertion are copied; the remaining nodes are *shared* between the old and new trees. Figure 13.1 illustrates the effect of inserting 8 into a tree containing the integers 1, 2, 3, 4, 5, 6, 7, and 9.

Thus the cost of insertion is directly proportional to the depth at which insertion occurs. (Insertion by selective updating would be faster, but its cost would also be directly proportional to the insertion depth.)   □

As Figure 13.1 implies, the actual representation of trees (and other recursive types) in a functional language is similar to the linked representation that might be chosen by an imperative programmer. (An important difference is that the pointers would be manipulated explicitly by the imperative programmer, but are hidden from the functional programmer.) An expression like 'node (...)' is actually an allocator, creating a heap object.

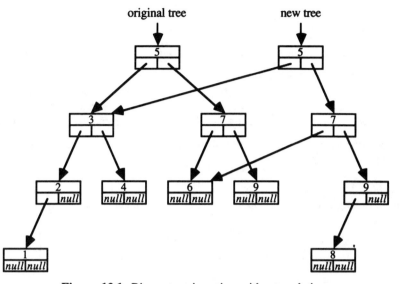

Figure 13.1 Binary tree insertion without updating.

The style of programming illustrated by Example 13.4 results in rapid allocation of heap storage. How can it be reclaimed? An explicit deallocator would clearly have a side effect (and might leave dangling references), and so is unsuitable for a functional language. Instead the implementation must deallocate heap objects automatically when they become inaccessible. Thus the programmer is freed from the concerns of storage management. Moreover, sharing cannot affect the behavior of a functional program (as it would in an imperative program – see Section 3.4.2). The functional programmer can therefore ignore sharing, and can think of the values of type tree as trees rather than directed graphs – a useful simplification.

The example shows that recursive values such as lists and trees can be manipulated with reasonable efficiency in a functional language. The same is not true of arrays. Two trees that differ in a single component can share much of their structure, but two arrays that differ in a single component cannot. Therefore any function that returns a modified array must copy it in its entirety. This is prohibitively expensive if the function modifies a single component. For this reason, few functional languages support arrays; and those few try to compensate by providing array operations that modify many components at once.

Lists are the most ubiquitous composite values in functional programs. ML's parameterized list type is defined as follows:

datatype τ list = nil | cons **of** (τ * τ list)

ML provides convenient notation for expressions that construct lists:

$$x :: xs \quad\; = \text{cons } (x, xs)$$
$$[a, ..., z] = a :: ... :: z :: \text{nil}$$

A variety of useful functions on lists are predefined, such as:

`hd`	:	$\text{List}(\tau) \to \tau$	(first element of a list)
`tl`	:	$\text{List}(\tau) \to \text{List}(\tau)$	(remaining elements of a list)
`length`	:	$\text{List}(\tau) \to \text{Integer}$	(length of a list)
`@`	:	$\text{List}(\tau) \times \text{List}(\tau) \to \text{List}(\tau)$	(concatenation of two lists)

We can also easily define other useful functions on lists, as the following example illustrates.

Example 13.5

The following ML functions return the sum and product, respectively, of a list of integers:

```
fun sum (nil)        = 0
  | sum (n::ns)      = n + sum (ns)

and product (nil)    = 1
  | product (n::ns) = n * product (ns)
```

The following ML operator returns the list of integers m through n:

```
fun op through (m, n) =
            if m > n
            then nil
            else m :: (m+1 through n)
```

(The keyword **op** in the function definition specifies that `through` will be a binary operator, i.e., a function identifier that will be written between its two actual parameters in a function call.)

We can use the above functions to define the factorial function in an unusual way:

```
fun factorial (n) = product (1 through n)
```

$\square$

As illustrated by Example 13.5, iteration is often expressed by applying functions to lists. In some functional languages functions like `sum`, `product`, and `through` are predefined, thus encouraging this style of programming.

Iteration over lists is so important that several languages (such as Miranda, but not ML) provide special notation for it – the *list comprehension*. This is derived from conventional mathematical set notation.

If `ints` is a list of integers, we can extract a list of even integers from `ints` by writing:

$$[\text{n} \mid \text{n} \mathrel{<-} \text{ints}; \text{n mod 2} = 0] \tag{13.1}$$

(Compare with the mathematical set notation $\{n \mid n \in ints; n \bmod 2 = 0\}$.) Note that the occurrence of n to the left of the symbol '<-' is a binding occurrence, its scope being the list comprehension itself. Similarly, we can construct a list of integers, each one greater than the corresponding integer in ints, by writing:

$$[\text{n+1} \mid \text{n} \; \text{<-} \; \text{ints}] \qquad (13.2)$$

(Compare with the mathematical set notation $\{n+1 \mid n \in ints\}$.) If ints is the list [1, 9, 8, 8, 1, 0], then (13.1) will yield the list [8, 8, 0], and (13.2) will yield the list [2, 10, 9, 9, 2, 1].

Note that, despite the analogy with set notation, we are talking about *lists*. There is no suggestion that duplicate components are removed, or that the order of components is unimportant. A list comprehension is just convenient notation for iteration over a list.

Example 13.6

Imagine that ML is extended with list comprehensions. Then the following function returns the sum of the squares of the first n integers:

```
fun sumsq (n) = sum [i * i | i <- 1 through n]
```

We could program the Quicksort algorithm as follows:

```
fun sort (nil) =
        nil
  | sort (n::ns) =
        sort [i | i <- ns; i < n]
        @ [n]
        @ sort [i | i <- ns; i >= n]
```

(A version of Quicksort in Standard ML will be given in Section 15.1.2.) □

13.1.3 Higher-order functions

Functional languages treat functions as first-class values: they can be passed as parameters, returned as function results, built into composite values, and so on. This has a major impact on programming style.

A function whose parameters and result are all nonfunctional is called a *first-order* function. A function that has a functional parameter or result is called a *higher-order* function. We frequently exploit higher-order functions to make code reusable, by abstracting over those parts of it that are specific to a particular application. More radically, functions can be used to represent data in novel ways.

Allowing a function to return another function as its result opens up many interesting possibilities, which are heavily exploited in functional programming. The simplest way to generate a new function is by composing two existing functions; this was illustrated in Example 7.8.

Let us now study some more examples.

Example 13.7

Consider the following function that returns the nth power of the real number b. (We assume for simplicity that n is nonnegative.)

```
fun power (n, b) =
        if n = 0
        then 1.0
        else b * power (n-1, b)
```

The type of `power` is Integer × Real → Real. In other words, `power` is a function that, when applied to a pair consisting of an integer and a real number, will return a real number. For example, 'power (2, x)' returns the square of x.

Now consider the following closely related function:

```
fun powerC (n) (b) =
        if n = 0
        then 1.0
        else b * powerC (n-1) (b)
```

The type of `powerC` is Integer → (Real → Real). In other words, `powerC` is a function that, when applied to an integer *n*, will return another function; the latter is a function that, when applied to a real number, will return the *n*th power of that real number. For example, 'powerC (2) (x)' returns the square of x.

The advantage of `powerC` is that we can call it with only one argument. For example:

```
val sqr  = powerC (2)
and cube = powerC (3)
```

Here both `sqr` and `cube` are functions of type Real → Real.   □

The function `powerC` of Example 13.7 is called a *curried* version of `power` (after the logician Haskell Curry, who studied such functions). The technique of calling a curried function with fewer than the maximum number of arguments is called *partial application*.

The following ML predefined function:

$$\text{filter} : (\tau \rightarrow \text{Truth-Value}) \rightarrow (\text{List}(\tau) \rightarrow \text{List}(\tau))$$

is a higher-order function. When applied to a function *f*, it yields a new function that filters the components of a given list; only those components *x* for which *f(x)* yields *true* are retained in the result list. Thus 'filter (odd)' yields a function, of type List(Integer) → List(Integer), that maps the list [2, 3, 5, 7] to the list [3, 5, 7].

The following ML predefined function:

$$\text{map} : (\sigma \rightarrow \tau) \rightarrow (\text{List}(\sigma) \rightarrow \text{List}(\tau))$$

is also higher-order. When applied to a function *f*, it yields a new function that applies *f* separately to each component of a given list. Thus 'map (sqr)' yields a function, of type List(Integer) → List(Integer), that maps the list [2, 3, 5, 7] to the list [4, 9, 25, 49]; and 'map (odd)' is a function, of type List(Integer) → List(Truth-Value), that maps the list [2, 3, 5, 7] to the list [*false, true, true, true*].

Example 13.8
Let us parameterize the sorting function of Example 13.6 with respect to the item comparison function:

```
fun generic_sort (precedes) =
    let
        fun sort (nil) =
                nil
          | sort (x::xs) =
                sort [i | i <- xs;
                        precedes (i, x)]
                @ [x]
                @ sort [i | i <- xs;
                        not (precedes (i, x))]
    in
        sort
    end
```

This function is of type $(\tau \times \tau \rightarrow \text{Truth-Value}) \rightarrow (\text{List}(\tau) \rightarrow \text{List}(\tau))$. It is not itself a sorting function. It is a generic function that, when applied to an appropriate comparison function, generates a specific sorting function. Here are two examples:

```
val ascending_int_sort  = generic_sort (op <)
and descending_int_sort = generic_sort (op >)
```

Each of the functions generated here is of type $\text{List}(\text{Integer}) \rightarrow \text{List}(\text{Integer})$, and sorts a list of integers. (Recall that the operators '<' and '>' denote functions, each of type Integer $\times$ Integer $\rightarrow$ Truth-Value.)

Here is a more complicated example, where the values to be sorted are tuples, and the comparison function is explicitly programmed:

```
type date = int * int * int;

fun before ((y1,m1,d1): date, (y2,m2,d2): date) =
            if y1 <> y2 then y1 < y2
            else if m1 <> m2 then m1 < m2
            else d1 < d2;

val date_sort = generic_sort (before)
```

In the last example, the argument to generic_sort is a function, of type Date $\times$ Date $\rightarrow$ Truth-Value, that tests whether the first date is earlier than the second. (Note, incidentally, that this function is defined by pattern matching, on triples of type Date.) The result of generic_sort is therefore a function, of type $\text{List}(\text{Date}) \rightarrow \text{List}(\text{Date})$, that sorts a list of dates. □

Example 13.9
The functions sum and product of Example 13.5 are structurally very similar. They differ only in the binary operator applied to components of a nonempty list, and in the value to which an empty list is mapped. We can define a function, reduce, that

generates these and many similar functions on lists:

```
fun reduce (binaryop, unity) =
        let
            fun f (nil)    = unity
              | f (x::xs) = binaryop (x, f (xs))
        in
            f
        end
```

This function is of type $(\tau \times \sigma \to \sigma) \times \sigma \to (\text{List}(\tau) \to \sigma)$.

We can now use `reduce` to generate our `sum` and `product` functions:

```
val sum     = reduce (op +, 0)
and product = reduce (op *, 1)
```

We can also generate many similar functions, such as the following function that concatenates a list of strings:

```
val implode = reduce (op ^, "")
```

where '`^`' is the string concatenation operator.   □

As these examples illustrate, when we abstract over functions we very often also want to abstract over types. There is little advantage in being able to reuse a sorting function to sort lists of integers into a variety of different orders; there is much advantage in reusing it to sort many different types of list. Nearly every functional language therefore has a polymorphic type system, or is dynamically typed.

The previous examples share the common characteristic that the higher-order functions could, in principle, be removed by macroexpansion at compile-time. Although functions are returned as results, the number of different function values generated is predictable. But functions can also be used much more dynamically, to represent data rather than algorithms.

Example 13.10

Let us study an unusual way of representing lists by functions.

First consider the functions '`@`' (list concatenation) and `rev` (list reversal).

```
fun op @ (nil, ys)    = ys
  | op @ (x::xs, ys) = x :: (xs @ ys)
and rev (nil)    = nil
  | rev (x::xs) = rev (xs) @ [x]
```

The '`@`' function clearly recurses to a depth equal to the length of its first argument, so the cost of concatenating '`rev (xs)`' and '`[x]`' is proportional to the length of `xs`. Since `rev` itself recurses to a depth equal to the length of its argument, the cost of reversing a list of length n is proportional to n^2.

In fact it is possible to reverse a list in linear time, i.e., time proportional to n. One way is to represent lists by functions. We represent the list `xs` by the following function:

```
fn zs => xs @ zs
```

i.e., the function of a list `zs` that prefixes `xs` to `zs`. We can recover `xs` from this function simply by applying it to the empty list.

Now consider the composition of two such functions:

$$
\begin{aligned}
&\texttt{(fn zs => xs @ zs) o (fn zs => ys @ zs)} \\
={}&\texttt{fn zs => xs @ (ys @ zs)} \\
={}&\texttt{fn zs => (xs @ ys) @ zs}
\end{aligned}
$$

which is another function in the same form, representing the list '`xs @ ys`'. So composing two such functions models concatenation – but more cheaply, since function composition takes constant time.

We can define a linear-time reversal function that returns its result represented by a function of this form:

```
fun revF (nil) =
         id      (* the identity function represents the empty list *)
  | revF (x::xs) =
         revF (xs) o (fn ys => x :: ys)
               (* this represents rev (xs) @ [x] *)
```

Finally, we can derive an ordinary list simply by applying the result to the empty list:

```
fun rev (xs) = revF (xs) (nil)
```

□

Example 13.11

A weightier example is the representation of 'exact' real numbers by functions. Various representations have been proposed for exact real numbers, but all must permit the calculation of an approximation to any desired precision. It is therefore natural to represent an exact real number by a function from the desired precision to a suitable approximation. The approximation can be represented by an arbitrary-precision rational number, and the desired precision can conveniently be represented by an integer p on a logarithmic scale. Thus, if f is the function representing the real number r, we guarantee that $| f(p) - r | \le 2^{-p}$. For example, the real number $\pi = 3.14159\ldots$ might be represented by the function $\{\ldots, 1 \mapsto 3, 2 \mapsto 6/2, 3 \mapsto 13/4, 4 \mapsto 25/8, \ldots\}$.

It is not difficult to define the arithmetic operations in terms of this representation. For example, to compute a sum accurate to within 2^{-p}, we must compute the summands to within $2^{-(p+1)}$:

```
fun realsum (f1, f2) =
            fn p => rationalsum (f1 (p+1), f2 (p+1))
```

Of course, this arithmetic on exact real numbers is far slower than floating-point arithmetic, but the answers are guaranteed to be accurate. The extra cost is worthwhile for ill-conditioned problems, which cannot be solved at all using floating point.   □

13.1.4 Lazy evaluation

We have already encountered the concept of lazy evaluation, in Section 5.3. It is a parameter mechanism whereby an argument to a function is evaluated at its first use, rather than at the moment when the function is activated. If the argument is never used, it is never evaluated, with a possible saving in computer time. Thus we can pass an unevaluated expression into a function.

The usefulness of lazy evaluation is greatly increased if we also allow unevaluated expressions as components of composite values. Such expressions may eventually be evaluated, but only if and when they are selected from the composite values. This extension implies that functions not only can receive unevaluated arguments, but also can return partially unevaluated results.

A remarkable consequence is that we can build *infinite* composite values. In particular, we can build infinite lists, whose tails remain unevaluated. These are called *lazy lists*.

Standard ML uses eager evaluation. However, the dialect Lazy ML does support lazy evaluation. In the examples of this subsection, we shall assume the semantics of Lazy ML in order to illustrate the implications of lazy evaluation.

Example 13.12
Consider the following Lazy ML function:

```
fun from (n) = n :: from (n+1)
```

which generates a list of all integers not less than n. Of course, this list is infinite (if we ignore the computer's limited range of integers). With eager evaluation, this function would never terminate. But with lazy evaluation, the recursive call will be built into the list, and will be evaluated only if and when the tail of the list is selected.

The following function returns the first prime in a given (nonempty) list of integers:

```
fun firstprime (n::ns) =
        if prime (n)
        then n
        else firstprime (ns)
```

Composing these, the following expression computes the first prime not less than m:

```
firstprime (from (m))
```

In principle, this expression first computes an infinite list of integers, and then tests the first few integers in this list until it finds a prime. In practice, the list always remains partially evaluated. Only when `firstprime` selects the tail of the list does a little more evaluation of the list take place.   □

This example illustrates that the infinity of a lazy list is only potential. A lazy list is an active object that is capable of computing as many of its own components as are required.

A major benefit of lazy evaluation is that it supports a new kind of modularity: the separation of *control* from *calculation*. The idea is to break an iterative or recursive computation into a pure calculation part, which computes all the necessary values and builds them into a composite value (such as a lazy list), and another part that traverses all or part of this composite value, thus determining the flow of control. Very often the calculation can be expressed more simply once control information is removed. Often the same calculation part can be reused with different control parts, or a control part can be reused with different calculation parts. (See also Exercise 13.10.)

Example 13.13
Consider the problem of computing square roots by the Newton–Raphson method. This can naturally be decomposed into a calculation part that computes approximations, and a control part that decides when the process has converged sufficiently. Arbitrarily many approximations can be computed, so it is natural to build them into a lazy list. The following Lazy ML function returns a list of converging approximations for the square root of x:

```
fun approxsqrts (x) =
        let
           fun from (approx) =
                   approx :: from (0.5
                      * (approx + x/approx))
        in
           from (1.0)
        end
```

The following is a control function that interprets convergence as a sufficiently small absolute difference between successive approximations:

```
fun absolute (eps) (approx1::approx2::approxs) =
        if abs (approx1-approx2) <= eps
        then approx2
        else absolute (eps) (approx2::approxs)
```

Now we can compose the square root function as follows:

```
val sqrt = absolute (0.0001) o approxsqrts
```

We could reuse the same list of approximations with a different control function. For example, we could use relative difference rather than absolute difference to test for convergence; or we could choose the fourth approximation regardless; or we could plot all the approximations on a graph; or we could format them for debugging. (See also Exercise 13.11.)

Conversely, we could reuse any one of these control functions with any numerical algorithm that generates a sequence of converging approximations. □

The same idea can be exploited in search algorithms. The search space is calculated and built into a composite value such as a tree, and the search strategy is then expressed as a function on this tree. When both the computation of the search space and the search strategy are complex, separating the two can be a significant simplification. The explicit representation of the search space as a tree also makes it easy to add functions that manipulate the search space. For example, we could limit the search to a fixed depth by discarding deeper branches; or we could order branches so that regions of the search space in which the solution is likely to lie are explored first.

Lazy evaluation does not fit well into an imperative language. With lazy evaluation, the programmer has little control over evaluation order. A function that builds a composite value has no influence on the order in which its components are evaluated – this is determined by the computation that *uses* the composite value. Without control over evaluation order, side effects can have very surprising consequences.

Example 13.14

Imagine a version of ML with both lazy evaluation and variables. The following function would attach the numbers 1, 2, ... to the components of a given list:

```
fun numbered (xs) =
        let
            val n = ref 0;
            fun number (x) =
                        (n := !n + 1; (!n, x))
        in [number x | x <- xs]
        end
```

We might expect that this function, when applied to the list [a, b, c], would return [(1, a), (2, b), (3, c)]. This assumes that the list components are evaluated from left to right. But with lazy evaluation, the list components could be evaluated in any order, depending on the order in which they are subsequently used; so the components could be numbered in any way.   □

Example 13.15

Suppose that the function print prints its argument as a side effect, but otherwise acts like the identity function. Consider the following function, which we might expect to print all the components of a given list:

```
fun printall (xs) = [print (x) | x <- xs]
```

Since the calls of print are built into a lazy list, it is possible that nothing will be printed at all! Any printing happens only when and if components are selected from the result of printall. This might happen at any later time, or perhaps never. The most we can assert about the behavior of this function is that some components of xs might be printed, at some later time, in any order. This is not very useful, and helps to explain why conventional debugging aids are not much used with lazy functional languages.   □

The consensus among lazy functional programmers is that side effects should be confined to very small and carefully written modules (such as the input–output functions), and that these modules should present a purely functional interface (free of side effects) to the remainder of the program. In this way the strange effects illustrated by these examples can be avoided.

13.1.5 Modeling state

At first sight it might appear that functional languages cannot model state, and that problems with inherent state (e.g., maintaining the balance of a bank account) cannot be solved functionally. Actually we *can* model state in functional languages, but we do so indirectly, without using storage.

Recall Example 13.2, where we translated a definition of the factorial function from Pascal into ML. We modeled the changing contents of a Pascal variable by the changing arguments to a recursive function. More generally, we can model the state of an object by a function with the object's current value as an argument.

Example 13.16
We can model a bank account by a recursive function with the current balance as an argument:

```
datatype request =
                deposit of int
              | withdrawal of int;

fun account (balance, deposit amount) =
        account (balance + amount) ...
    | account (balance, withdrawal amount =>
        account (balance - amount) ...
```

Thus there is no difficulty in modeling *local* state. But how can `account` communicate its evolving state to the rest of the program? To solve this problem we focus on the *communications* with a bank account. Viewing communication as message passing, we can define the possible messages by giving their types, `request` as above and `reply` as follows:

```
datatype reply =
                updatedbalance of int
              | cash of int
              | overdrawn
```

But how are messages communicated to and from an account?

Suppose that the requests arrive at an `account` in a *channel*, and that the replies are sent to a channel. A channel carries a sequence of messages, so it is tempting to represent it by a list of messages. A process, such as a bank account, is then represented by a function from an input channel to an output channel. Given a sequence of requests, it computes the sequence of replies. Of course, it must be possible to create a channel and pass it as an argument to a process before any of the messages in it have been evaluated – but this is exactly what lazy evaluation allows! We therefore represent a channel by a lazy list of messages; selecting a component from the list causes the process to wait for that component to be evaluated. We can now define `account` as follows:

```
fun account (balance,
                deposit amount :: requests) =
```

```
        updatedbalance (balance+amount)
         :: account (balance + amount, requests)

| account (balance,
        withdraw amount :: requests) =
    if balance >= amount
    then cash amount :: account (
            balance - amount, requests)
    else overdrawn
            :: account (balance, requests)
```

On each recursive activation, this function waits for a message from the request channel, updates its balance, and places a message on the reply channel. The bank account can now communicate with any part of the program to which its channels are passed.   □

This approach to communication is quite general. For example, any program may be regarded as sending requests to the operating system and receiving replies from it, and so may be modeled by a function from a list of operating-system replies to a list of operating-system requests. Even an interactive program may be represented as a function from a list of the user's inputs to a list of the program's outputs. So a functional program can model arbitrary state, and interact in an arbitrary way with an imperative operating system.

Despite its generality, this approach does have drawbacks. For example, consider a bank account communicating with two independent user processes such as a payroll process and a cash machine. The order in which requests arrive from the two user processes is nondeterministic, and can affect behavior – the bank account may permit a withdrawal from the cash machine if it arrives after a deposit from the payroll process, but not if it arrives before. But functional programs are always deterministic. So although we can express each process functionally, we cannot express the way in which they are connected. It is possible to add nondeterministic primitives to a functional language so that this can be done, but this leads to theoretical difficulties and so is not wholly satisfactory either.

Another problem is that this way of modeling state is hardly natural. In an imperative language, it is a simple matter to update a global variable from anywhere in its scope. In an object-oriented language, it is equally simple to send an updating request to a global object. In a functional language it is necessary to produce a list of requests, pass them to the function that models the state, take the replies, and pass them back to the source of the requests. This can lead to a lot of 'plumbing' – programming whose only purpose is to arrange this flow of data. It can also lead to a loss of modularity: a function can communicate with the operating system (or other processes) only through its arguments and result, and so the calling module must be aware of this communication. Alleviating these drawbacks is an area of active research.

13.2 Pragmatics

13.2.1 Transformation and proof

A strong motivation for studying functional languages has been their suitability for program transformation and formal proof. Functional programs are easy to reason about and transform because one particular basic proof rule is easy to understand and apply: *identifiers may be freely replaced by their values.*

Take the expression '**let val** $I = E$ **in** E' **end**'. We can obtain an equivalent expression by substituting E for each free occurrence of I in E' – but only if side effects are absent, and (surprisingly) only if the language uses lazy evaluation.

Example 13.17
Using our proof rule we may reason that:

```
    let val x = 2 in x + x end
=   2 + 2                              – because x may be replaced by 2
=   4
```

That the proof rule is valid only in the absence of side effects is illustrated by:

```
    let val x = print (2) in x + x end
≠   print (2) + print (2)
```

because the former prints 2 once, while the latter does so twice.

That the proof rule also depends on lazy evaluation is illustrated by:

```
    let val x = m div n in 3 end
=   3
```

and this is valid only if the definition is interpreted lazily – n might be 0! □

In languages (such as Standard ML) with side effects and/or eager evaluation, identifiers may be replaced by their values only under carefully defined conditions. Since this is such a basic proof rule, the restriction means that the theorems we prove are true only under corresponding conditions. For example, consider the map function again. In a purely functional language we can conclude that:

```
    map (f o g) = map (f) o map (g)
```

But in ML we can draw this conclusion only under the condition that calls of f and g can be reordered. Checking such conditions at each proof step is a considerable burden. It is a significant advantage that this is unnecessary in a purely functional language.

Example 13.18
Consider once more the list reversal function rev:

```
fun rev (nil)    = nil
  | rev (x::xs) = rev (xs) @ [x]
```

As shown in Example 13.10, using `rev` makes the cost of reversing a list of length n proportional to n^2.

An alternative algorithm is to shift elements successively from the front of one list to the front of a second list. If the second list is initially empty, we obtain the reverse of the first list:

```
fun shift (nil, zs)    = zs
  | shift (y::ys, zs) = shift (ys, y::zs);

fun rev' (xs) = shift (xs, nil)
```

Using `rev'` makes the cost of reversing a list of length n proportional to n. This is a great improvement. But, while the definition of `rev` is 'obviously' correct, the same cannot be said of the definition of `rev'`. So let us prove that `rev'` denotes the same function as `rev`.

The idea underlying `rev'` is that the shifting function is supposed to satisfy the following equation:

$$\text{shift (ys, zs)} = \text{rev(ys) @ zs} \tag{13.3}$$

We can prove (13.3) by induction over the length of the list `ys`.

Firstly, we prove (13.3) in the case that `ys` is the empty list:

```
    shift (nil, zs)
=   zs                    – by definition of shift
=   nil @ zs              – by a property of concatenation
=   rev (nil) @ zs        – by definition of rev
```

Secondly, we prove (13.3) in the case that `ys` is the nonempty list `x::xs`. Our inductive hypothesis is that (13.3) is true for `ys = xs`:

```
    shift (x::xs, zs)
=   shift (xs, x::zs)       – by definition of shift
=   rev (xs) @ (x::zs)      – by the inductive hypothesis
=   (rev (xs) @ [x]) @ zs   – by a property of concatenation
=   rev (x::xs) @ zs        – by definition of rev
```

Thus, by induction, (13.3) is true for any list `ys` (and for any list `zs`). Finally we can deduce that, for any list `xs`:

```
    rev' (xs)
=   shift (xs, nil)        – by definition of rev'
=   rev (xs) @ nil         – by (13.3)
=   rev (xs)               – by a property of concatenation
```

thus proving that `rev'` denotes the same (mathematical) function as `rev`. □

13.2.2   Efficiency

Functional languages have a reputation for inefficiency. This is not the place for a detailed discussion of this point, but let us briefly consider whether functional languages are *inherently* less efficient than imperative ones. There are several apparent reasons why this might be so:

(a) Since functions are first-class values, local data must be allocated on the heap, and deallocated automatically by the implementation. This is in order to avoid dangling references.

(b) Lazy evaluation implies that every time a function argument is used, and every time a component is selected from a composite value, it must be checked in case it turns out to be an unevaluated expression. Such checks are unnecessary in languages with eager evaluation (including all imperative languages).

(c) The preferred functional programming style uses many intermediate composite values.

Do these imply that functional language implementations must always be significantly slower than imperative ones? Things are not quite what they seem:

(a) Heap management techniques are improving rapidly, and allocating all data on the heap is not really inefficient.

(b) Early implementations of lazy evaluation were expensive. Recent ones are much less so. Moreover, optimizing compilers can generate improved code in many cases. For example, if a function is shown to be strict (see Section 5.3), then its argument can safely be evaluated eagerly.

(c) Intermediate composite values can often be eliminated by program transformation, and the transformations involved are easy enough to be done by optimizing compilers.

It would therefore be rash to assert that functional language implementations will always be slower than imperative ones, even on sequential machines. Dramatic improvements have taken place: early implementations were 100–1000 times slower, but more recent implementations are only 3–5 times slower, and further improvements can be predicted.

13.2.3   Concurrency

No overview of functional programming would be complete without a discussion of concurrency, which has been one of the driving forces behind the development of the field. Functional languages are thought to be very suitable for concurrent implementation. Shared values need no special protection, since they can never be updated. As a result, explicit synchronization constructs are unnecessary in a functional language, and in a distributed implementation values may be copied freely without danger of copies becoming inconsistent. Moreover, concurrent functional programs are deterministic, since the concurrent processes can never interfere with each other, and this greatly simplifies reasoning and testing. (In some concurrent applications nondeterminism is desirable, but more often our motivation for interest in concurrency is simply to improve performance.)

The behavior of a functional program does not depend on whether any particular expression is evaluated concurrently with the rest of the program or not. Many researchers aim to allow the compiler to decide which expressions should be evaluated concurrently, rather than requiring the programmer to make such decisions. This is comparable to allowing a Fortran compiler to decide what concurrent processing of large arrays is possible in a given program. However, a functional language compiler can in principle take advantage of irregular concurrency, as well as the very regular concurrency exploited by array processors. An advantage of this approach is that a deterministic program can be recompiled and run, without change, on a variety of concurrent (and sequential) architectures. Of course, the programmer must avoid choosing an inherently sequential algorithm.

There are certainly difficult problems to solve before a good concurrent implementation can be achieved. There are hidden overheads in delegating an expression evaluation to a different processor: the data needed to evaluate the expression must be communicated from one processor to the other, and the expression's result must be communicated back. If the expression takes little time to evaluate, the communication overheads can easily swamp the time saved by delegating the expression evaluation. The problems of keeping these overheads reasonably low must be solved by the implementation without the programmer's assistance. Finding good techniques for doing so is an area of active research.

13.3   Further reading

There are several good introductions to functional programming available. Bird and Wadler (1988) teach a purely functional language, with lazy evaluation, similar to Miranda, placing strong emphasis on proofs of correctness and program transformation. Wikström (1987) covers the purely functional subset of Standard ML, emphasizing programming methodology; a definition of Standard ML is included as an appendix. Abelson *et al.* (1985) describe Scheme, a dialect of Lisp that supports higher-order functions and (to a limited extent) lazy evaluation, but also provides variables and side effects. They explore the potential of a hybrid functional–imperative style, concentrating heavily on the modularity of their programs. None of these books assumes prior knowledge of programming.

Two books that cover programming, transformation, proof, and implementation are Henson (1987) and Field and Harrison (1988). Henson has a greater emphasis on transformation and proof, while Field and Harrison stress implementation.

Exercises 13

13.1   In ML, the operator o composes any two compatible functions, as in 'not o odd'. Give *three* reasons why o cannot be programmed in Pascal.

13.2   The obvious algorithm to compute b^n (where $n \geq 0$) is to multiply b by itself n times. This algorithm is implemented in Pascal, using both iteration and recursion, in Example 10.2. A better algorithm is suggested by the following equations:

$$b^0 \quad = 1$$
$$b^{2n} \quad = (b^2)^n$$
$$b^{2n+1} \quad = (b^2)^n \times b$$

Implement this better algorithm, using both iteration and recursion.

13.3   Define further functions on the type shape (Example 13.3): (a) to compute a given shape's perimeter; (b) to determine whether a given point is inside a given shape centered at a given point. Use pattern matching.

13.4   Draw a diagram, along the same lines as Figure 13.1, that shows the effect of evaluating 'ints1 @ ints2', where ints1 is the list [2, 3, 5, 7] and ints2 is the list [11, 13, 17].

13.5   (a) Define an ML function that maps an unordered integer list to an ordered binary tree, using the function insert of Example 13.4. (b) Define a function that maps an integer binary tree to an integer list formed by a left–root–right traversal. (c) Form the composition of these functions. What does it do?

13.6   You are given employees, a list of employee records. Each record has a field name (a string), a field age (an integer), a field gender (*female* or *male*), and a field status (*managerial, clerical,* or *manual*). Write list compre-hensions to compute the following: (a) a list of all female employees; (b) a list of all male employees over 60 years old; (c) a list of the names of all managers. (d) Write an expression that computes the mean age of all female clerical employees.

13.7*   (a) Consider a list comprehension of the form:

$$[\ E_1 \mid I <-\ E_2\ ]$$

This takes the existing list given by the expression E_1. From this list it computes a new list, each component of which is determined by evaluating E_2 with the identifier I bound to the corresponding component of the exist-ing list. Show how the same effect can be achieved in Standard ML, using only functions. (*Hint:* Use the predefined function map.) (b) Repeat with a list comprehension of the form:

$$[\ E_1 \ | \ I <- E_2 \ ; \ E_3 \ ]$$

which is similar, except that only components of the existing list for which the expression E_3 yields *true* are considered. (*Hint:* Use the functions `map` and `filter`.)

13.8 Use `generic_sort` (Example 13.8) to generate functions suitable for sorting lists like that of Exercise 13.6. The lists are to be sorted (a) by name; (b) primarily by status and secondarily by name.

13.9 Explain the following functions generated by `reduce` (Example 13.9):

```
reduce (op or, false)
reduce (repl, "*")
```

where the operator `or` denotes disjunction of truth values, and `repl` is the string replicating function (e.g., 'repl (3, "*")' yields "***").

13.10 By replacing the calculation part and/or the control part of Example 13.12, write expressions to compute the following: (a) the first power of 2 not less than m; (b) a list of all prime numbers between m and n.

13.11 Implement some of the control functions suggested in Example 13.13.

CHAPTER FOURTEEN

The Logic Programming Paradigm

All the other programming paradigms covered in this book are based on the notion that a program implements a mapping. In an imperative language, the program typically is a command that reads inputs from files and writes outputs to files. The outputs are functionally dependent on the inputs, so the program may be viewed abstractly as implementing a mapping from inputs to outputs. In a functional language, the program typically is a function, and thus obviously implements a mapping.

Logic programming is based on the notion that a program implements a relation, rather than a mapping. Since relations are more general than mappings, logic programming is potentially higher-level than imperative or functional programming. In this chapter we first briefly examine some of the general concepts underlying logic programming. Then we look at the most popular logic programming language, Prolog.

14.1 Logic programming

Consider two sets of values S and T. R is a **relation** between S and T if, for every $x \in S$ and $y \in T$, $R(x, y)$ is either *true* or *false*. If $R(x, y)$ is *true*, we say that R holds between x and y.

For example, '>' is a relation between numbers, since for any pair of numbers x and y, $x>y$ is either *true* or *false*. (By convention, we write '$x>y$' rather than '$>(x, y)$'.) Another simple example is the relation 'flows through' between rivers and countries: 'the Clyde flows through Scotland' is *true*, but 'the Columbia flows through California' is *false*.

Figure 14.1 illustrates several different relations between two sets $S = \{u, v\}$ and $T = \{a, b, c\}$. A double-headed arrow connects each pair of values between which a given relation holds. For example, the relation R_1 holds only between u and a and between v and c.

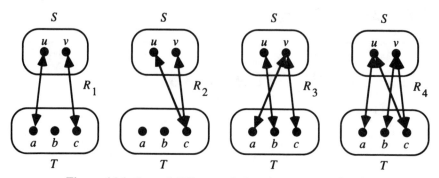

Figure 14.1 Several different relations between sets S and T.

Compare Figure 2.3, which illustrated *mappings* between sets S and T. Every (total) mapping in $S \rightarrow T$ has the property that each x in S maps to exactly one y in T. The relations R_1 and R_2 in Figure 14.1 happen to have a similar property; indeed, they correspond to the two mappings in Figure 2.3. More generally, however, a relation between S and T may hold between a given x in S and *many y* in T. R_3 and R_4 are such relations. A mapping is in general a *many-to-one* relationship, whereas a relation is in general a *many-to-many* relationship.

Imperative and functional programming are essentially about implementing mappings. Having implemented a mapping m, we can make requests like:

> Given a, determine the value of $m(a)$.   (14.1)

A request like (14.1) will always have a single answer.

Logic programming is about implementing relations. Having implemented a relation R, we can make requests like:

> Given a and b, determine whether $R(a, b)$ is *true*.   (14.2)
> Given a, find all y such that $R(a, y)$ is *true*.   (14.3)
> Given b, find all x such that $R(x, b)$ is *true*.   (14.4)
> Find all x and y such that $R(x, y)$ is *true*.   (14.5)

A request like (14.2) will have a single yes/no answer, but a request like (14.3), (14.4), or (14.5) might have many answers (or none). Moreover, requests (14.3) and (14.4) show that a relation makes no distinction between inputs and outputs. Requests like these are characteristic of logic programming, and explain why it is potentially higher-level then imperative or functional programming.

For simplicity, the above discussion has concentrated on *binary relations*, i.e., relations between pairs of values. We can also talk about *unary relations*, written $R(x)$, *ternary relations*, written $R(x, y, z)$, and so on.

Example 14.1
Let Point = Real × Real be the set of all points on the xy plane.

Consider the relation $origin(p)$, signifying that point p is the origin. This is a unary relation on the set Point. It can be defined as follows:

origin$((x,y))$ if and only if $x = 0$ and $y = 0$.

Now consider *inside*(p, r), signifying that point p lies inside the circle of radius r centered at the origin. This is a binary relation between Point and Real. It can be defined as follows:

inside$((x,y), r)$ if and only if $x^2 + y^2 < r^2$.

Finally consider *collinear*(p_1, p_2, p_3), signifying that points p_1, p_2, and p_3 all lie on a straight line. This is a ternary relation. (See Exercise 14.1.)

Note that we can define relations in terms of other relations. *Origin* and *inside* were defined in terms of the relations '=' and '<' on real numbers. □

No logic programming language can exploit the full power of mathematical logic, for that formalism is unimplementable. We can use it to specify problems that are incomputable. For example, Fermat's last theorem could easily be specified as follows:

fermat(n) if and only if:
there exist $a, b, c \in \{1, 2, \ldots\}$ such that $a^n + b^n = c^n$.

but this 'program' cannot be implemented.

Logic programming languages restrict us to **_Horn clauses_**, i.e., clauses of the form:

A_0 if A_1 and ... and A_n.

Each A_i is a simple assertion of the form $R_i(\ldots)$ where R_i is a relation name. Informally, this clause means that, if $A_1, \ldots,$ and A_n are all *true*, then we can infer that A_0 is also *true*. But we cannot conversely infer that A_0 is *false* just because some A_i turns out to be *false*. A Horn clause is written in terms of 'if' rather than 'if and only if'. There might well be another clause in the program that allows us to infer that A_0 is *true*.

In the special case where $n=0$, a Horn clause simplifies to a *fact*:

A_0.

This clause unconditionally states that A_0 is *true*.

A logic program is a collection of Horn clauses. The restriction to Horn clauses ensures implementability, and allows the implementation to be tolerably efficient.

Computation consists of testing a given assertion (*query*) A. If we can infer from the clauses of the program that A is *true*, then we say that A *succeeds*. If we cannot infer that A is *true*, then we say that A *fails*. This does not mean that A is definitely *false*; it means simply that A cannot be inferred to be *true* from the clauses of the program.

The testing of a query A can be implemented by a technique called *resolution*:

- If the program contains a fact 'A_0.' such that A_0 matches A, then we immediately conclude that A succeeds.

- If the program contains a clause 'A_0 if A_1 and ... and A_n.' such that A_0 matches A, then we proceed by testing A_1, ..., and A_n separately as (sub)queries. If all succeed, then we conclude that A succeeds. If one of the A_i fails, then we must *backtrack*, i.e., give up the attempt to use this particular clause and try another clause instead.

Only when we have exhausted all clauses whose left-hand sides match A can we conclude that A fails.

Relations are abstractions over assertions. We can define a relation R by (one or more) clauses of the form '$R(...)$ if ....'; and we can invoke it from clauses of the form '... if ... $R(...)$ ....'. Relations in a logic language thus play much the same role as procedures and functions in imperative and functional languages. Backtracking, however, gives logic programming a distinctive flavor, and is responsible for much of its power and expressiveness. But backtracking has a cost: it is expensive in time and storage space.

We now explore the logic programming paradigm in more detail by looking at a particular language, Prolog.

14.2   Case study: Prolog

Prolog was not really designed as such. Rather, it gradually evolved during the 1970s, mainly at the Universities of Marseille and Edinburgh, as an experimental artificial intelligence tool. Owing to the lack of a standard definition, several dialects of Prolog evolved, differing even in their basic syntax! Fortunately, the Edinburgh dialect is now widely accepted as a standard.

Prolog received a major boost in 1981, when the Japanese Institute for New Generation Computing Technology selected logic programming as its enabling software technology, and launched a ten-year project to provide a complementary hardware technology in the shape of fast logical inference machines.

A Prolog program is basically a collection of Horn clauses defining relations, as explained in the previous section.

14.2.1   Values, variables, and terms

Prolog's values are numbers, atoms, and structures. Lists are a particular kind of structure, and strings are a particular kind of list.

Atoms are primitive values that have no properties other than the ability to distinguish one from another. They are used to represent real-world objects that are primitive as far as the current application is concerned. Examples of atoms are red, green, and blue, which might represent colors, and jan, feb, etc., which might represent months.

Structures are tagged tuples. For example, structures like date(2000,jan,1) and `date(1989,mar,26)` might be used to represent dates. In the notation of Section 2.3, the values of these structures are *date* (2000, *jan*, 1) and *date* (1989, *mar*, 26), respectively. The tags serve to distinguish structures that happen to have the same components but represent distinct real-world objects, e.g., `point(2,3)` and `rational(2,3)`. The components of a structure can be any values, including (sub)structures; thus structures are hierarchical. The following structure is illustrated in Figure 14.2(a):

```
person(name("Susanne","Watt"),
       female,
       date(1978,may,5))
```

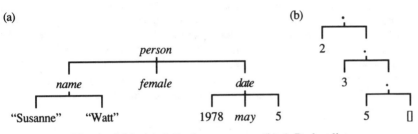

Figure 14.2 (a) A Prolog structure. (b) A Prolog list.

Lists are just a subset of the structures. The atom `[]` represents the empty list, and '`.(x,xs)`' represents the list whose head is *x* and whose tail is the list *xs*. Alternative notations for lists are provided:

$$[x \mid xs] \quad = \quad .(x, xs)$$
$$[a, ..., z] \quad = \quad .(a, ... (z, [\,])...)$$

The list `[2,3,5]` is illustrated in Figure 14.2(b).

A *string* is a list of integers. (Individual characters are represented by integers.) Thus the string literal `"Susanne"` is shorthand for a list of seven integers.

Prolog is an *untyped* language. Numbers, atoms, and structures can always be used interchangeably. Thus we can construct heterogeneous lists containing these different sorts of value. We can also compare different sorts of value using the equality relation '=', but such a comparison will always yield *false*.

(Note that *untyped* is not the same as *dynamically typed*. In an untyped language, values such as numbers and structures are different but comparable. In a dynamically typed language, any attempt to compare such values would be a run-time type error.)

A Prolog expression, or *term*, is a variable, numeric literal, atom, or structure aggregate. Terms occur as arguments to relations; a simple assertion is of the form $R(T_1, ..., T_n)$, where each T_i is a term.

A Prolog variable (written with an initial uppercase letter to distinguish it from atoms and tags) denotes a fixed but unknown value, of any type. Thus Prolog variables correspond to mathematical variables, *not* the updatable variables of an imperative language. A variable is declared implicitly by its occurrence in a clause, and its scope is just the clause in which it occurs.

14.2.2   Clauses and relations

A Prolog program defines a collection of relations. Each relation is defined by one or more clauses, written in the following notation:

$$A_0 :- A_1, \ldots, A_n.$$

(The symbol ': -' means 'if', and the symbol ', ' means 'and'.)

A_0 *matches* an assertion A if there is a substitution of terms for variables that makes A_0 and A the same. For example, 'age (P, Y)' matches 'age ("David", 42)' under the substitution of "David" for P and 42 for Y; and 'age (P, Y)' matches 'age ("Susanne", A)' under the substitution of "Susanne" for P and A for Y. Clearly, having the same relation name and having the same number of terms are necessary conditions for two assertions to match.

The scope of every relation name is the entire program. It is not possible in Prolog to define a relation with a narrower scope, such as an auxiliary relation used in only one part of the program.

Example 14.2
The following Prolog facts together define a unary relation star on celestial bodies. Each celestial body is represented by an atom (e.g., sun).

```
star(sun).
star(sirius).
star(betelgeuse).
...
```

and similarly for other stars. Now consider the following queries:

- star(sun)?   This will yield the answer yes (i.e., succeed).
- star(jupiter)?   This will yield the answer no (i.e., fail).

The following Prolog facts together define a binary relation orbits between celestial bodies:

```
orbits(mercury,  sun).
orbits(venus,    sun).
orbits(earth,    sun).
orbits(mars,     sun).
orbits(moon,     earth).
orbits(phobos,   mars).
orbits(deimos,   mars).
...
```

and similarly for the other planets and their satellites. Now consider the following queries:

- `orbits(mars, sun)?`   This will yield the answer yes.
- `orbits(moon, sun)?`   This will yield the answer no.
- `orbits(phobos, B)?`   This asks which body or bodies Phobos orbits; it will yield the single answer B = `mars`.
- `orbits(B, mars)?`   This asks which body or bodies orbit Mars; it will yield the two answers B = `phobos` and B = `deimos`.
- `orbits(B, venus)?`   This will yield the answer no, since there is no value for B that would make this assertion succeed.

The following clause defines a unary relation `planet`:

```
planet(B)   :-   orbits(B, sun).
```

i.e., a body B is a planet if it orbits the Sun. Consider the following queries:

- `planet(mars)?`   This will yield the answer yes.
- `planet(P)?`   This will yield the answers P = `mercury`, P = `venus`, P = `earth`, P = `mars`, etc.

The following clause defines a unary relation `satellite`:

```
satellite(B)   :-   orbits(B, P),   planet(P).
```

i.e., a body B is a satellite if it orbits some body P and that same P is a planet. Consider the following queries:

- `satellite(phobos)?`   This will yield the answer yes.
- `satellite(S)?`   This will yield the answers S = `moon`, S = `phobos`, S = `deimos`, etc.

Finally, the following clause defines a unary relation `solar`:

```
solar(sun).
solar(B)   :-   planet(B).
solar(B)   :-   satellite(B).
```

i.e., (a) the Sun is a member of the solar system; (b) a body B is a member of the solar system if it is a planet; (c) a body B is a member of the solar system if it is a satellite. Consider the following queries:

- `solar(sun)?`   This will yield the answer yes.
- `solar(moon)?`   This will yield the answer yes.
- `solar(sirius)?`   This will yield the answer no.
- `solar(B)?`   This will yield the answers B = `sun`, B = `mercury`, B = `venus`, B = `earth`, B = `mars`, B = `moon`, B = `phobos`, B = `deimos`, etc.

                                           □

The query '`satellite(S)?`' in Example 14.2 has the following meaning in predicate logic:

Does there exist S such that *satellite(S)*?

In general, each variable that occurs in a query is existentially quantified.

The clause defining `satellite` has the following meaning in predicate logic:

> For all B:
> > *satellite(B)* if
> > > there exists P such that *orbits(B, P)* and *planet(P)*.

In general, each variable that occurs on the left-hand side of a clause is universally quantified ('for all ...: ...'), and each variable that occurs only on the right-hand side of a clause is existentially quantified ('there exists ... such that ...'). Quantification is always implicit in Prolog. This accounts for the fact that the scope of each variable is the clause in which it occurs.

Not all relations defined in Prolog have such straightforward logical meanings. The following example illustrates one way in which Prolog departs from our logical intuition.

Example 14.3

The relations of Example 14.1 might be expressed in Prolog as follows. Assume that the point (x,y) is represented by the structure `pt (x, y)`.

```
origin(pt(X,Y))      :-   X = 0,   Y = 0.
inside(pt(X,Y), R)   :-   X*X+Y*Y < R*R.
```

Now consider the following queries:

- `origin(pt(0,2))?`   This will yield the answer `no`.
- `origin(P)?`   This will yield the answer `P = pt(0,0)`.
- `inside(pt(1,2), 3)?`   This will yield the answer `yes`.
- `inside(pt(1,2), R)?`   This query is erroneous.

The last query attempts to ask for the radii of all circles that enclose the point (1,2). It amounts to finding every value for R such that `5 < R*R`, but Prolog's built-in relation '<' works only when both its arguments are known numbers. In consequence, the relation `inside` works only when both its arguments are known.   □

Relations on lists are typically recursive, since lists are themselves recursive structures.

Example 14.4

The following clauses define a binary relation `element(X, L)`, signifying that the value X is an element of the list L:

```
element(X, [Y|Ys])   :-   X = Y.
element(X, [Y|Ys])   :-   element(X, Ys).
```

i.e., (a) X is an element of a list with head Y and tail Ys if X is equal to Y; and (b) X is an element of a list with head Y and tail Ys if X is an element of Ys. Consider the following queries:

- `element(3, [2,3,5])?`   This will yield the answer yes.
- `element(4, [2,3,5])?`   This will yield the answer no.
- `element(V, [2,3,5])?`   This will yield the answers V = 2, V = 3, and V = 5.
- `element(4, [])?`   This will yield the answer no.

The last query fails simply because there is no clause that matches it.

The following clauses define a ternary relation `addlast(X, L1, L2)`, signifying that by adding X to the end of list L1 we obtain the list L2:

```
addlast(X, [], [X]).
addlast(X, [Y|Ys], [Y|Zs])  :-  addlast(X, Ys, Zs).
```

i.e., (a) by adding X to the end of the empty list we obtain the list `[X]`; and (b) by adding X to the end of the list `[Y|Ys]` we obtain the list `[Y|Zs]`, if by adding X to the end of the list Ys we obtain the list Zs. Consider the following queries:

- `addlast(7, [], L)?`   This will yield the answer L = [7].
- `addlast(7, [2,3,5], L)?`   This will yield the answer L = [2,3,5,7].
- `addlast(V, L, [2,3,5])?`   This will yield the answer V = 5, L = [2,3].
- `addlast(V, L, [])?`   This will yield the answer no.

The following clauses define a ternary relation `append(L1, L2, L3)`, signifying that by concatenating the lists L1 and L2 we obtain the list L3:

```
append([], Ys, Ys).
append([X|Xs], Ys, [X|Zs])  :-  append(Xs, Ys, Zs).
```

i.e., (a) by concatenating the empty list and the list Ys we obtain the list Ys; and (b) by concatenating the lists `[X|Xs]` and Ys we obtain the list `[X|Zs]`, if by concatenating the lists Xs and Ys we obtain the list Zs. Consider the following queries:

- `append([2,3], [5,7], L)?` This will yield the answer L = [2,3,5,7].
- `append([2,3], L, [2,3,5,7])?`
      This will yield the answer L = [5,7].
- `append(L1, L2, [5,7])?`   This will yield answers giving all possible ways of splitting the list [5,7], i.e.:
  - (1) L1 = [], L2 = [5,7]
  - (2) L1 = [5], L2 = [7]
  - (3) L1 = [5,7], L2 = []

Thus the relation `append` can be used to concatenate two given lists, or to remove a given list from the front (or back) of another, or to find all ways of deconcatenating a given list. In an imperative or functional language, we would need to write several functions to accomplish all these computations.   □

14.2.3   The closed-world assumption

An assertion *A* might fail. This does not mean that *A* is definitely *false*; it simply means that we cannot infer from the clauses of the program that *A* is *true*. In fact, very few assertions in Prolog are definitely *false*. (The exceptions are trivial assertions like 'chalk = cheese' and '2 > 3'.) When an assertion is tested, therefore, success means *true* and failure means either *unknown* or *false*.

As this is rather inconvenient, Prolog bends the rules of logic by ignoring the distinction between *unknown* and *false*. In other words, an assertion is assumed to be *false* if it cannot be inferred to be *true*. This is called the *closed-world assumption* – the Prolog processor assumes that the program encodes all relevant information about the 'world' (i.e., the application domain).

In Example 14.2, a query like 'orbits(halley, sun)?' would yield the answer no, simply because we omitted to assert anything at all about Halley's comet. A query like 'comet(halley)?' would also yield the answer no, simply because there are no clauses defining a unary relation comet.

This of itself is not too serious. Prolog programmers are perfectly aware that the closed-world assumption obliges them to encode all relevant information. However, Prolog compounds the problem by providing a form of negation. If *A* is an assertion, then 'not (*A*)' is an assertion that negates the *assumed* truth value of *A*. Thus the negation of *unknown* is taken to be *true*! Using negation, it is easy to write clauses that are truly misleading.

Suppose that we add the following clause to Example 14.2:

```
comet(B)   :-   not(star(B)),   not(planet(B)),
                not(satellite(B)).
```

then the query 'comet(halley)?' will now yield the answer yes, but only by coincidence; the query 'comet(apollo)?' will also yield the answer yes! Of course, the query 'orbits(halley, sun)?' will still yield the answer no.

14.2.4   Control

In principle, the order in which resolution is done should not affect the set of answers yielded by a query (although it will affect the order in which these answers are found). In practical logic programming, however, the order is very important.

The main consideration is the possibility of nontermination. Suppose that we add the following relation to Example 14.2:

```
neighbor(A, B)   :-   neighbor(B, A).
neighbor(A, B)   :-   planet(A),   orbits(B, A).
```

In principle, queries like 'neighbor(earth, moon)?' and 'neighbor(moon, earth)?' should both yield yes. If we consistently apply the nonrecursive clause first, these queries will give the correct answers. But we consistently apply the recursive clause first, these queries will loop forever, due to repeated application of the recursive clause.

Consider testing an assertion A using the clause '$A_0 : - A_1, A_2.$', where A_1 will loop forever but A_2 will fail. If we test A_2 first, it will fail and we can immediately conclude that A fails. (This is consistent with a predicate logic interpretation of the clause.) But if we test A_1 first, it will loop forever and the computation will make no further progress.

Thus the actual behavior of a logic program depends on the order in which resolution is done. To allow the programmer control over the computation, Prolog defines the resolution order precisely. The assertions on the right-hand side of a clause are tested in order from left to right. If there are several clauses defining the same relation, then these are tried in order from first to last. As a consequence, every Prolog program is deterministic. If a query has multiple answers, we can even predict the order in which these answers will be found.

Backtracking is very space- and time-consuming. If we know in advance that a query will have only one answer (say), then it would be wasteful to allow the Prolog processor to continue searching for more answers once the first answer has been found.

In Example 14.2, we know that a query like 'orbits(deimos, P)?' will have just one answer, but the Prolog processor does not know that (since we cannot declare that orbits is a many-to-one relation). So even when the answer P = mars has been found, the Prolog processor will search all the remaining clauses in a fruitless attempt to find other answers.

Prolog provides a kind of sequencer, called the *cut*, that suppresses backtracking whenever it is encountered. Suppose that we are testing an assertion A using the clause '$A_0 : - A_1, !, A_2.$'. If A_1 fails, then the Prolog processor backtracks and tries to find another clause for A, as usual. But if A_1 succeeds, the processor accepts the first answer yielded by A_1, passes the cut, and goes on to test A_2. Passing the cut has the effect that, if A_2 subsequently fails, then the processor immediately concludes that A itself fails – the processor makes no attempt to find any further answers from A_1, and makes no attempt to find any further clauses for A.

Or suppose that we are testing an assertion A using the clause '$A_0 : - !.$'. If A_0 matches A, the Prolog processor will make no attempt to use any further clauses for A.

Example 14.5
Suppose that a telephone directory is represented by a structure of the form entry(*name, number, rest of directory*), or by the atom empty. Assume that no two entries contain the same name. The following directory structure is illustrated in Figure 14.3:

```
entry("David",6041,
    entry("Helen",4967,
        entry("Bill",6034,
            entry("John",4454,
                entry("Gill",4967,empty))))))
```

The following clauses define a relation lookup(Directory, Name, Number), signifying that Directory contains an entry for Name with Number:

```
lookup(entry(Name1,Num1,Rest), Name1, Num1).
lookup(entry(Name1,Num1,Rest), Name2, Num2)   :-
     lookup(Rest, Name2, Num2).
```

Let *dir* be the structure illustrated in Figure 14.3. The query 'lookup(*dir*, "David", Number)?' will yield the single answer Number = 6041. But to find this answer, the Prolog processor examines every entry in *dir*!

Queries like this can be answered more efficiently if we cut off the search as soon as we have a match:

```
lookup(entry(Name1,Num1,Rest), Name1, Num1)   :-   !.
lookup(entry(Name1,Num1,Rest), Name2, Num2)   :-
     !,  lookup(Rest, Name2, Num2).
```

Although the cuts do not affect the answers yielded by queries like the above, they do eliminate possible answers to other kinds of query. For example, with the first version of lookup, the query 'lookup(*dir*, Name, 4967)?' would yield *two* answers, Name = "Helen" and Name = "Gill"; with the second version of lookup, the same query would yield only one of these answers. (See also Exercise 14.4.)   □

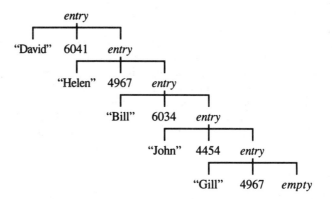

Figure 14.3 A Prolog structure representing a telephone directory.

The cut is an *ad hoc* feature, added to Prolog to make execution of queries tolerably efficient. The cut cannot be understood in terms of predicate logic, but only in terms of the particular way in which the Prolog processor performs resolution. It often has unexpected effects, as illustrated by Example 14.5. In these respects the cut shares the drawbacks of low-level sequencers in more conventional programming languages.

14.3 Further reading

This chapter has given only a very brief outline of the logic programming paradigm. For a much fuller account of logic programming in general, and of Prolog in particular, see Malpas (1987).

Exercises 14

14.1 Define the ternary relation `collinear` (see Example 14.1) in Prolog.

14.2 Refer to Example 14.4. (a) Give an alternative definition of `addlast` in terms of `append`. (b) Define a relation `last(L, X)`, signifying that X is the last element of the list L. (c) Define a relation `reverse(L1, L2)`, signifying that L2 is the reverse of the list L1. (d) Define a relation `ordered(L)`, signifying that the list of integers L is in ascending order.

14.3 Refer to Example 14.5. With each version of the relation `lookup`, and with the directory *dir* of Figure 14.3, what answers would you expect from the following queries? Explain these answers.

```
lookup(dir,  "David",  9999)?
lookup(dir,  "Susanne",  Number)?
lookup(dir,  Name,  6041)?
lookup(dir,  Name,  Number)?
```

Repeat with the following third version of `lookup`. (The built-in relation '`\=`' succeeds if and only if its operands are unequal. Its operands must both be known values.)

```
lookup(entry(Name1,Num1,Rest),  Name1,  Num1).
lookup(entry(Name1,Num1,Rest),  Name2,  Num2)  :-
    Name1 \= Name2,   lookup(Rest, Name2, Num2).
```

Define a relation `insert(Directory, NewName, NewNumber, NewDir)`, signifying that `NewDir` is the directory obtained by adding to `Dir` an entry for `NewName` and `NewNumber` (or failing if `Directory` already contains an entry for `NewName`).

14.4 Use cuts to improve the efficiency of queries in Example 14.2. Make reasonable assumptions about which kinds of query are most likely, and note which kinds of query will have their answers affected by your cuts.

CHAPTER FIFTEEN

Conclusion

A basic understanding of programming language concepts and paradigms is needed by all software engineers, not just programming language specialists. This is because programming languages are our most fundamental tools. They influence the very way we *think* about software design and construction, about algorithms and data structures.

This chapter draws together ideas from the preceding chapters to examine two problems. Firstly, how should we select a programming language for a specific software project? Most of us are frequently involved in making such selections. Secondly, how should we design programming languages? Few of us are likely ever to design a complete new language, but we might well be involved in designing extensions to a language. We should at least be able to analyse critically the design of an existing language.

This concluding chapter is less technical and more subjective than the rest of the book. There is plenty of scope for differences in informed opinion on the merits of different languages, and on how languages should be designed. (And there is even more scope for blind prejudice!) So the opinions expressed here are the author's own, although hopefully well founded.

15.1 Language selection

15.1.1 Issues

At some stage in every software project, the choice of programming language becomes an important decision. There are many considerations to be taken into account, both technical and nontechnical, both strategic and tactical.

Here is a checklist of important strategic issues that arise when a programming language is considered for use in a project. Strategic issues are issues of software design and integration.

- *Abstraction:* Does the language provide effective support for the concept of abstraction? Abstraction allows us to separate, in our minds, *what* a module is to do (and, indeed, *why* it is needed) from *how* it will be implemented. This separation of concerns is an essential intellectual tool for designing large programs. Relevant concepts here are procedures, functions, abstract types, and objects.
- *Programming in the large:* Does the language support the orderly development of large programs? The language should allow programs to be constructed from modules that have been written and verified separately, possibly by different programmers. Separate compilation (as in Ada) is a practical necessity for large programs; but independent compilation (as in Fortran and C) is at best an evil necessity. Full inter-module type checks are more (not less) important than intra-module type checks. For example, a procedure call is *most* likely to be ill-typed if the called procedure is in a different module and was written by a different programmer. (See the discussion of separate *vs* independent compilation in Section 10.3.7.)
- *Software reuse:* Does the language support effective software reuse? If it does, the present project can be accelerated by reusing previously written tried-and-tested modules. The present project will also be more profitable if it produces new modules suitable for future reuse.

Here now is a checklist of tactical issues. These are concerned with the details of programming in the proposed language.

- *Modeling:* Does the language provide types, and associated operations, that are suitable for modeling objects in the project's application area? Examples would be records and files in data processing; real numbers and arrays in scientific computation; strings in text processing; and lists, trees, and tables in language translation. If the language itself lacks the needed types, does it allow the programmer to define new types and operations that accurately model objects in the application area? Relevant concepts here are abstract types and object classes.
- *Level:* More generally, is the language truly high-level, encouraging the programmer to think in terms related to the application area? Or is it relatively low-level, forcing the programmer to think all the time about coding details?
- *Security:* Is the language designed in such a way that programming errors are likely to be detected quickly – preferably at compile-time, or at worst at run-time? For example, experience suggests that weak type rules, numerous coercions, and default declarations tend to encourage sloppy programming habits and delay error detection; but strong type rules and requiring all entities to be declared help to speed up detection and elimination of many, even most, careless programming errors.
- *Efficiency:* Is the language capable of being implemented efficiently? Some features such as dynamic type checking and dynamic binding are inherently inefficient. If the application demands very high efficiency in a critical section of code, and if the language itself does not support low-level programming, do the language and its compiler support *secure* interfacing to code written in a lower-level language? For example, it should be possible to call procedures written in the lower-level language without undue risk of interface errors.
- *Compiler:* Is a good-quality compiler available for the language? That is a compiler that enforces all the language rules, reports errors accurately, generates correct and

efficient object code, and generates comprehensive run-time checks (at least as an option) to trap any errors that cannot be detected at compile-time. Linking this with the previous issue, the fact that a language is *capable* of being implemented efficiently does not guarantee that a given compiler *actually* implements it efficiently. For example, many compilers implement procedure and function calls badly, and some programmers believe that calls are inherently expensive (and try to avoid them). But this is a myth, and should not be allowed to discredit good programming methods, like abstract types and object-oriented programming, that tend to lead to many small procedures and functions. Instead, the compiler should be closely scrutinized for quality in this critical area.

- *Familiarity:* Are the programmers already familiar with the language? If not, is suitable training available, and will the investment in training justify itself in the present and future projects?

None of the strategic issues and (surprisingly) few of the tactical issues are specific to any particular application area. This suggests that any reasonable language that passes muster on the nonspecific issues might well be acceptable in most application areas. This might explain why Pascal has proved equally satisfactory (and equally unsatisfactory) in such a wide variety of applications.

Example 15.1
Suppose that we have undertaken a project to implement a word processor. Using the above checklist, let us assess Pascal's suitability for this project.

- *Abstraction:* By modern standards Pascal's abstraction mechanisms are minimal: procedures and functions only.
- *Programming in the large:* Standard Pascal does not support modules or separate compilation. This will hinder the development of even a medium-sized system like the word processor. The programmer(s) will have to develop informal 'modules' (groups of constants, types, variables, procedures, and functions); integration will consist of textually merging these 'modules'.
- *Software reuse:* The lack of modules and generics seriously impedes software reuse in Pascal.

- *Modeling:* In Pascal it is quite easy to define the composite types, such as lists and dictionaries, likely to be needed in the word processor. However, the lack of flexible strings, and more generally the lack of abstract types, are likely to be a hindrance.
- *Level:* Pascal is a high-level language, except for its reliance on pointers for defining recursive types.
- *Security:* Pascal's static binding and static typing make it a secure language in most respects. But there are dangerous loopholes: variant records can be selectively updated, and the deallocator dispose can leave dangling references.
- *Efficiency:* Pascal is capable of being implemented very efficiently.
- *Compiler:* There is a wide choice of low-cost good-quality Pascal compilers.
- *Familiarity:* Most professional programmers are familiar with Pascal, or can quickly be trained in it.

In summary, Pascal would be a possible but far from ideal choice of programming language for this project. It is worth noting that many Pascal-like languages, including Ada (and the major dialects of Pascal itself), specifically address the defects of Pascal highlighted by this example. □

15.1.2   Comparison

When we compare different languages in detail, it becomes clear that the contrasts between programming paradigms are far greater than the differences between individual languages. For example, Pascal contrasts more sharply with ML than with other imperative languages such as Ada and C. So let us compare an imperative language, a functional language, and a logic language, by means of a single example.

Such a comparison of very different languages must be done with great caution. Different languages are well suited to different classes of problem. It is perfectly possible, by a careful choice of example, to make any reasonable paradigm or individual language seem superior to all others.

Nevertheless, sorting is a ubiquitous problem, and it does illuminate the style of programming encouraged by various languages. So let us examine the *Quicksort* algorithm as it might be programmed in Ada, ML, and Prolog. The requirement is to sort a sequence of items into ascending order.

Example 15.2
Here is an Ada version of the Quicksort algorithm. It is a recursive procedure, `sort`, with the array of items to be sorted as an *in out* parameter.

```
type Item is ...;
type ItemSequence is
        array (Integer range <>) of Item;

procedure sort (items : in out ItemSequence) is
    left, right : Integer;
begin
    if items'first < items'last then
        partition (items, left, right);
        sort (items(items'first..right));
        sort (items(left..items'last));
    end if;
end;
```

The procedure `sort` is rather easy to understand. First it partitions the array, segregating the smaller items from the larger ones, by calling an auxiliary procedure, `partition`. Then it calls itself recursively to sort each of the partitions. (Note that `items'first` and `items'last` denote the lower and upper bounds of `items`.)

The procedure `partition` selects one of the items as a *pivot*, then segregates all the items in the array `items` around the pivot such that no item in the subarray `items(items'first..right)` is greater than the pivot, and no item in the subarray `items(left..items'last)` is less than the pivot:

```
procedure partition (items : in out ItemSequence;
                      left, right : out Integer) is
   l : Integer := items'first;
   r : Integer := items'last;
   pivot : constant Item := items(l);
   procedure swapitems is new swap (Item);
begin
   loop
      while items(l)<pivot loop l:=l+1; end loop;
      while pivot<items(r) loop r:=r-1; end loop;
      exit when l > r;
      swapitems (items(l), items(r));
      l := l+1;   r := r-1;
      exit when l > r;
   end loop;
   left := l;   right := r;
end;
```

(See Example 10.11 for a definition of the generic procedure swap.)

The procedure partition contains the details of rearranging the items within the array. These rather low-level details make this part of the Ada version tricky to write and quite hard to understand.

On the other hand, this version of Quicksort is very efficient. The items are sorted in place, with only a small storage overhead (for local variables). As a valuable piece of software likely to be reused frequently, the effort of writing it efficiently will pay for itself many times over.

The Quicksort procedure would be even more reusable if it were generic – see Exercise 15.2.   □

Example 15.3

Here is an ML version of Quicksort. It is a recursive *function*, sort, whose argument is a *list* of items to be sorted, and whose result is the sorted list of items. Lists are used because arrays are awkward to handle in a functional language. (See Section 13.1.2.) This gives the following version of Quicksort a very different flavor from the Ada version in Example 15.2.

```
fun sort (nil) =
        nil
  | sort [singleitem] =
        [singleitem]
  | sort (firstitem::otheritems) =
        let val (smallitems, bigitems) =
                partition (firstitem, otheritems)
        in
           sort (smallitems) @ [firstitem]
             @ sort (bigitems)
        end
```

The function `sort` selects the first item as the pivot, and partitions the other items into two sublists: those less than the pivot, and those not less than the pivot. Then it recursively sorts the two sublists, and finally concatenates the sorted sublists and the pivot in the correct order. Note that the sorting and concatenation of the sublists can be programmed as an ordinary expression – there is no need to name the intermediate lists.

The auxiliary function `partition` takes a pivot and a list of items, and returns a pair of lists into which the items have been distributed around the pivot:

```
fun partition (pivot, nil) =
        (nil, nil)
  | partition (pivot, first::others) =
        let val (smalls, bigs) =
                  partition (pivot, others)
        in
          if first < pivot
          then (first::smalls, bigs)
          else (smalls, first::bigs)
        end
```

The ML version is easy to write and easy to understand. However, it is considerably slower than the Ada version, because all items are copied into auxiliary lists. For the same reason, it uses a lot of auxiliary storage. In practice, the language processor will reclaim this auxiliary storage, sooner or later, but the process of reclaiming storage itself incurs overheads in time and storage space.

The `sort` function is monomorphic, because the function, '`<`', used to compare items is itself monomorphic. The function will sort only integers. We can make `sort` polymorphic if we parameterize it with respect to the comparison function – see Exercise 15.3. □

Example 15.4
Here is a Prolog version of the Quicksort algorithm. It is in the form of a *relation* between lists of items.

The following clauses define a binary relation `sort(Items, SortedItems)`, signifying that the result of sorting the list `Items` is the list `SortedItems`:

```
sort([], []).
sort([SingleItem], [SingleItem]).
sort([FirstItem|OtherItems], SortedItems) :-
        partition(FirstItem, OtherItems,
                  SmallItems, BigItems),
        sort(SmallItems, SortedSmallItems),
        sort(BigItems, SortedBigItems),
        append(SortedSmallItems,
               [FirstItem|SortedBigItems],
               SortedItems).
```

The following clauses define an auxiliary relation `partition(Pivot,`

Items, Smalls, Bigs), signifying that Smalls is a list of those items in Items that are less than Pivot, and Bigs is a list of those items in Items that are not less than Pivot:

```
partition(Pivot, [], [], []).
partition(Pivot, [First|Others],
          [First|Smalls], Bigs) :-
      First < Pivot,
      partition(Pivot, Others, Smalls, Bigs).
partition(Pivot, [First|Others],
          Smalls, [First|Bigs]) :-
      not(First < Pivot),
      partition(Pivot, Others, Smalls, Bigs).
```

The Prolog version is structurally similar to the ML version in Example 15.3. However, Prolog has no functions, and therefore expressions cannot be composed using function calls. So it is necessary to name all intermediate lists: the two lists resulting from the partition step (SmallItems and BigItems), and the two lists obtained by sorting them (SortedSmallItems and SortedBigItems). This makes the Prolog version somewhat clumsier than the ML version.

Although Prolog is untyped, the relation sort holds only between lists of numbers. This is because the built-in relation '<' works only on numbers. Moreover, there is no way to parameterize the relation sort with respect to the ordering relation – Prolog is a first-order logic programming language, and it is not possible to pass a relation as an argument to another relation. □

15.2   Language design

15.2.1   Selection of concepts

The main purpose of this book has been to show that a large variety of programming languages can be understood in terms of a relatively small number of concepts. Nevertheless, these concepts are probably too numerous to be incorporated in a single language. The language designer's first problem, therefore, is a judicious selection of concepts. What to omit is just as important a decision as what to include.

Of the basic concepts studied in Chapters 2–5, the concepts of values (primitive and composite), bindings, and abstraction are so fundamental that they are sure to be present in every programming language. Storage might seem to be equally fundamental. However, the (pure) functional and logic languages demonstrate that this concept is not indispensable: many useful problems can be solved entirely in terms of functions or relations. A *general-purpose* language needs variables and commands; but the non-imperative parts of the language should be rich enough to allow the programmer to work entirely within them whenever appropriate.

In the 1990s it is hard to envisage a realistic language that does not support encapsulation in some form. Programmers can exploit the concept of encapsulation to decompose large programs into modules. This is an essential tool for managing the complexity of large programs. Even smaller programs benefit from a modular structure, and a lack of encapsulation is now seen as a weakness in any programming language. The language designer has several kinds of module to choose from. Abstract types and objects are suitable for simple programming languages, but packages (which are more general, and can be used to implement abstract types and objects) are probably needed in general-purpose languages.

An important goal of software engineering is reuse. When designing and constructing a new program, we want to be able to select 'off the shelf' modules that have previously been developed and thoroughly verified. Reusable modules must be self-contained, and in particular should make no unnecessary assumptions about the types of data that they manipulate. Thus a language intended for serious software engineering should support some form of generics, inheritance, or polymorphism. Currently these concepts tend to be associated with imperative, object-oriented, and functional languages, respectively, but it is not clear why this should be so. Language designers have limited experience with these concepts, which developed in the late 1970s, and consequently they are less well understood than the more basic concepts that have been in use since the 1950s.

Concurrency is also important in some applications. But concurrent programming is significantly more difficult than sequential programming, and is justified only when large efficiency gains are possible (e.g., when an inherently parallel algorithm can be implemented on a multiprocessor), or when the application is naturally concurrent or real-time (e.g., an operating system or process controller). The language designer can reasonably omit concurrency in a language not intended for such applications.

15.2.2   Regularity

How should concepts be combined to design a programming language? Simply piling feature upon feature is not a good approach, as PL/I vividly demonstrated. Even smaller languages sometimes betray similar symptoms. Fortran and Cobol offer baroque input–output facilities, but every programmer encounters situations where these facilities are not exactly what he or she requires. Surely it is preferable to provide a small set of basic facilities, and allow programmers to build more elaborate facilities on top of these as required? Abstract types and objects support and encourage this approach.

To achieve maximum power with a given number of concepts, the programmer should be able to combine these concepts in a regular fashion, with no unnecessary restrictions or surprising interactions. The semantic principles discussed in this book help the language designer to avoid irregularities.

The type completeness principle (Section 2.5.3) suggests that all types in the language should have equal status. For example, parameters and function results should not be restricted in type. Nevertheless, many languages restrict function results to be primitive; this forces the programmer, in a situation where a function with a composite result would be natural, to resort to a procedure that stores the composite result in an argument variable. Imagine programming complex arithmetic in a language where we cannot write functions (such as addition) with complex results!

The abstraction principle (Section 5.1.3) invites the language designer to consider abstraction over each semantically meaningful syntactic class. Nearly all languages have functions, abstracting over expressions, and/or procedures, abstracting over commands. The language designer should also consider abstraction over declarations (e.g., Ada generics) and over types (e.g., ML parameterized types).

The correspondence principle (Section 5.2.3) states that for each form of declaration there exists a corresponding parameter mechanism, and *vice versa*. This principle helps the language designer to select from the bewildering variety of possible parameter mechanisms. To the extent that the language complies with this principle, the programmer can perform certain program transformations easily and reliably: transforming a block into an abstraction, and *vice versa*.

The qualification principle (Section 4.5.3) invites the language designer to consider including a block in each semantically meaningful syntactic class. Many languages have block commands, but few have block expressions, and still fewer have block declarations.

15.2.3   Simplicity

Simplicity should always be a goal of language design. The programming language is the programmer's most basic tool, and must be thoroughly mastered. The language should help the programmer to solve problems: it should allow solutions to problems to be expressed naturally, and indeed should help the programmer to discover these solutions in the first place. A large and complicated language *creates* problems by being difficult to master. Tony Hoare has expressed this point succinctly: large and complicated languages belong to the problem space, rather than to the solution space.

Pascal demonstrates that a language designed with limited aims can be very simple. Indeed its success was due largely to its simplicity. It incorporates a small but judicious selection of concepts; it is easily and quickly mastered, and yet powerful enough to solve a wide variety of problems.

Nevertheless, the goal of simplicity is in conflict with the demands of a truly general-purpose language. Such a language will be used in a wide variety of application areas, including those demanding concurrent and real-time programming. It will be used to construct large programs consisting of numerous modules written by different programmers, and to construct libraries of modules likely to be reused in many programs. Such a language must incorporate most of the concepts studied in this book, and is bound to be much more complicated than Pascal.

To resolve this conflict, the most promising approach is to compartmentalize the language. An individual programmer then has to master only those parts of the language needed to solve the problem on hand. For this approach to work, the language designer must avoid any unexpected interactions between different parts of the language, for then an unwary programmer might stray into unknown territory.

PL/I has been heavily and justifiably criticized for failing to control its complexity. A notorious example is the innocent-looking expression '25 + 1/3', which might easily be written by a programmer familiar only with the rules of integer arithmetic. This expression yields 5.3! The reason is that PL/I defines evaluation of this expression in terms of its complicated (and counterintuitive) rules for fixed-point arithmetic, which entail truncation of the least *and most* significant digits!

Ada has also been criticized for its size and complexity. In many respects, however, Ada makes a reasonable job of controlling its complexity. For example, a Pascal programmer converting to Ada is unlikely to get into trouble with exceptions, even if unaware of their existence. In the absence of a handler, an Ada program raising an exception will simply halt with an appropriate diagnostic message, just as the corresponding Pascal program would do. On the other hand, the unwary programmer is liable to be confused by the mere existence of overloading in Ada. If he or she declares an integer function and then calls it in a context where a real result is expected (which is legal in Pascal, due to the availability of an integer-to-real coercion), the resulting error message might well be phrased in terms of a failure to identify an overloaded function!

Even ML, a very much simpler language, has traps for the unwary programmer who chooses to rely on type inference. Consider the function definition:

fun f (g) = **if** g (true) **then** g (1) **else** g (2)

This seems reasonable, since the function call 'f (id)' could sensibly be evaluated. However, the function definition will fail its type check because ML's type inference rules cannot find a type for g: its type would have to be both Truth-Value → Truth-Value and Integer → τ. Another danger in ML's type inference is that the type inferred for a function might be different from the one intended by the programmer. Such a discrepancy might be buried in the middle of a large program, and thus escape notice.

What overloading and type inference have in common is a lack of redundancy. The Pascal programmer redundantly has to specify the type of every entity, and redundantly may declare only one entity with a given identifier within a given scope; the compiler then simply checks the usage of these entities against rigid type rules. With overloading or type inference, information not supplied explicitly by the programmer must be deduced by the compiler. This is error-prone, since a slight programming error might radically affect what the compiler deduces.

To return to our theme of controlling complexity, the language designer cannot, and should not attempt to, anticipate all facilities that the programmer will need. Rather than building too many facilities into the language, the language should allow programmers to identify the facilities they need and implement them in the language itself. The key to this is abstraction. Each new function, in effect, enriches the language's repertoire of expressions; each new procedure enriches its repertoire of commands; and each new abstract type or object class enriches its repertoire of types.

We can illustrate this idea in the area of input–output. Fortran, Cobol, and PL/I are notable for their baroque input–output sublanguages. Being built-in and inextensible, they make a vain attempt to be comprehensive, but often fail to provide exactly the facilities needed in a particular situation. By contrast, Ada has no built-in input–output at all. Instead there are several standard input–output packages, which cater for most needs. But a programmer who does not need these packages can ignore them, and a programmer who needs different facilities can design a new input–output package. Neither pays any penalty (e.g., in terms of compiler complexity) for the existence of the standard input–output packages.

Taken to its logical conclusion, this approach suggests a small core language with powerful abstraction mechanisms, together with a rich environment of standard modules. The language could provide a small number of primitive types, together with ways of defining new primitive and composite types, and associated operations. The environment could include modules for strings, lists, arrays, input–output, and so on. See Figure 15.1. The effect is that necessary complexity is transferred from the programming language itself to its environment. Furthermore, programmers can smoothly extend the environment by adding new modules for such things as trees, tables, dictionaries, different input–output facilities, and so on. Smalltalk illustrates this approach very well. (See also Exercise 15.5.)

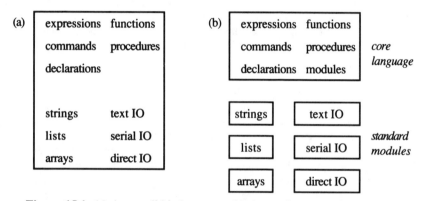

Figure 15.1 (a) A monolithic language. (b) A core language plus modules.

15.2.4   Syntax

This book has deliberately concentrated on semantic concepts, because they are of primary importance in designing, understanding, and using programming languages. Syntactic issues are of secondary importance – but by no means unimportant! So a brief discussion is certainly appropriate here.

Numerous articles have been written on surface syntactic issues. Should semicolons separate or terminate commands? Should keywords be abbreviated? Should control structures be fully bracketed? And so on. Undoubtedly these aspects of a language's syntax affect the number of syntactic errors made by programming novices, but experienced programmers have little trouble in adapting to the conventions of a new language.

The overriding criterion for a language's syntax is that programs should be *readable*. A program is written once but read many times, both by its author and by other programmers. So the language designer should choose a syntax that permits and encourages programmers to write programs fit to be read by others. Programmers should be free to choose meaningful identifiers (an obvious point, perhaps, but one ignored in Fortran and Basic). Keywords should generally be preferred to unfamiliar symbols. It should be easy to mingle commentary with the program text, and to lay out the text in such a way as to suggest its syntactic (and semantic) structure.

A deeper point is that the syntax should be transparent. It should be obvious from a syntactic form what semantic concept is being invoked. The syntactic forms and semantic concepts should be (more or less) in one-to-one correspondence.

The same syntactic form should not mean different things in different contexts. For example, the Pascal syntactic form '**var** *I* : *T* ' violates this dictum. In one context this is a new-variable declaration, binding *I* to a newly created variable. In another context the same form is a variable parameter specification, binding *I* to an *existing* variable.

A single syntactic form should not confuse two distinct concepts. For example, Pascal and Ada record types confuse the distinct concepts of Cartesian product and disjoint union. This makes it awkward for the programmer to define a plain disjoint union type. In Pascal, moreover, the fact that a union behaves like a record leads to insecurity, due to selective updating of the tag field; in Ada this insecurity is avoided, but at the cost of restrictions that are hard to learn and understand. By contrast, ML's so-called datatypes clearly and directly support the concept of disjoint union, and its record types separately support the concept of Cartesian product.

Each concept should preferably be supported by a single syntactic form. Providing alternative forms for the same concept makes the language larger and more complicated, and is rarely justified. A fairly harmless example was the existence of the notation '*E* **where** *D* **end**' as an alternative to '**let** *D* **in** *E* **end**' in an earlier version of ML. More seriously, Ada has a bad tendency to allow the programmer to achieve a given effect in several different ways. For example, given the procedure declaration:

```
procedure draw_box (x, y, width, depth : Integer);
```

this procedure can be called not only in the conventional positional notation:

```
draw_box (0, 0, 4, 2);
```

but also in keyword notation:

```
      draw_box (x=>0, y=>0, width=>4, depth=>2);
  or  draw_box (depth=>2, width=>4, x=>0, y=>0);
  or  ...
```

The advantage of keyword notation is that the user of the procedure does not have to remember the parameter order. The disadvantage is that the flexible order of actual parameters, together with the possibility of mixing positional and keyword notation and the existence of default arguments, makes the rules for interpreting procedure calls very much more complicated.

A program is essentially a semantic structure, specifying how a computation should be performed. The syntax is merely a notation by which the programmer selects the semantic concepts to be used in that computation. The most important properties of the syntax is that it should be easy to learn, and make programs easy to understand.

15.2.5   The programming language life cycle

Each new language passes through a number of stages from its initial design to routine use by programmers:

- The requirements for the new language are identified. What is its intended application area? Will it be used to write long-lived reusable software, or short-lived 'throw away' programs?
- The language's syntax and semantics are designed. As discussed above, the primary decisions are which semantic concepts to select, and how to combine them to make the language regular and simple, yet powerful. Design of the syntax is secondary, and should be left until last.
- A formal or informal specification of the new language is prepared. If informal, the specification must be clearly written and, as far as possible, complete, consistent, and unambiguous.
- Using the specification, an initial implementation of the new language is constructed. The new language is tested by programmers.
- The specification, implementation, and programmers' experience all provide feedback to the designer, drawing attention to any unsatisfactory aspects of the new language. The design can then be improved.
- If the new language is successful, improved implementations are constructed, textbooks are written, and a community of programmers is built up. In due course, the language might become a national or international standard. It might also undergo revision as the need is perceived.

The perceptive reader might notice analogies between the above and the familiar software life cycle: requirements, design, specification, prototyping, implementation, testing, documentation, and maintenance. In fact, we have identified a *programming language life cycle*.

15.3   Further reading

The Quicksort algorithm (implemented in Examples 15.2, 15.3, and 15.4) is fully described in Hoare (1962).

Useful commonsense advice on language design has been offered by Hoare (1973) and Wirth (1974). Both Hoare and Wirth place strong emphasis on simplicity, security, efficiency (at both compile-time and run-time), and readability. Hoare recommends that the language designer should select and consolidate concepts already invented and tested by others, and avoid the temptation to introduce new and untried concepts. Wirth emphasizes the importance of making the inherent cost of using each concept clearly visible to the programmer.

The present author advocates an integrated approach to language design, specification, and implementation. A central role is played by a formal specification of the new language, which should be the designer's first task. Writing the specification helps the designer to discover inconsistencies, irregularities, and unnecessary complexities in the new language. The same specification acts as a basis for prototyping, and eventually full implementation, of the language. It also acts as a definitive source for the preparation of language manuals and textbooks. For a more detailed discussion see Watt (1986).

Exercises 15

15.1* Assess your favorite programming language against the checklist in Section 15.1.1, in the context of a software project in which you have recently been involved. Are there any issues in language selection that you would add to the checklist?

15.2 Make the Ada `sort` procedure of Example 15.2 generic, with respect to the type of items being sorted, and with respect to the item comparison function.

15.3 Make the ML `sort` function of Example 15.3 polymorphic, and parameterize it with respect to the item comparison function.

15.4* Assess each of the following language's compliance with the abstraction principle: Fortran, Cobol, Pascal, Ada, Smalltalk, ML, and Prolog. Consider expressions, commands, declarations, types, and any other relevant syntactic classes.

15.5* Consider the approach to managing language complexity suggested at the end of Section 15.2.3, and illustrated in Figure 15.1. It might be argued that this is a recipe for chaos. A monolithic language at least forces all programmers to work with a common set of facilities. A core language plus modules encourages programmers to invent and use their own facilities, encouraging egotistic programming and impeding program portability. Develop this argument, and also develop a counterargument.

Answers to Selected Exercises

This appendix gives answers, sometimes only in outline, to about half of each set of exercises.

Answers 2

2.1

Suit = {*club, diamond, heart, spade*}
Rank = {2, ..., 14}
Card = Suit × Rank
Hand = {1, ..., 7} → Card
Turn = Card + Unit

2.3 (a) A *serial file* with components of type T may be viewed as a list in T^*. However, the process of reading a serial file effectively splits it into two lists: components already read, and components still to be read. Thus $T^* \times T^*$.

(b) A *direct file* with components of type T is essentially a mapping in $\{1, ..., m\} \to T$, assuming that components are indexed by positive integers up to a maximum of m.

(c) A *relation* is a set of tuples or records. If each tuple has two components, of types S and T, then we have $\wp\ (S \times T)$. (Alternative answers are $S \to \wp T$ and $T \to \wp S$.)

2.4 (a) The predefined Ada operator **not** and the following constant array:

```
non : constant array (Boolean) of Boolean
        := (false => true, true => false);
```

both represent the same mapping, *(false ↦ true, true ↦ false}*, so '**not** b' and 'non (b)' always yield exactly the same result.

(b) The following Ada function and constant array:

```
subtype Small is Integer range 1..7;

function factorial (n : Small) : Integer is
begin
   if n = 1 then
      return 1;
   else
      return n * factorial (n-1);
   end if;
end

fac : constant array (Small) of Integer
      := (1 => 1, 2 => 2, 3 => 6, 4 => 24,
          5 => 120, 6 => 720, 7 => 5040)
```

both represent the same mapping, $\{1 \mapsto 1, 2 \mapsto 2, 3 \mapsto 6, 4 \mapsto 24, 5 \mapsto 120, 6 \mapsto 720, 7 \mapsto 5040\}$, so 'factorial (i)' and 'fac(i)' always yield exactly the same result.

A variable array can be selectively updated, whereas a constant array or function abstraction represents a fixed mapping. A function abstraction contains an algorithm, and so might behave in certain ways (e.g., nontermination, side effects) that are impossible when accessing a component of an array, which is a passive data structure.

2.5 The set of values of type Screen would be $\{0, ..., 511\} \times \{0, ..., 255\} \to \{0, 1\}$, i.e., exactly the same as type Window. An array s of type Screen could be indexed directly by a record p of type Position, as in 's[p]', whereas an array of type Window must always be indexed by two separately computed integers, as in 'w[p.x,p.y].

2.6 The sets $S \to (T \to U)$ and $(S \times T) \to U$ are isomorphic. For each mapping $f: S \to (T \to U)$, there is a mapping $g: (S \times T) \to U$ such that $f(x)(y) = g(x,y)$; and *vice versa*.

The two array types are isomorphic. In Pascal they are treated as equivalent; in Ada they are not.

(In general, two sets are *isomorphic* if and only if there is a one-to-one correspondence between the values in one set and the values in the other.)

2.7 The sets $S \to$ Truth-Value and $\wp S$ are isomorphic. For each set $s: \wp S$, there is a mapping $f: S \to$ Truth-Value such that $f(x) = (x \in s)$; and *vice versa*. In fact, 'set of S' in Pascal is usually implemented in the same way as 'packed array [S] of Boolean'.

2.11 In Ada a file variable is declared with a type that implies the type of the file components. Say that f is declared as an integer-file variable. Then, e.g., 'open (f, ..., "DATA")' opens the actual (filestore) file named DATA and makes f refer to it; and 'write (f, 5)' writes an integer to the file to which f refers. The identity of the actual file named DATA is determined only when the open procedure is called, so there can be no type check on the actual file until then. Thus the open procedure call must be type-checked dynamically. (Indeed, the actual file might not even exist at compile-time.) However, calls to the write procedure can be type-checked statically, e.g., 'write (f, "May")' would fail its type check.

2.12 Pascal conforms poorly with the type completeness principle:

Type	*constant*	*operand*	*operator result*	*argu-ment*	*function result*	*compo-nent*
primitive	•	•	•	•	•	•
record/array				•		•
string	•	•		•		•
set		•	•	•		•
file						•
pointer	•			•	•	•
reference				•		
abstraction				•		

Ada conforms with the principle in respect of its first-class values:

Type	*constant*	*operand*	*operator result*	*argu-ment*	*function result*	*compo-nent*
primitive	•	•	•	•	•	•
composite	•	•	•	•	•	•
pointer	•	•	•	•	•	•
reference				•		
abstraction						

ML conforms fully with the principle:

Type	*constant*	*operand*	*operator result*	*argu-ment*	*function result*	*compo-nent*
primitive	•	•	•	•	•	•
composite	•	•	•	•	•	•
reference	•	•	•	•	•	•
function	•	•	•	•	•	•

Answers 3

3.2   (a) If strings are static arrays, the length of each string variable is fixed when the program is written. Shorter strings can be accommodated, but only using some programmer-defined convention such as a sentinel character. Comparison and concatenation would probably have to be programmed explicitly – even if these operations were provided for arrays generally, they would not respect the sentinel-character convention.

(b) If strings are dynamic arrays, the length of each string variable is fixed when it is created at run-time. Otherwise the above points still apply.

(c) If strings are flexible arrays, the length of each string variable changes on every assignment. Comparison and concatenation, if provided for flexible arrays generally, would work for strings too.

3.3   Lifetimes of variables:

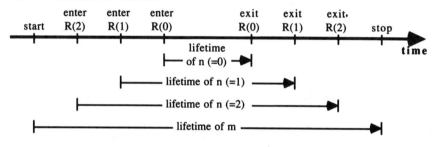

3.4   Lifetimes of variables:

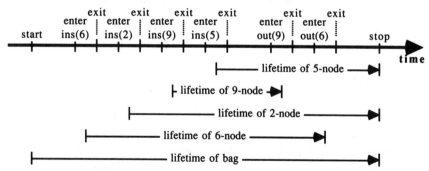

3.10   The loop '**repeat** C **until** E' is exactly equivalent to:

```
C;
if not (E) then
    repeat C until E
```

The loop '**repeat** C_1 **while** E **do** C_2' is exactly equivalent to:

```
C₁;
if E then
   begin
   C₂;
   repeat C₁ while E do C₂
   end
```

3.13   Forbid a function body to update any nonlocal variable (either directly or through a variable parameter). Forbid a function body to call any nonlocal procedure (either directly or through a procedural parameter), since there is a possibility that the procedure might cause side effects.

The latter condition is stronger than strictly necessary: the nonlocal procedure would not necessarily cause side effects. However, the restrictions would not significantly reduce the expressive power of Pascal functions (at least for those programmers who prefer to avoid side effects).

Answers 4

4.2   Environments:
① { x ↦ 99 }
② { x ↦ 99, Nat ↦ type }
③ { x ↦ 99, Nat ↦ type, m ↦ variable, n ↦ variable }
④ { x ↦ 99, Nat ↦ type, m ↦ variable, f ↦ function abstraction,
      n ↦ value parameter }
⑤ { x ↦ 99, Nat ↦ type, m ↦ variable, n ↦ variable,
      f ↦ function abstraction }
⑥ { x ↦ 99, Nat ↦ type, m ↦ variable, n ↦ variable,
      f ↦ function abstraction, w ↦ procedure abstraction,
      i ↦ value parameter }
⑦ { x ↦ 99, Nat ↦ type, m ↦ variable, f ↦ function abstraction,
      w ↦ procedure abstraction, i ↦ value parameter, n ↦ 6 }
⑧ { x ↦ 99, Nat ↦ type, m ↦ variable, n ↦ variable,
      f ↦ function abstraction, w ↦ procedure abstraction }

4.5   One possibility is to change the syntax of an Ada function definition to:

function *I* (*FP₁*; ...; *FPₙ*) **return** *T* **is** *F*

where *F* designates the function that *I* is to denote. *F* could be either an ordinary function body, or the identifier of an existing function.

4.6   A Pascal function body defines its result by an assignment of the form '*I* : = *E*', where *I* is the function identifier; thus the function body cannot be separated from the function definition of *I*. If the assignment were replaced by a command such as '**return** E', however, the function body would become a self-contained block expression.

4.7   In the ML recursive value definition '**val rec** $I = E$', we must evaluate E before we know what I denotes, and this cannot be done if E contains I as a subexpression. But there is no problem if E is of the form '**fn** (...) => ... I ...', since the function body is not evaluated until the function is actually called.

4.8   The filenames are completely unrelated to the identifiers in a program; their scopes do not overlap.

The command '`reset (f, 'EMPS')`' opens the file denoted by EMPS in the file environment *at the time the command is executed*, not at the time the command was compiled. This is dynamic binding.

A standard Pascal program cannot use filenames. Its only means of communicating with actual (filestore) files is through program parameters; the program can be 'called' with actual files as arguments. Thus there is no dynamic binding in standard Pascal.

Answers 5

5.1   If a function body were simply an expression, Pascal's expression repertoire would need to include conditional expressions (to compensate for the loss of conditional commands), block expressions (to allow local declarations), aggregates (to compensate for the loss of assignments to construct composite values); also, constants and functions of any type should be permitted.

5.2   (a) It would not make sense to apply the abstraction principle to literals, since they contain no details to abstract from, and cannot be parameterized. (b) It would make sense to apply the abstraction principle to types – see Sections 6.2 and 7.3.2.

5.3   For example, a parameterless function that returns a random number, or a parameterless function that returns the current time of day. A parameterless function like these must work by inspecting a global variable that is updated behind the scenes, either by the function itself or by some other means.

5.4   Value parameters work by assignment. In Pascal a file value may not be assigned.

5.7   Using ML-like syntax:

> **fun** if_then_else (b: bool, x: τ, y: τ) =
>   **if** b **then** x **else** y

With eager evaluation, all arguments would be evaluated. But with normal-order or lazy evaluation, either the second or the third argument would remain unevaluated.

5.12   (a) Eager evaluation:

$$F \ (E') \ \equiv \ subst \ (E, X, value \ of \ E')$$

(b) In the example given, blind substitution would lead to an unintentional identifier clash. Instead we must systematically replace the inner binding occurrence of n, and all corresponding applied occurrences of n, by a different identifier:

```
let
   val n = 2;
   fun f (x: int) =
         let val n' = 7 in n' * x end
in
   f (n+1)
end
```

before doing the substitution. Thus the result of substitution will be:

```
let
   val n = 2;
in
   let val n' = 7 in n' * (n+1) end
end
```

Answers 6

6.2   (a) Use the following single declarations:

```
const pi = 3.1416;

function norm (x : Real) : Real;  ...;
function sin (x : Real) : Real;  ...;
function cos (x : Real) : Real;  ...
```

Disadvantages: pi and norm are not hidden; the grouping is informal; the constant definition must be separated from the function definitions.

(b) Using an ML-like block declaration:

```
local
   const pi = 3.1416;
   function norm (x : Real) : Real;   ...
in
   function sin (x : Real) : Real;   ...;
   function cos (x : Real) : Real;   ...
end
```

6.4   (a) Complex might have operations:

```
zero, one, i :  Complex
      complex :  Real × Real → Complex
         +, - :  Complex → Complex
   +, -, *, / :  Complex × Complex → Complex
  re, im, abs :  Complex → Real
```

Possible representation: a pair of real numbers (real and imaginary parts).
(b) Money might have operations:

```
    zero :  Money
   cents :  Integer → Money
 dollars :  Real → Money
    +, - :  Money → Money
    +, - :  Money × Money → Money
    *, / :  Money × Real → Money
       / :  Money × Money → Real
```

Possible representation: an integer (sum of money in cents).
(c) Date might have operations:

```
date :  Integer × Month × {1, ..., 31} → Date
+, - :  Date × Integer → Date
   - :  Date × Date → Integer
```

Possible representation: a triple in Integer × Month × {1, ..., 31}.
(d) Fuzzy might have operations:

```
yes, no, unknown :  Fuzzy
             not :  Fuzzy → Fuzzy
         and, or :  Fuzzy × Fuzzy → Fuzzy
```

Possible representation: *yes*, *no*, or *unknown*.

6.6   (a) Counter object as an Ada package:

```
package counter_object is
   procedure zero;
   procedure increment;
   function count return Natural;
end counter_object;
```

```
package counter_object body is

    n : Natural;

    procedure zero is
    begin
        n := 0;
    end;

    procedure increment is
    begin
        n := n+1;
    end;

    function count return Natural is
    begin
        return n;
    end;

end counter_object;
```

(b) Counter class as an Ada generic package:

```
generic package counter_class is
    procedure zero;
    procedure increment;
    function count return Natural;
end counter_class;
```

Otherwise as in (a).

6.7 Advantages of automatic initialization: it guarantees that the object always has a defined state; the user does not have to remember to call an initialization procedure. Disadvantage: not every object has a unique obvious initial state, so several initialization procedures, or a parameterized initialization procedure, might be preferable to automatic initialization.

6.10 The generic package body of Example 6.10 might be completed as follows:

```
package body queue_class is
    items : array (1..capacity) of Character;
    size, front, rear :
            Integer range 0..capacity;

    procedure append
                (newitem : in Character) is
    begin
        if size < capacity then
            size := size + 1;
            rear := rear mod capacity + 1;
            items(rear) := newitem;
```

```
            else
               ...;   -- queue is full
            end if;
         end;

         procedure remove
                    (olditem : out Character) is
         begin
            if size > 0 then
               olditem := items(front);
               size := size - 1;
               front := front mod capacity + 1;
            else
               ...;   -- queue is empty
            end if;
         end;

      begin
         size := 0;  front := 1;  rear := 0;
      end queue_class;
```

The generic package body of Example 6.11 would be similar, except for replacement of the free type identifier Character by the type parameter Item.

6.11   (a) Outline of Ada generic package declaration and body:

```
      generic
         type Item is private;
      package set_type is
         type Set is limited private;
         ...
      private
         type SetNode;
         type Set      is access SetNode;
         type SetNode is record
                           member : Item;
                           rest : Set;
                         end record;
         empty : constant Set := null;
      end set_type;

      package body set_type is

         function single (anitem : Item)
                          return Set is
         begin
            return new SetNode' (anitem, null);
         end;
```

```
function member (anitem : Item;
                  aset : Set)
                        return Boolean is
   s : Set := aset;
begin
   while s /= null and then
         s.member /= anitem loop
      s := s.rest;
   end loop;
   return (s /= null);
end;

   ...

end set_type;
```

Here a set is represented by a list of distinct items. The assumption is that the operations '=' and '/=' are available for type Item — this is in fact the minimum assumption.

(b) Outline of Ada generic package declaration and body:

```
generic
   type Item is (<>);    -- a discrete primitive type
package set_type is
   type Set is limited private;
   ...

private
   type Set is array (Item) of Boolean;
   empty : constant Set := (Item => false);
end set_type;

package body set_type is

   function single (anitem : Item)
                        return Set is
   begin
      return Set' (anitem => true,
               others => false);
   end;

   function member (anitem : Item;
                     aset : Set)
                        return Boolean is
   begin
      return aset(anitem);
   end;

   ...

end set_type;
```

Here a set is represented by an array indexed by items. The membership test is far more efficient. The price paid by the user is that the generic package is less general: it can be instantiated to handle sets of discrete primitive values, but not sets of strings, sets of records, etc.

Answers 7

7.2 A procedure with parameter type S may be overloaded with a procedure with parameter type S' only if S and S' are distinct. (As usual, S and S' may be Cartesian products.) Overloading of procedures is always context-independent.

Any procedure call of the form 'write (i/j)' is ambiguous if i and j are of type Integer.

7.3 A literal of type T may be overloaded with a literal of type T' only if T and T' are distinct. Overloading of literals is always context-dependent.

The proposed overloading of integer literals would make expressions like '7/3' ambiguous.

7.4 (a) The list reversing function has type $\text{List}(\tau) \rightarrow \text{List}(\tau)$. (b) The list concatenation function has type $\text{List}(\tau) \times \text{List}(\tau) \rightarrow \text{List}(\tau)$. See Example 13.9 for definitions of these two functions.

(c) The function to return the ith component of a given list has type $\text{List}(\tau) \times \text{Integer} \rightarrow \tau$:

```
fun indexed (l, i) =
        if i = 1
        then hd (l)
        else indexed (tl (l), i-1)
```

7.5 The function map has type $(\sigma \rightarrow \tau) \times \text{List}(\sigma) \rightarrow \text{List}(\tau)$:

```
fun map (f, l) =
        case l of
           nil => nil
         | cons(h,t) =>
               cons (f (h), map (f, t))
```

The function filter has type $(\sigma \rightarrow \text{Truth-Value}) \times \text{List}(\sigma) \rightarrow \text{List}(\sigma)$:

```
fun filter (f, l) =
        case l of
           nil => nil
         | cons(h,t) =>
               if f (h)
```

```
            then cons (h, filter (f, t))
            else filter (f, t)
```

7.6   Parameterized set type in ML:

```
        abstype τ set = τ list
        with
            val empty = nil;
            fun single (anitem: τ) =
                    [anitem]
            and union (set1: τ set, set2: τ set) =

                    ...

            and member (anitem: τ, aset: τ set) =
                    case aset of
                        nil =>
                            false
                      | cons(first,rest) =>
                            if anitem = first
                            then true
                            else member (anitem, rest)

            ...
        end
```

The constant empty has type Set(τ), the function single has type $\tau \rightarrow$ Set(τ), the function union has type Set(τ) $\times$ Set(τ) $\rightarrow$ Set(τ), the function member has type $\tau \times$ Set(τ) $\rightarrow$ Truth-Value, etc.

7.7   The function negation has type ($\tau \rightarrow$ Truth-Value) $\rightarrow$ ($\tau \rightarrow$ Truth-Value); cond has type ($\sigma \rightarrow$ Truth-Value) $\times$ ($\sigma \rightarrow \tau$) $\times$ ($\sigma \rightarrow \tau$) $\rightarrow$ ($\sigma \rightarrow \tau$).

7.8   The function insert has type $\sigma \times$ ($\tau \times \sigma \rightarrow \sigma$) $\times$ List(τ) $\rightarrow \sigma$. The functions sum1 and sum2 have type List(Integer) $\rightarrow$ Integer; they are in fact the same function.

Answers 8

8.3   The hypothetical loop 'repeat C_1 while E do C_2' is a single-entry single-exit control structure because the subcommands C_1 and C_2 each has a single entry and a single exit, and so does the loop as a whole.

       The Ada loop 'loop C end loop;' (where C contains one or more simple *exit* sequencers) is a single-entry multi-exit control structure because the subcommand C has multiple exits (although the loop as a whole has a single exit).

8.5 This is slightly awkward in Ada, but easy if the language were extended with an all-purpose escape allowing exit from *any* command:

```
search:
begin
   for amonth in Month loop
      for aday in Day loop
         if matches (..., ...) then
            keydate :=
                   (m => amonth, d => aday);
               escape search;
            end if;
         end loop;
      end loop;
      keydate := default date;
end;
```

8.6 In the following, 'escape loopbody' would achieve the effect of C's *continue* sequencer:

```
loop
   loopbody:
   begin
      ...
      ... escape loopbody;
      ...
   end;
end loop;
```

8.7 Procedure get_weather_data with result codes:

```
type ResultCode is
        (ok, data_error, end_error);

procedure get_weather_data
              (result : out ResultCode) is
   get_result : ResultCode;
begin
   for amonth in Month loop
      begin
         get (rainfall(amonth), get_result);
         case get_result is
            when data_error =>
               put ("..."); ...;
               skip_data_item; ...;
```

```
        when ok =>
            null;
        when others =>
            result := get_result; return;
      end case;
    end;
  end loop;
  result := ok;
end;
```

Main program with result codes:

```
procedure main (result : out ResultCode) is
  g_w_d_result : ResultCode;
begin
  get_weather_data (g_w_d_result);
  case g_w_d_result is
    when end_error =>
      put ("Incomplete data"); return;
    when ok =>
      null;
    when others =>
      result := g_w_d_result; return;
  end case;
  process_weather_data;
  result := ok;
end;
```

Result-code tests and handlers are italicized above. They swamp the normal-case code. The exception handlers in Example 8.5 are more concise, and also better separated from the normal-case code.

8.8   Revised package declaration:

```
generic
  capacity : in Positive;
package queue_class is
  procedure append (...);
  procedure remove (...);
  exception queue_full, queue_empty;
end queue_class;
```

Refer to the package body in the answer to Exercise 6.10 (above). At the comment *'queue is full '* insert the command '**raise** queue_full;'. At the comment *'queue is empty'* insert the command '**raise** queue_empty;'.

Answers 9

9.6   (*Note:* this is not Ada !)

```
procedure add (a, b : in Matrix;
                 sum : out Matrix) is
begin
   for i in 1 .. n loop
      declare
         k : Integer := i;
      begin
         start for j in 1 .. n loop
            declare
               l : Integer := j;
            begin
               start
                  sum(k,l) := a(k,l) + b(k,l);
            end;
         end loop;
      end;
   end loop;
end;
```

There are n^2+n+1 processes altogether. These could be active simultaneously, but it is more likely that processes created for early elements of the matrix will have terminated by the time later ones are started (because $t << T$ in practice). In a more realistic application, the computation would be much longer ($t \approx T$).

Special processors (such as the ICL Distributed Array Processor) have been designed for this kind of application. They are effective because, having one process preloaded in each processor, T is comparatively small while t can be large.

9.7   Using **start** again:

```
procedure traverse (atree : Tree; ...) is
begin
   if atree.left /= null then
      start traverse (atree.left, ...);
   end if;
   if atree.right /= null then
      start traverse (atree.right, ...);
   end if;
   ...;    -- process t.datum here;
end;
```

There is one call of `traverse` for every node in the tree, giving a total of n processes. The elapsed time between the first call on `traverse` and the last is proportional to $\log_2 n$, the depth of the tree. For the sequential program the elapsed time is proportional to n.

The concurrent version could not do any processing that depended on the results of traversing the subtrees. (Why?) Assuming that an ordinary procedure call takes 20μs and a process takes 20ms to start, how big must the tree be to show any speedup from the concurrency? Is this a practical proposition?

9.8   (a) To allow for indivisible operations.

(b) For example, without mutual exclusion, if process A stores 256 in I while process B is storing 255 in I, and store is accessed byte by byte, the end result could be 511.

(c) The same example would be OK if the values involved were 1 and 2, the data were stored in a single byte, and the store serialized byte accesses.

(d) The invariant is $0 \le waits(s) \le signals(s) + initial(s)$. The *wait* operation blocks the process until it can complete without violating the invariant. The *signal* operation unblocks a blocked process (if there is one), according to a fair scheduling rule such as first-come-first-served.

(e) A general semaphore has arbitrary initial value, represented by an integer. To implement a general semaphore G, using binary semaphores G.B, G.S, and an integer G.I, the following code is often displayed:

(i)   `wait(G):`

```
    wait(G.B);
    G.I := G.I - 1;
    if G.I < 0 then
        signal(G.B);   wait(G.S);
    else
        signal(G.B);
    end if;
```

(ii) `signal(G):`

```
    wait(G.B);
    G.I := G.I + 1;
    if G.I <= 0 then
        signal(G.S);
    end if;
    signal(G.B);
```

Actually, there is a logical error in these algorithms. Can you see what it is?

9.9   Assume the declaration:

```
    v : shared Integer;
```

(a) Hansen form:

```
region v do
   while v > 0 loop
      v := v - n;
   end loop;
   (* v ≤0 *)
   await P(sqrt(-v));
   ...
end region;
```

(b) Hoare form:

```
region v do
   while v > 0 loop
      v := v - n;
   end loop;
end region;
region v (* v ≤0? *) await P(sqrt(-v));
   ...
end region;
```

How could the uncertainty as to the value of v be resolved in version (b)?

Answers 10

10.1 All except (b) would have effects dependent on the Stack representation. The effect of command (d) would be sharing in the pointer implementation, but copying in an array implementation. The others would even fail their type checks if the implementation were changed to an array.

10.2 Since Stack is limited, only (b) is legal. If Stack were not declared to be limited, (d) and (e) would be legal, but their effects would be implementation-dependent.

10.5 Instantiation and call of the generic procedure can be achieved anywhere by means of a block command:

```
declare
   procedure swapint is new swap (Integer);
begin
   swapint (a(i), a(i+1));
end;
```

Instantiation and call of a generic function cannot be achieved in a similar manner because Ada has no block *expression*.

10.6 Generic instantiations are restricted to declarations in order to allow the Ada compiler the choice of generating distinct object code from each instantiation. This might well be the best implementation strategy for generics with type parameters, such as Examples 10.10 and 10.11.

Answers 11

11.1 (b)

```
n : constant := 5;
...
type Process_Id is range 1 .. n;
type Resource_Id is range 1 .. n;
...

use serialized_output;
use banker;

procedure main is

    task type Philosopher is
        entry sign_in (id : in Integer);
        entry sign_out;
    end Philosopher;

    thinker :
            array (Resource_Id) of Philosopher;

    task body Philosopher is
        count        : Natural := 0;
        self         : Process_Id;
        left, right  : Resource_Id;
        my_forks     : Budget
                       := (Resource_Id => 0);
    begin
        accept sign_in (id : in Integer) do
            self  := Process_Id (id);
            right := Resource_Id (id);
            left  := right mod n + 1;
            my_forks(right) := 1;
            my_forks(left)  := 1;
            notify_claim (my_forks, self);
        end sign_in;
        loop
            acquire (right, self);
            acquire (left, self);
```

```
                  count := count + 1;
                  -- now philosopher self eats meal # count
                  relinquish (right, self);
                  relinquish (left, self);
                  -- now philosopher self finishes meal # count
                  exit when count = 20;   -- e.g.
              end loop;
              accept sign_out;
          end Philosopher;

      begin
          for id in 1 .. n loop
              thinker(id).sign_in(id);
          end loop;
          -- now they all are sitting at table and may eat
          for id in 1 .. n loop
              thinker(id).sign_out;
          end loop;
      end main;
```

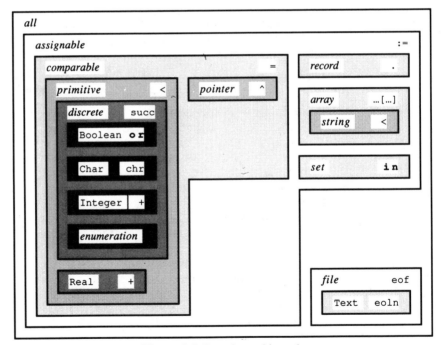

Figure A.1 Pascal type hierarchy.

Answers 12

12.2 The Pascal type class hierarchy is shown in Figure A.1, showing a typical operation for each type class.

This differs from the Smalltalk class hierarchy in that Pascal composite types (records, arrays, sets, and files) have components of *fixed* types, due to static typing. Also, each box with an italic label represents a *family* of types, not a single type. Thus (e.g.) we cannot simply create a variable of type *primitive*, and apply the operation '<' to it; in Smalltalk we can do this with the corresponding class Magnitude.

12.3 (a) Here is a definition of an object class Line, a subclass of Point. It uses the inherited hidden variables x and y (representing its midpoint), and additional hidden variables l (its length) and a (its angle of inclination).

```
placeat: xnew and: ynew \
 length: lnew angle: anew
    x <- xnew. y <- ynew. l <- lnew. a <- anew

length
    ^ l

inclination
    ^ a

rotateby: ashift
    a <- a + ashift

draw
        draw on the screen a line with length l, inclination a,
           and midpoint at coordinates x, y
```

Here is a definition of object class Rectangle, a subclass of Line. It uses the inherited hidden variables x and y (its center), l (its length), and a (its angle of inclination), and an additional hidden variable h (its height).

```
placeat: xnew and: ynew \
 length: lnew height: hnew angle: anew
    x <- xnew. y <- ynew.
    l <- lnew. h <- hnew. a <- anew

height
    ^ h

draw
        draw on the screen a rectangle with length l, height h,
           inclination a, and center at coordinates x, y
```

(b) Here is a definition of object class Picture, a subclass of Set:

```
draw
    self do: [ :element | element draw ]
```

(The variable self always refers to the receiver object. In this case, self is a Set object.)

Answers 13

13.3 (a)
```
fun perimeter (point)      = 0.0
  | perimeter (circle r) = 2.0 * pi * r
  | perimeter (box(l,h)) = 2.0 * (l + h)
```
  (b)
```
fun inside ((x,y), (xc,yc), point) =
        false
  | inside ((x,y), (xc,yc), circle r) =
        sqr(x-xc) + sqr(y-yc) < sqr(r)
  | inside ((x,y), (xc,yc), box(l,h))  =
        abs(x-xc) < 0.5*l
            andalso abs(y-yc) < 0.5*h
```

13.5 (a)
```
fun treed (nil)    = null
  | treed (n::ns) = insert (n, treed (ns))
```
  (b)
```
fun listed (null) =
        nil
  | listed (node(left,n,right)) =
        listed (left) @ [n] @ listed (right)
```
  (c)
```
listed o treed    (* is an integer list sorting function *)
```

13.6 (a)
```
[empl | empl <- employees; empl.sex = female]
```
  (b)
```
[empl | empl <- employees;
  empl.sex = male andalso empl.age >= 60]
```
  (c)
```
[empl.name | empl <- employees;
  empl.status = managerial]
```
  (d)
```
let
    fun mean (ages) =
```

```
                       sum (ages) div length (ages)
          in
              mean [empl.age | empl <- employees;
                     empl.sex = female
                       andalso empl.status = clerical]
          end
```

13.7   (a)

```
          map (fn I => E₁)  (E₂)
```

(b)

```
          map (fn I => E₁) (filter (fn I => E₃) (E₂))
```

13.11 Using relative difference rather than absolute difference:

```
          fun rel (eps) (approx1::approx2::approxs) =
                 if abs ((approx1-approx2)/approx2)
                     <= eps
                 then approx2
                 else rel (eps) (approx2::approxs)
          ...
          val sqrt = rel (0.0001) o approxsqrts
```

Choosing the fourth approximation unconditionally:

```
          fun fourth (approx1::approx2::approx3
                       ::approx4::approxs) =
                 approx4
          ...
          val sqrt = fourth o approxsqrts
```

Answers 14

14.1

```
          collinear(pt(X1,Y1), pt(X2,Y2), pt(X3,Y3))  :-
              X1 \= X2,  X2 \= X3,
              (Y1-Y2)/(X1-X2) = (Y2-Y3)/(X2-X3).
          collinear(pt(X1,Y1), pt(X2,Y2), pt(X3,Y3))  :-
              X1 = X2,  X2 = X3.
```

14.2   (a)

```
          addlast(X, L1, L2)  :-  append(L1, [X], L2).
```

(b)

```
          last(X, [X]).
          last(X, [Y|Ys])  :-  last(X, Ys).
```

(c)

```
reverse(Xs, Zs)   :-
      shift(Xs, [], Zs).
shift([], Ys, Ys).
shift([X|Xs], Ys, Zs)   :-
      shift (Xs, [X|Ys], Zs).
```

(d)

```
ordered([]).
ordered([N]).
ordered([N1,N2|Nums])   :-
      N1 =< N2,   ordered([N2|Nums]).
```

Answers 15

15.2

```
generic
   type Item is private;
   type ItemSequence is
           array (Integer range <>) of Item;
   with function precedes (x, y : Item)
                                  return Boolean;
procedure sort (...);

procedure sort (...) is
   ...

   procedure partition (...) is
      ...
   begin
      loop
         while precedes (items(l), pivot) ...
         while precedes (pivot, items(r)) ...
         ...
      end loop;
      ...
   end partition;

begin
   ...
end sort;
```

15.3

```
fun generic_sort (precedes) =
    let
        fun partition (pivot, ...) =
                ...
                if precedes (first, pivot) ...
                ...
        fun sort (...) =
                ...
    in
        sort
    end
```

Bibliography

Abelson, H., Sussman, G.J., and Sussman, J. (1985) *Structure and Interpretation of Computer Programs*, MIT Press, Cambridge, Massachusetts; also McGraw-Hill, New York.

ANSI (1966) *American National Standard FORTRAN*, ANS X3.9-1966, American National Standards Institute, New York.

ANSI (1974) *American National Standard Programming Language COBOL*, ANS X3.23-1974, American National Standards Institute, New York.

ANSI (1976) *American National Standard Programming Language PL/I*, ANS X3.53-1976, American National Standards Institute, New York.

ANSI (1978) *American National Standard Programming Language FORTRAN*, ANS X3.9-1978, American National Standards Institute, New York.

ANSI/IEEE (1983) *American National Standard Pascal Computer Programming Language*, ANSI/IEEE 770 X3.97-1983, American National Standards Institute, New York.

Atkinson, M.P., and Buneman, O.P. (1987) Database programming languages, *ACM Computing Surveys* **19**, 105–90.

Bird, R.A., and Wadler, P.L. (1988) *Introduction to Functional Programming*, Prentice Hall International, Hemel Hempstead, England.

Birtwistle, G.M., Dahl, O.-J., Myhrhaug, B., and Nygaard, K. (1975) *Simula Begin*, Petrocelli Charter, New York.

Böhm, C., and Jacopini, G. (1966) Flow diagrams, Turing machines, and languages with only two formation rules, *Communications of the ACM* **9**, 366–71.

Booch, G. (1987) *Software Engineering with Ada*, 2nd edn, Addison-Wesley, Reading, Massachusetts.

Brinch Hansen, P. (1973) *Operating System Principles*, Prentice Hall, Englewood Cliffs, New Jersey.

Brinch Hansen, P. (1977) *The Architecture of Concurrent Programs*, Prentice Hall, Englewood Cliffs, New Jersey.

BSI (1982) *Specification for Computer Programming Language Pascal*, BS 6192, British Standards Institution, Milton Keynes, England; also IS 7185, International Standards Organization, Geneva.

Burns, A. (1985) *Concurrent Programming in Ada*, Cambridge University Press, Cambridge, England.

Bustard, D., Elder, J., and Welsh, J. (1988) *Concurrent Program Structures*, Prentice Hall International, Hemel Hempstead, England.

Cardelli, L., and Wegner, P. (1985) On understanding types, data abstraction, and polymorphism, *ACM Computing Surveys* **17**, 471–522.

Carriero, N., and Gelernter, D. (1989) Linda in context, *Communications of the ACM* **32**, 444–58.

Chandy, K.M., and Misra, J. (1988) *Parallel Program Design: a foundation*, Addison-Wesley, Reading, Massachusetts.

Conway, R., and Gries, D. (1979) *An Introduction to Programming: A structured approach using PL/I and PL/C*, 3rd edn, Winthrop, Cambridge, Massachusetts.

Coulouris, G.F., and Dollimore, J. (1988) *Distributed Systems: Concepts and design*, Addison-Wesley, Wokingham, England.

Cox, B. (1986) *Object-oriented Programming: an evolutionary approach*, Addison-Wesley, Reading, Massachusetts.

Dahl, O.-J., Myhrhaug, B., and Nygaard, K. (1970) Simula 67 common base language, N.S-22, Norwegian Computing Center, Oslo.

Department of Defense (1978) Requirements for high-order computer programming languages, Ada Joint Program Office, Department of Defense, Washington, DC.

DeRemer, F.L., and Kron, H.H. (1976) Programming-in-the-large versus programming-in-the-small, *IEEE Transactions on Software Engineering* **2**, 80–6.

Dijkstra, E.W. (1968a) Cooperating sequential processes, in *Programming Languages* (ed. Genuys, F.), Academic Press, New York, pp. 43–112.

Dijkstra, E.W. (1968b) Go to statement considered harmful, *Communications of the ACM* **11**, 147–8.

Dijkstra, E.W. (1968c) The structure of THE multiprogramming system, *Communications of the ACM* **11**, 341–6.

Dijkstra, E.W. (1976) *A Discipline of Programming*, Prentice Hall, Englewood Cliffs, New Jersey.

Ellis, T.M.R. (1982) *A Structured Approach to Fortran 77 Programming*, Addison-Wesley, Wokingham, England.

Field, A.J., and Harrison, P.G. (1988) *Functional Programming*, Addison-Wesley, Wokingham, England.

Findlay, W., and Watt, D.A. (1985) *Pascal: An introduction to methodical programming*, 3rd edn, Pitman, London; also Computer Science Press, Rockville, Maryland.

Gehani, N., and McGettrick, A.D. (eds.) (1988) *Concurrent Programming*, Addison-Wesley, Wokingham, England.

Ghezzi, C., and Jazayeri, M. (1987) *Programming Language Concepts*, 2nd edn, Wiley, New York.

Goldberg, A., and Robson, D. (1983) *Smalltalk-80: The language and its implementation*, Addison-Wesley, Reading, Massachusetts.

Habermann, A.N. (1973) Critical comments on the language Pascal, *Acta Informatica* **3**, 47–57.

Harbison, S.P., and Steele, G.L. (1987) *C: A reference manual*, Prentice Hall, Englewood Cliffs, New Jersey.

Harper, R., Milner, R., and Tofte, M. (1988) The definition of Standard ML (version 2), Department of Computer Science, University of Edinburgh, Scotland.

Henson, M.C. (1987) *Elements of Functional Languages*, Blackwell, Oxford, England.

Hindley, J.R. (1969) The principal type-scheme of an object in combinatory logic, *Transactions of the AMS* **146**, 29–60.

Hoare, C.A.R. (1962) Quicksort, *Computer Journal* **5**, 10–15.

Hoare, C.A.R. (1972) Notes on data structuring, in *Structured Programming* (eds. Dahl, O.-J., Dijkstra, E.W., and Hoare, C.A.R.), Academic Press, London, pp. 83–174.

Hoare, C.A.R. (1973) Hints on programming language design, in *Proceedings of ACM Symposium on Principles of Programming Languages*, ACM Press, New York.

Hoare, C.A.R. (1975) Recursive data structures, *International Journal of Computer and Information Sciences* **4**, 105–32.

Hoare, C.A.R. (1978) Communicating sequential processes, *Communications of the ACM* **21**, 666–77.

Hoare, C.A.R. (1981) The emperor's old clothes, *Communications of the ACM* **2**, 75–83.

Hoare, C.A.R. (1985) *Communicating Sequential Processes*, Prentice Hall International, Hemel Hempstead, England.

Hoare, C.A.R., and Wirth, N. (1973) An axiomatic definition of the programming language Pascal, *Acta Informatica* **2**, 335–55.

Horowitz, E. (ed.) (1987) *Programming Languages: A grand tour*, Computer Science Press, Rockville, Maryland.

Ichbiah, J. (ed.) (1979) Rationale for the design of the Ada programming language, *ACM SIGPLAN Notices* **14**, no. 6B (special issue).

Ichbiah, J. (ed.) (1983) *Ada Programming Language*, ANSI/MIL-STD-1815A, Ada Joint Program Office, Department of Defense, Washington, DC.

Jensen, K., and Wirth, N. (1974) *Pascal User Manual and Report*, Springer, Berlin.

Jones, G., and Goldsmith, M. (1988) *Programming in occam2*, Prentice Hall International, Hemel Hempstead, England.

Kernighan, B.W., and Ritchie, D.M. (1988) *The C Programming Language*, 2nd edn, Prentice Hall, Englewood Cliffs, New Jersey.

Knuth, D.E. (1974) Structured programming with goto statements, *ACM Computing Surveys* **6**, 261–302.

Landin, P.J. (1966) The next 700 programming languages, *Communications of the ACM* **9**, 157–64.

Ledgard, H.F., and Singer, A. (1982) Scaling down Ada, *Communications of the ACM* **25**, 121–5.

Liskov, B.H., and Zilles, S.N. (1974) Programming with abstract data types, *ACM SIGPLAN Notices* **9**, 50–9.

McCarthy, J. (1965) A basis for a mathematical theory of computation, in *Computer Programming and Formal Systems* (eds. Braffort, P., and Hirschberg, D.), North-Holland, Amsterdam, pp. 33–70.

McCarthy, J., Abrahams, P.W., Edwards, D.J., *et al.* (1965) *LISP 1.5 Programmer's Manual*, 2nd edn, MIT Press, Cambridge, Massachusetts.

McGettrick, A.D. (1978) *Algol 68: A first and second course*, Cambridge University Press, Cambridge, England.

Malpas, J. (1987) *Prolog: A relational language and its applications*, Prentice Hall International, Hemel Hempstead, England.

Meyer, B. (1988) From structured programming to object-oriented design: the road to Eiffel, *Structured Programming* **10**, 19–39.

Meyer, B. (1989) *Object-oriented Software Construction*, Prentice Hall International, Hemel Hempstead, England.

Milner, R. (1978) A theory of type polymorphism in programming, *Journal of Computer and System Science* **17**, 348–75.

Naur, P. (ed.) (1963) Revised report on the algorithmic language Algol 60, *Communications of the ACM* **6**, 1–20; also *Computer Journal* **5**, 349–67.

Parnas, D.L. (1972) On the criteria to be used in decomposing systems into modules, *Communications of the ACM* **15**, 1053–8.

Perrott, R.H. (1987) *Parallel Programming*, Addison-Wesley, Wokingham, England.

Pratt, T.W. (1984) *Programming Languages: Design and implementation*, 2nd edn, Prentice Hall, Englewood Cliffs, New Jersey.

Reynolds, J.C. (1985) Three approaches to type structure, in *Mathematical Foundations of Software Development* (eds. Ehrig, H., Floyd, C., Nivat, M., and Thatcher, J.), Springer, Berlin, pp. 97–138.

Rosser, J.B. (1982) Highlights of the history of the lambda-calculus, *Conference Record of 1982 ACM Symposium on Lisp and Functional Programming, Pittsburgh*, ACM, New York, pp. 216–25.

Strachey, C. (1967) Fundamental concepts in programming languages, *Proceedings of International Summer School in Computer Programming*, Copenhagen.

Tennent, R.D. (1977) Language design methods based on semantic principles, *Acta Informatica* **8**, 97–112.

Tennent, R.D. (1981) *Principles of Programming Languages*, Prentice Hall International, Hemel Hempstead, England.

Turner, D. (1986) An overview of Miranda, *ACM SIGPLAN Notices* **21**, 158–66.

van Wijngaarden, A., *et al.* (1976) *Revised Report on the Algorithmic Language Algol 68*, Springer, Berlin.

Watt, D.A. (1986) Language engineering, Computing Science Department, University of Glasgow.

Watt, D.A., Wichmann, B.L., and Findlay, W. (1987) *Ada: Language and methodology*, Prentice Hall International, Hemel Hempstead, England.

Welland, R.C. (1983) *Methodical Programming in COBOL*, Pitman, London.

Welsh, J., Elder, J., and Bustard, D.W. (1984) *Sequential Program Structures*, Prentice Hall International, Hemel Hempstead, England.

Welsh, J., Schneeringer, M.J., and Hoare, C.A.R. (1977) Ambiguities and insecurities in Pascal, *Software Practice and Experience* **7**, 675–96.

Wexelblat, R.L. (ed.) (1980) *ACM History of Programming Languages Conference, Los Angeles*, ACM Monograph, Academic Press, New York.

Wichmann, B.A. (1984) Is Ada too big? – a designer answers the critics, *Communications of the ACM* **27**, 98–103.

Wikström, Å. (1987) *Functional Programming using Standard ML*, Prentice Hall International, Hemel Hempstead, England.

Wilson, L.B., and Clark, R.G. (1988) *Comparative Programming Languages*, Addison-Wesley, Wokingham, England.

Winston, P.H., and Horn, B.K.P. (1984) *LISP*, 2nd edn, Addison-Wesley, Reading, Massachusetts.

Wirth, N. (1971) The programming language Pascal, *Acta Informatica* **1**, 35–63.

Wirth, N. (1974) On the design of programming languages, *Proceedings of IFIP Congress 74*, North-Holland, Amsterdam, pp. 386–93.

Wirth, N. (1977) Modula: a programming language for modular multiprogramming, *Software Practice and Experience* **7**, 3–35.

Wulf, W.A., and Shaw, M. (1973) Global variables considered harmful, *ACM SIGPLAN Notices* **8**, 80–6.

Zahn, C.T. (1974) A control statement for natural top-down structured programming, *Symposium on Programming Languages*, Paris.

Index